JONSON AND THE PSYCHOLOGY
OF PUBLIC THEATER

JOHN GORDON SWEENEY III

Jonson and the Psychology of Public Theater

To Coin the Spirit,
Spend the Soul

PRINCETON UNIVERSITY PRESS

Copyright © 1985 by Princeton University Press
Published by Princeton University Press, 41 William Street,
Princeton, New Jersey 08540
In the United Kingdom: Princeton University Press,
Guildford, Surrey

All Rights Reserved
Library of Congress Cataloging in Publication Data will be
found on the last printed page of this book

ISBN 0-691-06622-1

Publication of this book has been aided by a grant from the
Henry A. Laughlin Fund of Princeton University Press

This book has been composed in Linotron Caledonia

Clothbound editions of Princeton University Press books
are printed on acid-free paper, and binding materials are
chosen for strength and durability

Printed in the United States of America by
Princeton University Press
Princeton, New Jersey

To Debby

CONTENTS

PREFACE	ix
INTRODUCTION. The Self-Seeking Spectator	3
CHAPTER ONE. The Comical Satires	17
CHAPTER TWO. *Sejanus*: The People's Beastly Rage	47
CHAPTER THREE. *Volpone*: "Fooles, They Are the Onely Nation Worth Mens Envy, or Admiration."	70
CHAPTER FOUR. *Epicene*: "I'le Doe Good to No Man Against His Will."	105
CHAPTER FIVE. *The Alchemist*: "Yet I Put My Selfe on You"	125
CHAPTER SIX. *Bartholomew Fair*: Jonson's Masque for the Multitude	157
CHAPTER SEVEN. Beyond *Bartholomew Fair*	190
CONCLUSION. The Theater of Self-Interest	207
NOTES	229
INDEX	241

PREFACE

ANYONE familiar with Ben Jonson appreciates the importance of extratextual addenda. No writer I know has made better use of the epistle, prologue, epilogue, and induction in the tendentious arena of Poesy. One need not share, however, the Jonsonian impulse to badger, obfuscate, deter, delay, and defend. Here I wish only to describe briefly what is to follow and thank the people who helped the book along the way.

This book is a study of Ben Jonson's relationship with his audience in the public theater, as the relationship changed in the course of his career from the comical satires through *Bartholomew Fair*. Jonson was fascinated by the phenomenon of commercial theater and the "contract" between playwright and spectator implied in the act of paying to enter the theater. Thus the plays take up questions of theatrical authority; that is, who determines the nature of experience in the theater, and what is to be done about what Jonson took to be the threatening interests of a meanly self-gratifying audience? Because he was an extraordinarily self-conscious author, because he saw fully the ways in which the relationship between stage and gallery affected his role as poet, and because he was never entirely satisfied that the conflicting interests of stage and gallery could be resolved, his plays tend to be concerned with competition for the stage and for the power to enact one's own self-substantiating drama. I have sought to show how public matters such as the role of author and the place of theater in Renaissance England influenced, and in turn were influenced by, the private issues of Jonson's life. His plays are metaphors—representations of authorial conflict—and rhetorical instruments that repeatedly enact the conflict between stage and gallery; a playwright reenacts private conflicts as public art for, but also with, an audience. In the

PREFACE

fourteen years during which he wrote his finest plays, Jonson learned to accept the risks of this volatile commercial relationship, in part by sharing them with his spectators. He learned to give over his work to the judgment of his audiences as he learned to negotiate in ever more sophisticated ways the limits to their authority. Thus, at least in Jonson's theater, only through the acknowledgment of theater as transaction is its power to entertain fully realized.

FOR consistency, I have worked from the Herford and Simpson edition of Jonson's work, which retains the oddities and archaisms of the original, though there are fine modern editions of the more popular plays available. I have, however, modernized the *u/v* and *i/j* spellings and eliminated arbitrary italics.

Among those who have guided my work, I wish to thank first those who taught me about Jonson and Renaissance drama when I was a graduate student at the University of California at Berkeley: Jonas Barish, Stephen Orgel, Stephen Greenblatt, Joel Altman, and William Nestrick. I owe special debts to Jonas Barish, who directed the dissertation from which the book grew and whose own work on Jonson I greatly admire; and to Stephen Orgel, for his brilliant work on Jonson and the court masque, for his course in Shakespeare that made wonder a habit, and for his unstinting support in matters large and small at every step of my career. I wish to thank, also, two good friends from Berkeley: David Sundelson asked me one Sunday morning in Geneseo, New York, why Celia dropped her handkerchief in *Volpone*. The day was ruined, but chapter 3 is much better for it. And Peter Carlson's intellectual clarity and precision are remarkable to behold. Among the circumstances oddly appropriate to the genesis of this book is the fact that many of my early impressions of Jonson were developed and refined in conversation with Peter while we baked thousands of pretzels at Bill's Naked Lunch Stand.

Whatever psychological insight I have been able to offer

PREFACE

concerning Jonson's relationship with his audience gained immensely from the chance to study with Murray Schwartz in an NEH summer seminar at SUNY Buffalo. At the University of Georgia, Charles Clay Doyle and Charles Lower have been careful readers of the manuscript and kind supporters of my work. Nathan Dean and the Office of the Vice President for Research made travel and research funds available to me. And for many kinds of assistance I thank Coburn Freer. On more than one occasion of professional crisis, real and imagined, I have been the beneficiary of his massive calm. Finally, I wish to thank the editors of *ELH* and *English Literary Renaissance* for permission to reprint the portions of the book that first appeared in their journals.

JONSON AND THE PSYCHOLOGY
OF PUBLIC THEATER

> ita Daedalus inplet
> Innumeras errore vias vixque ipse reverti
> Ad limen potuit: tanta est fallacia tecti.
>
> Ovid, *Metamorphoses*

INTRODUCTION

The Self-Seeking Spectator

IF THE London grocer's attempt to buy his son Ralph a play called *The Knight of the Burning Pestle* is an extreme example of upstart egocentricity, it is also the sign of a remarkable relationship between stage and gallery in the public playhouses of Jacobean England. In 1607 the Theater was gone, but the Globe, heir to its timbers, had marked the thirtieth anniversary of the playhouse in England, and just as the stage was experiencing its adult strength in *Volpone, King Lear, Macbeth,* and *Antony and Cleopatra,* so, obviously, were its audiences. For years Ben Jonson had been snarling at disruptive spectators, and Lyly, Marston, and Chapman, none quite so given to single combat as Jonson, had been flattering and scolding. They had various targets: groundlings who understood little of what they saw and heard, "Criticks" who complained about everything that crossed the stage, "Politick Spies" whose business was translating stage action into libel and treason, and an assortment of fools and impostors whose chief interest in the theater was the opportunity it provided for the worst sorts of self-celebration. Things must have been tense in the playhouses of the early seventeenth century, for play after play went forth escorted by prologues and epilogues which confronted directly the issue of audience behavior. Clearly the theater was feeling the tensions generated throughout the culture by rapid social change, but in a sense it was also acting out the cultural drama that James Burbage had set in motion in 1575 when he signed for the loans he needed to build the Theater.

As Stephen Orgel points out in *The Illusion of Power,* the Theater changed the nature of the English stage:

INTRODUCTION

All at once theater was an institution, a property, a corporation. For the first time in more than a thousand years it had the sort of reality that meant most to a Renaissance society: it was *real* in the way that "real estate" is real; it was a location, a building, a possession—an established and visible part of society. And having a permanent place, it also had a regular attendance, a permanent audience: theaters create not only their dramas, but their audiences, as well.[1]

One of the most intriguing aspects of this new theater is the financial relationship it established with its audience. For the first time, each theatergoer paid a set fee at the door, "putting to his Seale preposterously," as Jonson observed in the induction to *Bartholomew Fair*, which is to say that a spectator paid for the goods, like a fool, before assessing their worth. This arrangement altered irrevocably the traditional relation of audience to stage. Before the public playhouse found its place in English society, theatrical production was the realm of a relatively small and select group of those who could afford to pay for it. Monarchs, mayors, nobles, guilds, and church committees held the purse strings, which allowed them to dictate in large measure the character of the theater. They determined the nature of a production by commission and participated in the event as a privileged audience. Fees might have been collected from the commons at tournaments and the hat passed for players in the town square, but these were means of finance ancillary to those provided by a king who commissioned a tournament for his lady or by an earl who maintained a troupe of players among his household servants. In short, there were commonly two theater audiences, one for whom or by whom an event was commissioned and another, "the multitude," whose participation was allowed but whose place, both physically and metaphysically, was on the fringe.[2]

Burbage gave an increasingly commercial culture its own theater. It is a measure of the astonishing rate of social change

THE SELF-SEEKING SPECTATOR

in the last quarter of the sixteenth century and a sign of the inexorable progress of capitalism that a common player was able to finance a theater less than four years after passage of the Act Restraining Vagabonds. The playhouse gave the playgoing public control of the stage, and in spite of governmental and religious attempts to take it back, for half a century "the beast multitude"[3] got, by and large, what it was willing to pay for.

The playhouse also created a number of new social roles: the theatrical impresario, like Henslowe, attempting everything from building theaters to making personal loans to players; the playwright emerging from relative obscurity to command respect and social standing as a poet; the player rising from vagabond to gentleman. Among the strangest offspring of the public playhouse, however, were its spectators. The playhouse freed its audience from the traditional forms of social and religious authority that had previously prescribed conduct in the theater; consequently, playwrights found themselves facing a large, diverse, and aggressive gallery, whose expectations were a mystery when they weren't an insult and whose behavior was occasionally a real threat to a performance. The only sure thing was that those who paid to enter the theater expected to be entertained. Needless to say, writing for such a group posed problems that writing for church or court theater did not. A playwright seeking, in the best humanist tradition, to make the stage a reflection of its audience had first to deal with the fact that the playhouse audience defied depiction. As a result, all too frequently, at least in the estimation of dramatists with serious moral and intellectual interests, theater stooped to the lowest common denominator, or, in Jonson's words, to "the concupiscence of dances and antics." For such writers, the Socratic ideal of knowing oneself, once a powerful justification of theater's role in society, was threatened by a parodic version of itself, embodied in spectators whose self-seeking extended no further than a tickling of their fancies.

Part scarecrow part scapegoat, this self-seeking spectator

focused the anxiety professional playwrights felt about their role in a new theater. Humanism had scrubbed self-seeking clean and given it a place in the vision of life as platonic quest, where it served as the motive behind pursuits as various as literature and martial arts. But humanism is ill-equipped to deal with a world where social and moral codes are no longer widely shared, where money, not scholarly ideals, does most of the talking. Here self-seeking becomes an ideal in itself. This is not to say that the Middle Ages were more pious than the Renaissance, only that Renaissance culture came to its own terms with the social paradoxes it inherited. For a poet working to make sense of ideals in a world of cash, the problem is one of self-definition—how to unite popular and humanist traditions, not just theoretically but on the stage as well, so that professional success might be enjoyed without the guilt of betraying tradition. When individual desire is divorced from social and moral idealism, there is chaos but also freedom, and the question is how to mediate the two. Though the struggle for Elizabethan and Jacobean playwrights was, for the most part, a thoroughly unplatonic one, there was a platonic side: as culture resolves itself into a mass of individual cells, language and meaning as shared social phenomena are called into question. Each monadic member of society seeks to impose his own vision on the world, some more aggressively than others; thus, a poet like Jonson finds himself confronting fundamental questions about the nature of human community. Recreation, and theater in particular, might be an essential element of communal life, but the playwright has to face daily the problem of defining his worth.

No writer working for a mass audience can avoid this problem entirely. Insofar as success cannot be assured beforehand, one takes his chances with the public. Writers respond to this volatility in various ways: some ignore it and go about their business as they see fit; some limit their audience; some fuss; some quit. Ben Jonson took up the question of his relationship to his audience publicly, in prologues, epilogues, and inductions; in letters to his readers; and in the plays themselves. In one sense his plays are a series of attempts to come to terms with his playhouse audience over some fundamental issues of theater, particularly the question of how it is to be valued. When traditional ways of valuing theater are threatened, as they were by commercial theater, playwright and audience quickly find themselves toe to toe. The question of value becomes one of authority; that is, who is to do the valuing and on what grounds. In the extreme, even meaning becomes a commodity, something to be haggled over in the transaction between stage and gallery. Today we take for granted the commercial aspect of theater; we think in terms of shared experience and community, not in terms of concessions made and contracts negotiated. But no theatrical event can go forward without some concessions to social decorum, and in the English playhouse at the beginning of the seventeenth century such decorum was a risky proposition. There, the price of admission to the theater bought more than we are accustomed to purchasing with our tickets—it bought an interest in the real and immediate competition for the stage. In time the struggle was resolved: the insurrection from the pit was quelled and now, for the most part, we sit meekly in the dark.

Clearly Ben Jonson was fascinated by the tumult in the playhouse. Questions of dramatic form and meaning were for him always questions of his approach to his audience. He used the stage to formulate propositions about his spectators and thought their response as much a part of the theatrical event as the stage action. Moreover, he took his audience personally, as a direct threat to his attempts to define himself as a poet. By nature wary of his audience, he saw fully the ways in which the changing relation between stage and spectator in a commercial theater impinged upon artistic prerogatives; therefore, he set about publicly defining and asserting his interests in the theater.

In short, Jonson was extraordinarily self-conscious about his role as a man of the theater engaged in making a place for drama in English society. This study will consider how his

INTRODUCTION

plays, particularly those from *Every Man Out of His Humor* through *Bartholomew Fair*, deal with their audiences and how the relationship between stage and gallery determines the nature of the theater. In this fifteen-year period of his career, Jonson's commitment to the stage changed radically, largely, I will argue, because he mastered certain conflicts inherent in his sense of theater by repeatedly enacting them on the stage.

Characteristically, Jonson refuses his spectators the conventional, unwritten guarantee of fictional experience, anonymity. For the most part, fiction is a private affair; seldom does the spectator himself become the spectacle. The relatively modern fictional media—books, film, and television—by their nature minimize personal confrontation. All are easily terminated experiences; when we put aside a book we need not fear the pursuit of an irate author. Theater, however, is a much more confrontational medium: an attempt to object to a play or to leave the theater might conceivably be countered from the stage. Even so, the mainstream of theatrical production since Shakespeare's time, relying on conventions such as the darkened hall, the stage curtain, and the proscenium arch, has actually increased audience anonymity by setting the theatrical space apart from the audience. In general, the conventions of fictional media falsify fictional experience, at least to the extent that they discount the aspect of confrontation between author and spectator. It is the unusual artist, Jonson, Shakespeare, Pirandello, Camus, who calls attention to this fact by making the nature of the artistic act itself the subject of his work.

In a sense, every artist confronts his audience in his fiction, but neither party often escalates the aspect of confrontation. Normally we do not deal with authorial self-interest because we assume, and are encouraged to assume, a common interest. Jonson's is one theater, however, which cherishes the moment of confrontation between author and spectator. His theater insists that all activity dealing with social man inevitably must face the question of authority and its natural concomitant, conflict. Author and spectator meet to judge one another, and the fictional experience mediates what is a potentially explosive situation. One of Jonson's special aptitudes was recognizing that his authority to judge his spectators resided in his willingness to indulge their judgment of himself. Yet, whether we think of it or not, this is certainly the case with all public utterance. Performing for any audience is, after all, a risky business. It comprises an act of self-definition and an assertion of one's social worth, but, to the extent that the value of such an act depends on validation by an audience, it involves an act of submission as well. In effect, then, an artist's own authority always rests upon his concession to the authority of others, and it is to the personal risks of this situation that Jonson was particularly alive.

This playwright asks us to participate in *significant* theater, theater that promises self-knowledge and realizes the instructive potential of fiction. He offers "words, above action: matter above words."[4] But in addition, Jonson's theater is immensely self-serving, and its self-consciousness about the way it works frustrates our attempts to participate freely. The editorial pieces appended to his plays are full of attempts to secure his position in the public playhouse by assigning to his audiences the roles least threatening to himself. He addresses his spectators in the prologues and epistles not so much to greet them as to examine them and to reveal the roles he expects them to play in his theatrical community. He identifies the subversive elements at the outset, the better to enlist the general will in controlling them. But of course this tactic depends on the willingness of an audience to create its roles; ironically, Jonson could count only on the subversives, that intractable portion of his audience which, like Wycherley's Sparkish, saw the theater as a place of self-exhibition:

> Gad, I go to a play as to a country treat; I carry my own wine to one, and my own wit to t'other, or else I'm sure I would not be merry at either. And the reason why we are so often louder than the players is because we think

we speak more wit, and so become the poet's rivals in his audience. For to tell you the truth, we hate the silly rogues; nay, so much that we find fault even with their bawdy upon the stage, whilst we talk nothing else in the pit as loud.[5]

Jonson's characteristic response to his own sparkish spectators was to expose and excoriate them through the mouths of his stage representatives, Asper, Horace, Balladino, and others, or to put them on stage as Fitzdottrells and Wouldbes, where they exposed themselves.

Thus, in the critical apparatus surrounding his plays, Jonson attempts repeatedly to tie the experience of his work to the moral and intellectual qualifications of the individual spectator, but his search for the "judging spectator"[6] becomes a way to exercise his own formidable powers of judgment. Asper's *furor poeticus* preceding *Every Man Out* is just a single instance of Jonson's willingness to confront an audience by judging them:

> Doe not I know the times condition?
> Yes, Mitis, and their soules, and who they be,
> That eyther will, or can except against me.
> None, but a sort of fooles, so sicke in taste,
> That they contemne all phisicke of the mind,
> And, like gald camels, kicke at every touch.
> Good men, and vertuous spirits, that lothe their vices,
> Will cherish my free labours, love my lines,
> And with the fervour of their shining grace,
> Make my braine fruitfull to bring forth more objects,
> Worthy their serious, and intentive eyes.
>   (Induction, 128-38)

Here Jonson requires his spectators to be self-conscious about their own performance in his theater by denying them the anonymity the theater ordinarily guarantees. Response to the play is no longer free expression of a personal experience in the theater, but an index of moral health. We cannot judge, in other words, without being judged ourselves. The real issue is who "owns" Jonson's play, who has the right to determine the value and meaning of his labor. He calls these "free labours," but clearly the fact that he feels a threat suggests that he is unwilling to surrender his claim. Through Asper he attempts to obviate the threat by anticipating it. We are encouraged to judge, then are shown that our judgment is only part of a larger context which qualifies it.

Even when Jonson appears relatively at ease with his audience, the desire to confront it and to force revealing "moral" choices is not far from the surface. One of the subtlest examples of this is the two-part preface to *Catiline*, the letters "To the Reader in Ordinarie" and "To the Reader Extraordinary."[7] These two pieces carry the familiar markings of Jonson's other editorial addenda, the assertion of security, imperturbability, even gracious accommodation and the desire to give his work freely to those who will have it. The tone is self-consciously direct, open, and apparently without malice or guile. But in fact these epistles represent as sophisticated and powerful an attempt to manipulate an audience as any Jonson made. The opening sentence seems to address anyone who picks up the book: "The Muses forbid, that I should restrayne your medling, whom I see alreadie busie with the Title, and tricking over the leaves: It is your owne." What could be more gracious and disarming? Any reader busies himself with the title and tricks the leaves, so to all of us Jonson apparently professes his disinterestedness and cedes his rights to the book. But he will not let go. He begins, instead, to manufacture for us a choice of responses, every one of which carries with it a personal evaluation. If we commend acts 1 and 2 and "dislike the Oration of Cicero," we are unmistakably dull and in need of forgiveness. In fact, if we do not appreciate Cicero's diatribe, we sin not against Jonson but against the greater authority of Cicero. Having preempted one possible criticism, Jonson narrows his sights to those who might approve the play. What follows is a quibbling etymological distinction between commendation and

INTRODUCTION

approbation. Commenders are not to be trusted because their judgment may be feigned, and commendation, in Jonson's view, is most frequently dissembled, "for the most commend out of affection, selfe tickling, an easinesse, or imitation." Each of these motives calls up the specter of mob behavior which so disturbed Jonson. True judgment, on the other hand, is a function of the wise, solitary, and free human intelligence secure in its knowledge of self. Simply on the basis of word play, to the exclusion of any test in the theater, judgment and approval become one and the same.

Jonson has attempted to negate the right of his audience to judge his work freely, a right which he had affirmed just several lines earlier. In the end he judges the audience on the basis of an abstract scale of knowledge which ties our response to the play to our qualifications to enter Jonson's theater. What is disturbing is that it discounts affective response (Jonson sneers at "affection") and unself-conscious participation. There is no thought given to theater's capacity, much less its responsibility, to create and control its audience's experience. Jonson urges on us an experience whose validity lies in a realm one self-conscious step away from the immediate response, in a realm defined by judgment, knowledge, and moral fitness. In the final lines of the first letter, Jonson leaves the "Reader in Ordinarie" to his exercise and to the thought that if he censures the play it is from ignorance and deceit, and if he commends the play it is most likely for no better reasons. Then, as if to assert that nothing has really changed since the opening sentence, he repeats his disdain for such judgmental squabbles, "If I were not above such molestations now." The "Beginne" which concludes the address is not an invitation but a dare.

The "Reader Extraordinary," on the other hand, is an appropriate judge for Jonson's work. His status as a "better man" is a function of both his approving response and the level of his moral and intellectual understanding. Such a person is Jonson's chosen audience for *Catiline*, and when he concludes, "To you I submit my selfe, and worke," not only does he belie the indifference with which he began the first epistle, he also admits the personal risk attendant upon publication of his work.

The clearest evidence of how deeply Jonson's agression toward his audience penetrates these avowedly benign epistles is to be found in the movement of the language: the sentences frequently seem to take back what they initially offer, just as the entire piece steals with one hand what the other gives. Jonson cannot leave "Be anything you will be" alone without qualifying it with a clause which, in this context, is a veiled threat, "at your owne charge." "Would I had deserv'd but halfe so well of it in translation, as that ought to deserve of you in judgment," begins as an act of self-effacement and reverence for Cicero, continues as a warning to the audience, and concludes with an insult, "if you have any." The sentence that follows, "I know you will pretend (whosoever you are) to have that, and more," is an acknowledgment of human nature, and not particularly accusing until that final sardonic twist, "and more." Perhaps the most telling equivocation is in the second address, however: "though Places in Court go otherwise" strikes a sour note in this otherwise flattering sentence. Undoubtedly the phrase is one of Jonson's grumbles about the inequity of the world, but again the context suggests another meaning, an oblique warning to the reader that he had better not include himself in this group solely on the basis of social standing.

This rhetorical shell game extends throughout the first epistle as the piece progressively revises our understanding of the words "medling," "busie," and "tricking" in the first sentence. Indifference, even jocularity, masks the hostility beneath these words, no one of which is primarily pejorative, but in light of what follows it is clear that Jonson is belittling those he takes to be intruding on his work. Similarly, Jonson's use of the word "exercise" to describe the activity of the ordinary reader commands no attention until it is compared

INTRODUCTION

with the experience offered the "Reader Extraordinary." The latter is entrusted with the work and with Jonson himself, revealing the "exercise" of the former to be empty and foolish.

What makes these epistles all the more subtle is that Jonson appears to be drawing a distinction that accurately reflects the complexity of reading experience. Certainly there is an entire range of readers; in fact, any one reader experiences an entire range of reading experience from browsing to intense engagement. Jonson's ordinary reader seems a fair representation of ordinary reading, while the characterization of the extraordinary reader might be said to touch those times when we participate more fully. Surely the reward of sympathetic reading is the feeling that the author is submitting himself to us, or at least revealing himself in a privileged way, the feeling, in other words, that we have earned a trust. Jonson makes us self-conscious about our role in this process, but he also strains the conventional relationship. He is fundamentally unwilling to allow us to read as we choose; he *demands* sympathetic readers and enforces the demand by making a moral and intellectual distinction between readers. This distinction may have reflected the reality of Jonson's audience, and fullness of response is unquestionably a function of will and capacity, but this tactic seems unfair or at least disingenous as a greeting to an audience, and it conflicts radically with other Jonsonian tenets:

> It is the faire acceptance, Sir, creates
> The entertaynment perfect: not the cates.[8]

> Our wishes, like to those (make publique feasts)
> Are not to please the cookes tastes, but the guests.[9]

In general, Jonson's epistles, prologues, and inductions, by insisting on the factors which qualify and minimize audience response, refuse to permit sympathy to be something a reader brings freely to his reading or viewing experience. It is as if Jonson has been forced to pick and choose his audience, con-

THE SELF-SEEKING SPECTATOR

ferring the fullness of his work only upon the select. Certainly any author determines, to some extent, the nature of his audience through his work; what is significant in Jonson's case is his desire to make this selection anterior to his work, to make his criteria of suitability a condition of participation. In the end he only intensifies our sense of the importance of judging and being judged in his theater.

On the face of it, such a theater is consistent with Jonson's theories about literature: theater ought to assert moral and ethical propositions, and, if it can *require* its audience to take them seriously, so much the better. But it is equally clear that he was frequently uncomfortable with this commitment. At times, moral and intellectual imperatives are complicated by personal motives; in other instances, the level of aggression seems inconsistent with any "higher purpose." In addition, Jonson's work is full of overtly self-interested action. There are appeals for royal favor, self-aggrandizing presentations of The Poet, and, of course, attacks on personal enemies. His two major professional quarrels figure extensively in his work; the first, with Marston and Dekker, spawned *Poetaster*, and the second, with Inigo Jones, dominated their twenty-six year collaboration and repeatedly found expression in print. Jonson, it seems, could never entirely distinguish the desire to create and sustain an audience from self-gratifying aggression. In other words, he could not easily extricate the impulse to instruct and entertain from the impulse to dominate, and his vocal spectators did not help.

Jonson's battles with the "Criticks" and the "Politick Spies" are but the most obvious manifestation of his problematic relationship with his audience. And that relationship is but a part of his profound ambivalence toward authority in general. For a man who professed extreme devotion to queen and king, he had a great deal of trouble making good the commitment in his personal life. He was locked up for an offense to King James in *Eastward Ho!* and threatened with jail for his refusal to practice the correct religion. He glorified Queen Elizabeth on the stage, yet transmitted, undoubtedly with

INTRODUCTION

delight, the rumors of her unusual anatomical features.[10] In *Epigrammes* he created an idealized Cecil, then crabbed to Drummond about the real Cecil's lack of hospitality. Jonson's shadowy involvement with the Gunpowder Plot epitomizes the problem: at the moment when he was emerging as the pageant poet of James's court, his Catholicism threatened to make his life very difficult indeed.

Herford and Simpson's comment on the intrigue of the Gunpowder Plot is curious: "It is clear that he felt in the matter altogether as a subject and an Englishman, not as a Catholic,"[11] as if the Catholic and the Englishman can be as easily distinguished in a man as on a page. But the fact is that Englishman and Catholic were not easily distinguishable for this man; neither were dutiful subject and arrogant poet nor entertainer and savage satirist. Ambivalence to authority[12] and the confusion of self-interest with social service and aggression with instruction all inform Jonson's work, and his plays, particularly those from *Sejanus* to *Bartholomew Fair*, represent his progressive coming to terms with his complex feelings about authority. Ben Jonson makes available to us an aspect of the artistic process rarely seen in its fullness, but he makes us pay for it.

ONE

The Comical Satires

> With no lesse pleasure, then we have beheld
> This precious christall, worke of rarest wit,
> Our eye doth reade thee (now enstil'd) our Crites;
> Whom learning, vertue, and our favour last,
> Exempteth from the gloomy multitude.

I

BEN JONSON took considerable care to make *Every Man Out of His Humor, Cynthia's Revels,* and *Poetaster* look like a trilogy on dramatic satire. The 1616 Folio presents these three plays as "comical satyres," and for all the satire in the rest of Jonson's drama, no other play bears on its title page a reference to the genre. Moreover, the plays are enclosed as a group by two formidable statements about Jonsonian satire, the induction to *Every Man Out*, which establishes the grounds of his commitment to the genre, and *Poetaster*'s Apologetical Dialogue, which cuts short that commitment as Jonson heads for *Sejanus* and the aloof regions of tragedy. In short, the comical satires ask to be taken as a phase of Jonson's career, but criticism has been slow to consider the offer seriously. O. J. Campbell's *Comicall Satyre and Shakespeare's Troilus and Cressida* is the exception, and perhaps the breadth of this study and the fact that the comical satires are neither the best nor the easiest to handle of Jonson's works have kept the field relatively clear.

Campbell treats the plays as Jonson's "program for the creation of dramatic satire to meet a persistent social and intellectual interest of his age,"[1] as a *public* phenomenon, discounting the private side of Jonson's artistic development and the ways in which his plays constantly address the question of his authority in the theater. This private side is what interests me, particularly since the step from *Every Man In His Humor* to *Every Man Out of His Humor* is an astonishing change in direction. Nothing in the record of his career suggests why, at this moment, Jonson was drawn to a "program" in the first place, or why, after *The Case is Altered* and *Every Man In His Humor*, two relatively straightforward and critically unencumbered plays, Jonson appended to this play such curiosities as an induction that runs to nearly four hundred lines and covers everything from Renaissance psychology to the history of dramatic theory; a chorus composed of two characters who sit onstage offering comments on the action that are far more distracting than useful; and, for the published version of the play, a *dramatis personae* rounded out by prose sketches of each character. Perhaps this was Jonson's response to early posturing in the Stage Quarrel; it could be that he simply wanted to do something new, to make a name for himself apart from more conventional comic writers. Whatever the case, *Every Man Out* represents a major change of psychic weather. It is not just a new choice of subject or genre but a radical shift in Jonson's relation to his audience. Its induction contains his first serious attempt to alter the conventional distance between stage and spectator by breaking the single-perspective plane in which "realistic" drama operates. It is a stunning moment when Asper looks with surprise to the audience and declares, "I not observ'd this thronged round till now./Gracious, and kind spectators, you are welcome" (Induction, 51-52). What began as an event confined to the stage as represented action suddenly has become self-consciously theatrical, acknowledging itself as drama enacted before an audience in the theater, "this thronged round." Nor is this a facile trick of the eye like many of the witty asides in other plays of the period. It goes to the heart of Jonson's artistic intent; the remainder of the induction examines in detail what the play hopes to accomplish in relation to its audience, that is, both how the spectators are to behave and what the play will offer them in return for their attention and understanding. Jonson negotiates a "contract" in which Asper promises "musicke worth your eares" and offers generously: "Let me be censur'd by th'austerest brow,/Where I want arte, or judgement, taxe me freely" (Induction, 60-61). This in return for "attentive auditors,/Such as will joyne their profit with their pleasure,/And come to feed their understanding parts" (Induction, 201-3).

Whatever interest they claim in their own right, the questions of theory and form raised in the induction also reflect Jonson's ambivalence toward the role of satirist. A serious conflict is represented in the tone of the induction, though it is difficult to say whether it is the result or the cause of the impulse to alter the conventional relationship between stage and gallery. On one hand, the induction attempts to establish a new level of intimacy between author and audience; on the other it attempts to justify the venting of a tremendous amount of aggression toward the same audience. The justification is based upon an apparently reasonable distinction between the judicious portion of the audience, those who earn the pleasure Jonson offers, and the fools who are to be scourged and driven from the theater. But scrutiny reveals the strain in the scheme to dichotomize the audience. Asper's brave declaration, "Let me be censur'd" receives the following qualification seventy-five lines later:

> Doe not I know the times condition?
> Yes, Mitis, and their soules, and who they be,
> That eyther will, or can except against me.
> None, but a sort of fooles, so sicke in taste,
> That they contemne all phisicke of the mind,
> And, like gald camels, kicke at every touch.
> Good men, and vertuous spirits, that lothe their vices,
> Will cherish my free labours, love my lines.
> (Induction, 128-35)

This is a subtle but momentous shift of the responsibility for judging the play. What Asper gives in the first place, he revokes in the second: we are free to judge, but if we judge negatively, the privilege is essentially revoked. This is a trap, a double bind of which neither Asper nor Jonson, I think, is aware; and it is repeated in Asper's final lines: "If we faile,/ We must impute it to this onely chance,/'Arte hath an enemy cal'd Ignorance." His failure, in other words, is our ignorance.

The nexus of this conflict is best revealed in Asper's use of one of Jonson's favorite metaphors for his theater, borrowed from Cicero, the *"speculum consuetudinis"*:

> Well I will scourge those apes;
> And to these courteous eyes oppose a mirrour,
> As large as is the stage, whereon we act:
> Where they shall see the times deformitie
> Anatomiz'd in every nerve, and sinnew,
> With constant courage, and contempt of feare.
> (Induction, 117-22)

The problem is that mirrors reflect the images of their beholders; thus, how is it that courteous eyes should see deformities? Though we ought to be wary of demanding scientific accuracy of poets, still Jonson has made a problem for himself, one that might be more easily dismissed as an imprecise metaphor were it not for the fact that this kind of inconsistency keeps surfacing throughout his work.

Jonson's unwitting complication of what are offered initially as simple judgmental problems and distinctions suggests that his attempts to dichotomize his audience served ends other than, or in addition to, the accurate reflection of the playhouse audience. He used his playhouse audience to reflect the confusion in his own mind over what seemed to him two irreconcilable aspects of his role as a dramatic satirist: the entertainer, with what that implied for him in terms of seduction, and the teacher, with what that implied in terms of brutal domination. The conventional rhetoric of *furor poeticus* and the cankered muse explains a good deal about how Jonson drew Asper's character, but it does not begin to explain the complex commitment Asper feels toward his attentive auditors. Though he mentions contributing to their "profit," he eventually transcends the world of discursive and didactic meaning, alluding instead to a sensual world beyond words: he will make music. For his attentive auditors, he says:

> Ile prodigally spend my selfe,
> And speake away my spirit into ayre;
> For these, Ile melt my braine into invention,
> Coine new conceits, and hang my richest words
> As polisht jewels in their bounteous eares.
> (Induction, 204-8)

And so rapt in this sensuous rhetoric is Asper that he forgets himself and delays unwittingly the opening of the play:

> But stay, I loose my selfe, and wrong their patience;
> If I dwell here, they'le not begin, I see.

One need not even mention the puns on "spend," "spirit," "coine," and "conceits," intended or not, to point out that this is a world of emotional intimacy. Hanging polished jewels in bounteous ears is for lovers, and this aspect of the satirist stands in direct opposition to the earlier violence: "I would give them pills to purge," and:

> Ile strip the ragged follies of the time,
> Naked, as at their birth . . . and with a whip of steele,
> Print wounding lashes in their yron ribs.

The two experiences Jonson imagines in the theater are extreme opposites, and while the induction attempts to deal with this opposition by splitting the audience, it never fully resolves the inconsistency. Here intimacy and hostility are inextricably linked, and the appearance of this conflict coincides, significantly, with Jonson's attempts to alter his relationship with his spectators.[2]

This confusion is part of the larger problem of authority in *Every Man Out*. Where do we place Jonson in relation to Asper and Macilente? Who takes responsibility for the values

THE COMICAL SATIRES

expressed in the play? In a play in which narrative and representational integrity are paramount, one might ask whether the question itself is appropriate, whether anyone can be said to speak for the author. In *Every Man Out*, however, we have the opposite problem, too many spokesmen. In addition to Asper and Macilente, Mitis, Cordatus, and Carlo Buffone play important roles in the chain of command, and perhaps what is most telling is the difficulty Jonson has in establishing a clear and consistent judgmental perspective. Asper is listed in the *dramatis personae* as the "presenter," whatever that means. The play itself never makes the attribution, and on the basis of the induction there is very little to distinguish him from the author. Mitis calls it "his," Asper's play. Asper's declaration:

>   Ile prodigally spend my selfe,
> And speake away my spirit into ayre;
> . . .Ile melt my braine into invention,
> Coine new conceits, and hang my richest words
> As polisht jewels in their bountcous eares

and his command of literary theory make it appear that he wrote the play and wants only the name to be the stage representative of the real author. Indeed his whole bearing is one of authorial presence. We are led to believe that Asper will go off after the induction to play his role in the drama, leaving his two friends Mitis and Cordatus to maintain his interests with the audience. Furthermore, after those two continue at some length the discussion of dramatic theory and history, we assume that the play will operate on two planes, the stage action and the commentary supplied by Jonson as a buffer between stage and gallery.

But Jonson immediately complicates this arrangement. When the confusion over who will speak the prologue threatens to suspend indefinitely the play's beginning, Carlo Buffone, a character who otherwise has no life beyond the limits of the main stage action, steps up to offer his own prologue—as if

THE COMICAL SATIRES

he need pay no attention to any distinction between the world of the play and the world of its audience:

> Here's a cup of wine sparkles like a diamond.
> Gentlewomen (I am sworne to put them in first)
> and Gentlemen, a round, in place of a bad prologue,
> I drinke this good draught to your health here,
> Canarie, the very Elix'r and spirit of wine.
>   (Induction, 330-34)

The notion of toast as prologue charmingly undercuts Asper's self-righteous rant, and as Carlo continues he announces that he knows the *real* author and gives a speech that identifies the author as Ben Jonson or the Ben Jonson caricature that would have passed current with the knowledgeable portion of the theatergoing public:

> This is that our Poet calls Castalian liquor, when hee comes abroad (now and then) once in a fortnight, and makes a good meale among Players, where he has *Caninum appetitum*: mary, at home he keepes a good philosophicall diet, beanes and butter milke: an honest pure Rogue, hee will take you off three, foure, five of these, one after another, and looke vilanously when he has done, like a one-headed Cerberus (he do' not heare me I hope) and then (when his belly is well ballac't, and his braine rigg'd a little) he sailes away withall, as though he would worke wonders when he comes home.
>   (Induction, 334-45)

It is a funny moment, but a dizzying one as well. It leaves one perplexed over what to do about Asper and the elaborate fiction Jonson has made for him, because Asper's and Carlo's "authors" are not at all the same; in fact, it is the latter who suddenly appears to have the greater claim on reality. There is a fundamental problem about Jonson's investment in these two characters that the rest of the play never confronts.

To complicate things even further, Mitis and Cordatus treat Carlo as if he were a real man who is to impersonate himself in the play, but Cordatus scathes him with the description of his character that Jonson put into the *dramatis personae* along with the descriptions of Mitis and Cordatus. Thus, Carlo seems to exist in Jonson's world, though we know he does not, and that world seems the same as the world of Mitis and Cordatus, though at other times it does not, which means that Asper, Carlo, and Ben Jonson all seem to exist in the same plane of reality, though they do not.

The induction tramples the conventional boundaries between stage and audience, playfully but thoroughly, and once the play begins matters only get worse. One is never quite sure in the course of the action how to take Macilente and Carlo. As satiric commentators they present a great deal of the action to us, but they are also characters in the play who are objects of the satire. This would not necessarily be a problem, were it not that the induction stresses so heavily the need to establish one's judgmental bearings. Nothing in Asper's theorizing prepares us for Carlo, who is very funny as he lovingly exposes the fools to full view but is dismissed by the commentators Mitis and Cordatus as a "violent rayler."

Macilente is also complex, insofar as he bears the burden of moral outrage in the play while envy sullies his personal integrity. Theoretically, Macilente's situation is not as difficult as Carlo's, because the play takes as its aim cleansing Macilente and thereby purging moral outrage of self-interest in the satirist, a conventional satiric plot. What really complicates our response to Macilente, however, is Jonson's inconsistent treatment of the character. We sense him making fun of Macilente for the extremity of his response to the condition of the world, even though Asper's diatribe in the induction seems not simply to justify but even to require the most extreme response to the world. Indeed Macilente's own opening speech makes powerful claims on our sympathy:

> *Viri est, fortunae caecitatem facilè ferre.*
> Tis true; but Stoique, where (in the vast world)
> Doth that man breathe, that can so much command

> His bloud, and his affection? well: I see,
> I strive in vaine to cure my wounded soule;
> For every cordiall that my thoughts apply,
> Turnes to a cor'sive, and doth eate it farder.
> There is no taste in this Philosophie,
> Tis like a potion that a man should drinke,
> But turnes his stomacke with the sight of it.
> I am no such pild Cinique, to beleeve
> That beggery is the onely happiness;
> Or (with a number of these patient fooles)
> To sing: My minde to me a kingdome is,
> When the lanke hungrie belly barkes for foode.
>
> (I, i, 1-15)

This is hardly the foundation on which to base the subsequent ironic treatment of the character. Macilente's points seem reasonable, and the snarls at Cinique and Stoique carry a lot of force. They argue that this is a character who feels real human emotions, who has normal expectations of life, and whose envy and rage are appropriate to the circumstances. Again we have a problem with frame of reference in a play that cannot make up its mind about what it values.

Add to this confusion of perspective Mitis and Cordatus, whose commentary on the action is a peculiar mix of common sense distinctions, about such things as the length of scenes and aptness of characterization, and scholarly references to literary antecedents. The general idea seems to be to preempt a range of criticism that Jonson anticipated from his spectators, as a way of keeping them in line. We are not allowed to forget for long that there is a shield between stage and spectator that deflects criticism or turns it back on the critic. We accord Mitis and Cordatus some respect on the basis of their personal knowledge of the author and by virtue of their being more intelligent and judicious than any but the most sophisticated of the playhouse spectators. And it must be said that they do serve the function of educating the audience in the lore of dramatic convention. But they are also pests, period-

THE COMICAL SATIRES

ically dissipating whatever emotional energy builds up on stage and, therefore, interfering with our immediate participation in the play. If they help Jonson instruct his audiences, they do so at the expense of our delight.

Sorting from all of this some conclusions about Jonson's sense of satiric theater at this point in his career is not easy, but it seems clear that *Every Man Out* presents a conflict between the satirist as reformer and the satirist as entertainer. In spite of Asper's confidence in his own theoretical mixture of profit and pleasure, there is no real dramatic resolution to the conflict. The play leaves us feeling that for all the stress on moral outrage, Macilente's envy is an appropriate response to the world and, further, that what is most fun about satire is not the reformation of its spectators but the parasitic feeding on vice and foolishness. Carlo puts it best: ". . . now is that leane bald-rib Macilente, that salt villaine, plotting some mischievous device, and lyes a soking in their frothy humours like a drie crust, till he has drunke 'hem all up" (V, iv, 24-27). As for Carlo himself, he may be a "violent rayler," but he is also very funny, just the kind of satirist in whom Jonson will invest more and more of his imaginative energy as his career progresses. There is already too much of Jonson in Carlo to let us take seriously the criticism directed at him in the character sketch—or to feel that anything more than silliness is going on when Puntarvolo seals Carlo's lips with wax at the end of the play. Puntarvolo is too grand a fool to command any sympathy for the loss of his dog.

So the play settles almost nothing; it is funniest when Carlo and Macilente team up against the fools without regard for moral righteousness. Perhaps the best example of the play's tendency to close off dramatic resolution is the appearance of the queen in the original conclusion. Maternal authority simply bails out both Macilente and Jonson, projecting the conflict into the future of *Poetaster*. The terms of Macilente's self-proclaimed absolution are very interesting, however:

> Never till now did object greet mine eyes
> With any light content: but in her graces,

All my malicious powers have lost their stings.
Envie is fled my soule, at sight of her,
And shee hath chac'd all black thoughts from my bosome,
Like as the sunne doth darkenesse from the world.
My streame of humour is runne out of me.
And as our cities torrent (bent t'infect
The hallow'd bowels of the silver Thames)
Is checkt by strength, and clearnesse of the river,
Till it hath spent it selfe e'ene at the shore;
So, in the ample, and unmeasur'd floud
Of her perfections, are my passions drown'd.[3]

As many times as I have read this, it still astonishes me. Macilente describes his envy as sewage, human excrement, certainly a powerful metaphor and made even more so by its surprising proximity to the queen. As Edmund Wilson points out, Jonson's work routinely associates words, satire, and literary production with excrement,[4] but this particular instance is significant for more than just its sensationalism. It reveals another perspective problem: whereas within the play the "streame of humour" was directed at characters who deserved befouling, here Macilente describes the humor directed against the queen herself as a mixture of sexual and coprophilic aggression. She causes the "torrent," and but for her purity and strength, the torrent might "infect" her "hallow'd bowels." Instead this "passion" spends itself at the shore—a dribbed shot.

What are we to make of this? It makes no sense unless the queen is to be identified somehow with the other objects of Macilente's envy. Surprising as this might sound, it is exactly the case, and the plays that follow *Every Man Out* fill in the details. We are shown progressively that for Jonson satire was inextricable from personal motives like envy that sully the ideal selfless dedication to morality. In fact, envy is the perfect expression of this complex personal investment, because it unites the extremes of desire and aggression. The queen's involvement is this: as *Every Man Out* and *Cynthia's Revels* demonstrate, maternal authority can save the satirist from his nasty self, while also offering a kind of protection from the largely male objects of envy who, though felt by the satirist to be depraved and foolish, frequently are felt to be stronger. But the amalgamation of all those fools, the body politic (and the audience in the public theater), is characterized throughout Jonson's career as a female body. The queen governs the commonwealth, but in a sense she is the possession, the spouse of all those powerful males who make up the citizenry. Thus, at some level she is identified with her subjects in a relationship that the satirist stands outside of, and this is what makes sense of Macilente's implied aggression against her. Jonson's satirist wants it both ways. He wants the queen's recognition as the privileged insider, the premier subject for having exposed all the others as phonies, but he also wants to stand completely free of the whole system. *Every Man Out* reveals the strain but cannot relieve it.

This line of reasoning also makes sense of what I consider another of the play's oddities. Macilente takes a peculiar turn in act 3 when, having shed his rags, he appears decked out as a courtier, thanks to Deliro's beneficence. This guise immediately saps some of his force as a satirist because he is no longer an outsider, though Jonson could have countered this problem by having Macilente use his new position to exploit the fools in new ways, while making it clear that the clothes themselves are just a means to an end. But Macilente really likes his new clothes; he is pleased with himself and his new role to the extent that he fails to hear what Fastidius has to say to him:

> What's that he said? by heaven, I markt him not:
> My thoughts, and I, were of another world.
> I was admiring mine owne out-side here,
> To thinke what priviledge, and palme it beares
> Here, in the court!
>
> (III, ix, 6-10)

He recovers a bit and bemoans the superficiality of court politics, but it is clear that something in Macilente has changed.

Instead of using his advancement as satiric leverage, he does just the opposite; as Mitis points out, "This Macilente, signior, begins to bee more sociable on a suddaine, me thinkes, then hee was before" (IV, viii, 14-15). Thus, the play deals with Macilente's envy by moving him up the social ladder, a movement completed by the queen's appearance. This is neither a moral nor a conventionally satiric solution. It argues that what the satirist really wants is to be just one of the boys. A strange conclusion, but one that has a great deal to do with Jonson's sense of himself as a poet in relation to the issue of social position. Preferment at court can buy one out of the need to complain about the world one lives in, at least insofar as that need is a function of envy.

II

Jonson chose in his next play, *Cynthia's Revels*, to ignore the conflict at the heart of *Every Man Out*. Instead he continued to consolidate authority, both in terms of satiric theater and, by implication, in terms of the commonwealth of man that he imagined he was living in. To put it another way, he continued to cling to the ample skirts of a matronly monarch.

Crites's role in Gargaphie is the dramatic realization of the relationship between poet and monarch implied in Macilente's epiphany. Jonson moves from the maverick satirist to the pageant poet who serves the monarch and receives in return the royal authority which substantiates his satiric vision. The shift solves not only the authority problem of the stage satirist, but also Jonson's own problem of joining meaning with authority in the theater.

In comparison with *Every Man Out*, *Cynthia's Revels* may suffer as interesting drama, but in terms of Jonson's own artistic goals it is a far more subtle and sophisticated piece of work. Satire and satirist function efficiently as tools in the implementation of the utopian commonwealth. The Asper-Macilente-Carlo disparity has been resolved, and the taint of personality in Macilente's envy has been distilled in the royal presence.

Jonas Barish's characterization of *Cynthia's Revels* as "a great fossilized dinosaur of a play"⁵ suggests the futility of attempting scholarly resuscitation at this late date, but even if the play never breathes on its own again, a few more words should be said of its passing. First of all, *Cynthia's Revels* ought to be released from the rack of drama criticism. One of Jonson's gifts to the history of theater is the proof that theater is not necessarily drama and that our conventional expectations of plot, action, and character, though near and dear, are also limited. *Cynthia's Revels* is simply not a play in any usual sense; indeed it can be shown that Jonson's aims were clearly anti-dramatic and that he meant to restrict our customary modes of response to fiction, not because he was perverse or young or unwitting but because his interest was elsewhere.⁶ As theater, *Cynthia's Revels* bears a remarkable resemblance to Jonson's mature court masques, but in the playhouse there was no king to serve as the primary audience or to "realize" the meaning of the masque, and there were no courtiers to bridge the barrier between spectators and actors by taking roles in the production. Thus, differences in theater convention centering in the nature of the audience required a radical adjustment of the form. Jonson's aims, however, were identical: to make viable myths for his audience, affording them *matter* by using the stage to make assertions about the nature of the spectator. It is easy to talk about *Cynthia's Revels* in terms of meaning, far easier than it is to talk about *Hamlet* or *Bartholomew Fair*. Jonson's second comical satire is an allegory of self-love which demonstrates the destructiveness of narcissism for both the individual and the commonwealth. What is interesting and problematical about the play is the enactment of this meaning.

Given the nature of his intention, it seems reasonable to assume that Jonson saw plot, character, and action as tools of exposition, and to use them effectively he had to restrict the audience's tendency to value action above words, words above matter. His first attempt at defeating dramatic illusion is in the induction, with the three boy actors squabbling over the prologue. The presentation of actors outside the context of their immediate roles sharply curtails the illusion that their roles in the play are "realistic," and here Jonson takes particular advantage of the fact that these are the Children of Queen Elizabeth's Chapel. To quote George Parfitt:

> The induction is a thoroughly lively piece of work, both in dialogue and in stage business. One of its obvious functions is to present the child actors *as* child actors, and I think Jonson does this not so much defensively (as a way of covering himself in case the production seems inadequate) as to indicate relationships between the performers' youthfulness and the outlook of certain characters in the body of the play. Certainly he conveys a strong impression of childlike behavior from the very start, with the energetic jealous quarrel as to which boy shall speak the prologue: a gap opens up between the humorous and natural squabbling and the high spirits of the actors, and the, presumably, serious business of the play. This not only creates some tension as to whether the play will be properly peformed but it is also a hint that parodic effects may be part of what we are to see.[7]

While it is very difficult to imagine an audience familiar with the children experiencing doubts about their ability to act the play, it is certainly true that the induction impairs our sense of dramatic seriousness. And when one of the boys, as revenge for his loss of the prologue, reveals "most of the plot,"[8] we might note, before jumping to conclusions about Jonson's sanity, that *Cynthia's Revels* has no plot to reveal, at least in the conventional sense of the term. What the child gives away is the argument: "Ile goe tell all the argument of his play aforehand, and so stale his invention to the auditorie before it come forth" (Induction, 35-37). The term "argument" is not strictly synonymous with plot, and the result is not to "stale" the author's invention but to clarify a complex allegorical sequence.

Just before the play itself begins, the boys mime a couple of spectator types:

> Now, sir, suppose I am one of your gentile auditors, that am come in (having paid my monie at the doore, with much adoe) and here I take my place, and sit downe: I have my three sorts of tabacco in my pocket, my light by me, and thus I beginne. By this light, I wonder that any man is so mad, to come to see these rascally Tits play here—They doe act like so manie wrens, or pismires.
>
> (Induction, 116-22)

Another impersonates an understanding member of the auditory:

> It is in the generall behalfe of this faire societie here, that I am to speake, at least the more judicious part of it, which seems much distasted with the immodest and obscene writing of manie, in their playes. Besides, they could wish, your Poets would leave to bee promoters of other mens jests, and to way-lay all the stale apothegmes, or olde bookes, they can heare of (in print, or otherwise) to farce their Scenes withall.
>
> (Induction, 173-80)

This individual raises some very Jonsonian objections to the standard fare of the Elizabethan stage, hoping for some assurance that *Cynthia's Revels* will avoid such mean practice. But one of the other boys puts him off with the warning that he had better look to his own role as a spectator: "Good, sir, but what will you say now, if a Poet (untoucht with any breath of this disease) find the tokens upon you, that are of the auditorie?" (Induction, 199-201). The obvious justification of this performance is some fun at the expense of certain spectators and whatever it may have done to discourage the more disruptive of Jonson's spectators from fussing during the play.

More importantly, however, the sketch begins what is to be the process of the entire play, actors presenting stereotyped characters while other stage actors comment on them. The process of the induction parallels the process of the play, and the analogy complicates any simple response to the subsequent stage action.

The mechanisms by which Jonson comments on stage action are far more sophisticated in *Cynthia's Revels* than in *Every Man Out*. One of the reasons Mitis and Cordatus frequently are perceived as pests is that they are offered as "spectators"; they have no part in the play proper, and their commentary, while it reflects the response of a certain kind of spectator, seems idiosyncratic, random, and disjointed across the span of the entire play. In a sense, Jonson recast Mitis and Cordatus as Mercury and Cupid, and the latter emerge as a measure of Jonson's progress from one play to the next. Cupid and Mercury act in the play, and they are the basis of the mythological perspective which encases the dramatic action and accents its abstract, allegorical nature. They carry the bantering of the children from the induction into the first act by lampooning each other. Jonson is making the best of the quick-witted and verbally polished children, but he is also revealing here a great deal of mythological background. The first two scenes of the play, the meeting of Cupid and Mercury and the Echo episode, lend scope and vitality to thematic development which might otherwise have been insufferable. Here is mythology for the masses. As the play continues, Mercury and Cupid acquire a number of roles: shortly after the children describe the two gods in the induction, two of the children appear as Cupid and Mercury who then disguise themselves as court pages. Eventually Mercury impersonates a French monsieur to face Amorphous in the courtly duel, and Cupid performs the first masque as Anteros. All of this is accomplished with our knowledge, and it soon becomes clear that in this play self-knowledge is tied to dramatic perspective much more clearly and consistently than it was in *Every Man Out*. With Mercury, Cupid, and Crites all under cover as authorial moles, comment on the action is easy for Jonson. Nearly every scene offers the double perspective of character and commentator, whether in the form of set pieces or asides. While it is certainly true that Jonson declined, by and large, the challenge of allowing his characters to reveal themselves, this is no cause for criticism. What was important to Jonson was efficient, persistent exposition of type characters within the context of a sophisticated allegory.

Jonson's vision might have been unusual, but it was by no means shallow. *Cynthia's Revels* is tremendously successful in its own terms, terms which Jonson made every effort to spell out. This play is a much grander effort than its predecessor, primarily because it envisions a commonwealth based on classical heroic virtue as embodied in a monarch and articulated in the theater. The vision of theater is especially grand, combining the formal mythic processes of the masque with satiric power to expose and eliminate subversive influences. Explaining to Crites why the fools in the play must be made to perform in the revels, Arete frames the social theory which united masque and satire in the playhouse:

> For (in troth) not so
> T'incorporate them, could be nothing else,
> Then like a state ungovern'd, without lawes;
> Or body made of nothing but diseases:
> The one, through impotency poore, and wretched,
> The other, for the anarchie absurd.
> (V, v, 28-33)

Heroic theater transforms its spectators by calling on them to enact their own best selves, thereby transforming themselves into virtuous members of the commonwealth. This is an amazing vision of theater as a *real* social force, and *Cynthia's Revels* is Jonson's attempt to translate the vision into theatrical practice.

This play is the true child of *Every Man Out*, advancing significantly Jonson's concept of satiric theater. But the implications for the satirist himself are not entirely happy. Satire lives on the energy generated in the violent collision of social authority and the individual satiric consciousness. Cynthia's smothering goodness dissipates this energy, freezing Asper's fury at the moment of unmasking. The shift to satirist as pageant poet is accomplished at a high cost to our laughter and our sense of excitement in the theater. It leaves the satirist only a repeated drama of self-effacement. Instead of defining himself, as Juvenal did, by kicking against that vile and irreducible portion of human nature, Jonson's satirist grows fat at the feet of Cynthia, like a dog.

III

Jonson paid for the formal success of *Cynthia's Revels* by foregoing a great deal of aggressiveness; yet, considering his nature, one might suspect that such continence would be short-lived. Indeed his very next play, *Poetaster*, begins to reveal the strain. *Poetaster* is commonly treated as a rerun of *Cynthia's Revels* for which Jonson graciously changed the names, Horace for Crites, Augustus for Cynthia. This accusation cuts two ways, toward the fact that *Poetaster* repeats a good deal of its predecessor's form without appreciably developing it and toward the conclusion that the play is not successful, even in its own terms. Jonson himself seems uncharacteristically dismissive toward his work in both the prologue and the Apologetical Dialogue, revealing that the play was a hurried attempt to preempt an enemy counterattack in the Stage Quarrel. Yet, in the context of Jonson's entire career, *Poetaster* offers more than a blurred retake of an earlier work. This play takes Jonson's drama from the relative tranquility of the comical satires, dominated by virtuous monarchs and happy endings, to the violent and vicious worlds of *Sejanus* and *Volpone*. Jonson soured on Gargaphie because that snug little world was also stifling. It denied the satirist the artistic and psychological complexity that Jonson was finding in himself, whereas *Poetaster* and the plays that follow present progressively more sophisticated means of dealing with such complexity. At some basic level, *Poetaster* runs out of control, but, like most work which escapes the conscious control of its author, it is interesting for what it reveals about personal conflict.

Thirty years ago Ernest Talbert argued that *Poetaster* was intended as Jonson's *ars poetica*, a debate on the nature of true poetry.[9] Talbert took the unusual position that Jonson treats Publius Ovid with sympathy to make a point about the danger posed to poetry and to the commonwealth by "politick spies" like Lupus. Although critics generally have taken Ovid as another of Jonson's satiric objects, I think Talbert is right. But the point is not simply that Lupus misleads Augustus and thereby demonstrates the social threat of the self-interested and ignorant spy. More significant is Caesar's refusal to consider Ovid's offense in the mitigating context offered by Horace. The emperor's pious decree seems bizarre alongside Ovid's wit and intensity and Horace's avuncular willingness to accommodate the young poet's indiscretion. Caesar comes off badly, if only for a moment. Horace supports the emperor but does not share his judgment, and, on the basis of what we see in the first four acts of the play, it is difficult to disagree with Horace. Until Augustus storms on stage in act 4, scene 6 and "offers to kill his daughter," the play has shunned questions of morality, preferring questions of foolishness and practicality. Although Caesar's ranting is easily justified in abstract terms, it seems inappropriate to the play itself, and Talbert's point about Lupus will not bear the weight of four acts.

Though Jonson never faces the problem squarely, it is clear that he has begun to sever the symbiotic bond between monarch and satirist that he had labored to establish in the two previous plays. *Sejanus* develops the split, finally opposing imaginative energy and theatrical power to moral authority and social order. Through Crites and Horace we sense that the commitment required of a satirist to his audience can be stifling, even if a portion of that audience is sober, majestic, and judicious, all of the qualities which Jonson publicly exhorted. Jonson invested a great deal of himself in Publius Ovid, not in spite of but because of that character's licentiousness, literally his freedom from moral restraint. Yet, in subtle ways, both *Poetaster* and *Sejanus* suggest that the freedom had to be bought at a considerable psychological price to their author. Volpone is a remarkable amalgam of Ovid and Horace, made possible only by the divorce of satirist and monarch and accomplished, or at least reflected, in the conflicts which Jonson played out in his earlier work.

As Robert Jones points out, by the time we reach Horace in the progression of comical satires, the Jonsonian satirist is a mere shadow of his former self.[10] The real creative energy in *Poetaster* lies with Ovid. There is a poignance in the relationship between Horace and Jonson that softens what many critics take to be an outrageous personal projection. We see a Horace who is exhausted, unsure of his social position, and, above all, restive. In the Trebatian dialogue, Horace reveals a very strange relationship to his work: his writing fills the hours of nights he cannot sleep, and he speaks of the public response to his work as if he can neither understand nor tolerate it:

> There are, to whom I seeme excessive sower;
> And past a satyres law, t'extend my power:
> Others, that thinke what ever I have writ
> Wants pith, and matter to enternise it;
> And that they could, in one daies light, disclose
> A thousand verses, such as I compose.
> What shall I doe, Trebatius? say.
>
> (III, v, 1-7)

What comes of this talk with Trebatius is the sense that satire is Horace's idiosyncratic means of dealing with the impulse to create. It is the only means available to him, and, for this reason, it is as much a trap as it is a means of self-expression.

The original Horatian satire is a very elusive piece of work, because the question of the relationship between the poet

Horace and the persona he fashioned for the satire is a complex one. We come away from this poem feeling that the character who reveals himself to Trebatius speaks for the poet, but that the poet stands behind his mask with a far more sophisticated sense of things. What Horace says about the satirist and his relationship to his audience is true, but the pitiable self-revelation and the enthusiasm he shows for Trebatius' suggestion that he abandon his work is a bit of a joke: "Peream male, si non optimum erat; verum nequo dormire."[11] This is a brilliant stroke: a distinguished poet opens his second volume of satire with the confession that he writes to cure his insomnia. Jonson accomplishes the same effect in the opening lines of *The Forest*, his own second volume of poetry:

> Why I Write Not of Love
>
> Some act of Love's bound to reherse,
> I thought to binde him, in my verse:
> Which when he felt, Away (quoth hee)
> Can Poets hope to fetter mee?
> It is enough, they once did get
> Mars, and my Mother, in their net:
> I weare not these my wings in vaine.
> With which he fled me: and againe,
> Into my ri'mes could ne're be got
> By any arte. Then wonder not,
> That since, my numbers are so cold
> When Love is fled, and I grow old.[12]

Jonson asks us to believe that he is tapped out, and yet if we continue through the book we encounter some of his finest love poetry. Beneath the jesting, *The Forest*, like Horace's satire, is never far from the crucial question of what it is to be a poet, what it is to mediate between the demands of one's audience and the demands of one's own psyche.

Horace is fascinating for his ability to examine such intensely personal problems from a distance, using the dramatic mode to pick them apart with amusement. He opens the dialogue with Trebatius by making himself a passive object of others' interest:

> Sunt quibis in satura videar nimis acer et ultra
> legem tendere opus; sine nervis altera, quidquid
> composui, pars esse putat similisque meorum
> mille die versus deduci posse. Trebati,
> quid faciam, praescribe.[13]

Sunt, "they are," but *videar*, "I seem, I am seen." Moreover, Horace poses his problem to his friend with no trace of personal response to this state of affairs. The point is that Horace the satirist has full control of a sophisticated set of responses, whereas Jonson, using Horace, does not. In *Poetaster*, Horace's satire all of a sudden acquires a context which robs it of its subtlety. The Horace of Jonson's play is a far cry from his historical namesake and even from a Jonsonian satirist like Asper, whose intense commitment to his work, if not reflected in subtlety, is reflected in passion. Perhaps Jonson meant the late addition of Horace's poem to compensate for his own Horace's lack of energy in the play, but what emerges is a kind of tragic figure, not a figure of immense wit and sophistication. Jonson's Horace *has* to write, satire is his innate mode of expression, and the fact that he has any audience at all, much less that he would offend them, seems a terrible accident. The commitment to satire which he reveals in the final seventy lines is very peculiar: he wishes evidently to write satire, "his stile," for himself, and only if attacked will he retaliate. What kind of satire is this? Presented in a context which drains away all of its original wit, the poem presents the satiric impulse as a handicap, a neurosis of some sort—a social phenomenon only by accident or by the perverse intrusion of the public on an essentially private event:

> My pleasure is in feet, my words to close,
> As, both our better, old Lucilius does:
> He, as his trustie friends, his bookes did trust

> With all his secrets; nor, in things, unjust,
> Or actions lawful, ran to other men:
> So, that the old mans life, describ'd was seene
> As in a votive table in his lines;
> And to his steps my Genius inclines.
>   (III, v, 49-56)

The identification of Jonson with Horace is a natural one, but the original version of *Poetaster*, minus the scene with Trebatius, is much less Horace's play than Ovid's. His scene with the bore Crispinus notwithstanding, Horace is largely peripheral until the conclusion of the play, whereas there is good reason to associate Ovid with the author of *Poetaster* from the start. It is striking that Ovid opens the play composing his elegy to Envie when Envie has just appeared in the prologue as a threat to the entire business of "The Arraignment." And the position that Ovid and the prologue take up against Envie is remarkably similar to that in which the "Author" finds himself in the Apologetical Dialogue. The addition to act 3 complicates things even more because what Horace works through with Trebatius as his straight man is similar in many ways to what Ovid works through in his poem. Ovid is pinched by the suggestion that his quill is "idle" and that his neglect of martial experience is unmanly. He answers that he seeks immortality, and to Envie's quotidian concerns he opposes a litany of poetic authority:

> Homer will live, whil'st Tenedos stands, and Ide,
> Or, to the sea, fleet Simois doth slide:
> And so shall Hesiod too, while vines doe beare,
> Or crooke sickles crop the ripened eare.
> Callimachus, though in invention lowe,
> Shall still be sung: since he in art doth flowe.
> No losse shall come to Sophocles proud vaine.
>   (I, i, 51-57)

Horace also talks of escape from the mundane, resolving to serve his genius in spite of public resistance just as Ovid serves immortality, and Horace carefully places himself in the line of revered Lucilius.

No fewer than four figures who can be associated with Jonson himself complain of hostile audiences: the prologue, Ovid, Horace, and the Author of the Apologetical Dialogue. Two of these, the prologue and Ovid, define this audience response as envy. Envy is one of Jonson's favorite cudgels, always close at hand when he berates his spectators. And no wonder—the accusation of envy is a doubly self-serving act. It is not a simple accusation but one that implicitly assumes that the accuser and the accused share the same values. The envious spectator no longer just dislikes a play; rather, he likes it so much that he envies the author, manifesting the malice born of covetousness. Furthermore, such a spectator can be charged with imposture for dissembling his true feeling. What Jonson creates, finally, is an image of the spectator protected by a multilayered shield of self-flattery.

Poetaster, then, makes some peculiar bedfellows in the matter of artistic authority. Horace and Ovid seem to share Jonson's own feelings about the gloomy multitude, but Ovid is brought into direct conflict with Caesar, to whom Horace makes his greatest commitment. Horace is caught uncomfortably between Ovid and Augustus on several scores, but we are asked to confront the conflict only once, at the moment in act 4, scene 6 when Horace and Mecoenas plead for the young poet. One scene later Horace explains himself to Lupus:

> Was this the treason? this, the dangerous plot,
> Thy clamorous tongue so bellow'd through the court?
> Hadst thou no other project to encrease
> Thy grace with Caesar, but this wolvish traine;
> To prey upon the life of innocent mirth,
> And harmelesse pleasures, bred, of noble wit?
> (IV, vii, 37-42)

Though Jonson keeps the issue away from the center of the play, it is clear that Horace is strung between his allegiance to Caesar and his commitment to the kind of poetry Ovid represents, torn in a way that Crites never is and Asper is only incipiently. In *Cynthia's Revels*, there is no discrepancy between the satirist's public and private commitments: the things owed to Caesar and the things owed to one's own muse are the same. *Poetaster*, however, identifies and develops just such a discrepancy. It starts when Jonson identifies his interests with Ovid at the outset of the play. Campbell, Waith, and Parfitt all caution that while Jonson appears sympathetic, or at least "ambiguous,"[14] toward the poet in the early acts, we ought not be misled: Ovid is nonetheless Jonson's archetypal profligate poet. The play, however, does not confirm this response to Ovid. Our introduction to the play is through the eyes of Envie:

> Nor would I, you should looke for other lookes,
> Gesture, or complement from me, then what
> Th'infected bulke of Envie can afford:
> For I am risse here with a covetous hope,
> To blast your pleasures, and destroy your sports,
> With wrestings, comments, applications,
> Spie-like suggestions, privie whisperings.
>
> (Induction, 19-25)

The prologue, with whom Jonson's interests are clearly identified, treads Envie under foot: "So spight should die,/Despis'd and scorn'd by noble industrie." The elegy Ovid composes and reads in the opening scene addresses itself immediately to the question of "noble industrie." Moreover, Envie's outstanding feature is her snake collection:

> Here will be the subject for my snakes, and me.
> Cling to my necke, and wrists, my loving wormes,
> And cast you round, in soft and amourous foulds,
> Till I doe bid, uncurle: Then, breake your knots,
> Shoot out your selves at length, as you forc't stings
> Would hide themselves within his malic't sides,
> To whom I shall apply you.
>
> (Induction, 5-11)

THE COMICAL SATIRES

The elegy picks up on this iconographic theme, "Envie, the living, not the dead, doth bite," and Horace repeats it in his dialogue with Trebatius:

> Yet, envy (spight of her empoisoned brest)
> Shall say, I liv'd in grace here, with the best;
> And, seeking in weake trash to make her wound,
> Shall find me solid, and her teeth unsound.
>
> (III, v, 119-22)

There is nothing here, or anywhere else in Jonson's work, to substantiate the idea that he took Ovid for a moral reprobate. Moreover, there is a good deal in this play to suggest the opposite. Ovid is the hero of the play for the first four acts—even more so if we exclude Horace's scene with Trebatius. He carries the reputation of a respected poet and an emerging master, and he enjoys the company of other substantial poets, such as Propertius and Horace himself. His defense of poetry is extremely Jonsonian, as is his perception of his audience. Beyond this, however, Jonson presents Ovid to us with no sign of the satiric framing necessary to cast him in an ironic light. I think it is accurate to say that until *Bartholomew Fair* Jonson never presents a satiric object without some commentary from another character to confirm the "humor." In *Cynthia's Revels*, for instance, Jonson is cautious about exposing Amorphous. He allows him to introduce himself in the scene with Echo but follows this immediately with a scene in which Crites leaves nothing in doubt. We meet Ovid, however, through his poetry, not through satiric asides, and the scene with his father only confirms the son's point of view. Ovid Senior reveals himself as a fool, particularly when he takes on Homer:

> Name me a profest poet, that his poetrie did ever afford him so much as a competencie. I, your god of poets there (whom all of you admire and reverence so much) Homer, he whose worme-eaten statue must not bee spewd against, but with hallowed lips, and groveling adoration, what was he? what was he?
>
> (I, ii, 78-83)

THE COMICAL SATIRES

The father drops out of the play early, but the authority he represents seems to get shunted off onto Caesar. The emperor cherishes certain kinds of poetry, but he shares with Ovid Senior the role of a repressive parent concerned to see that his child makes good. Ovid Senior may be a fool, but his impulse is the same as Caesar's: a man's work is valuable only insofar as it contributes in certain conventional ways to the commonwealth. In the end, Ovid Senior's misapprehension of Homer is no more foolish than Caesar's perception of Ovid Junior.

Vice is not a problem in *Poetaster* until Augustus makes it one. Things move easily until Caesar arrives; Ovid and Propertius, presented as talented and serious poets, mix freely with silly people like Crispinus, Chloe, and Albinus. So does Horace, unlike his prickly predecessor, Crites. His torture at the hands of Crispinus is farce, not really sustained satire, and it confirms in Horace a real vulnerability, born of gregariousness, to pests. All of a sudden, at the end of act 4, authority overreacts, and the play seems to change direction, heading for the kind of conclusion offered by *Every Man Out* and *Cynthia's Revels*, vastly different plays. Caesar takes the play over, introducing moral and social concerns which the play has not taken seriously to this point.

By virtue of his willingness to take issue with Caesar's judgment, however briefly, Horace sets himself up as the authority of the play, balancing the mutually exclusive worlds of Ovid and Augustus. The situation is far more subtle than a matter of opinion about the propriety of Ovid's masque. Horace's response opens up a new dramatic perspective. Within the play itself, Ovid and Augustus are locked in a clash of values, but Horace offers a context which resolves the problem, and, therefore, he steps momentarily outside the action of the play. His choice to support Caesar quickly reestablishes our sense of order, but it is clear that Horace has preempted Caesar's theatrical authority; that is, he has changed our relationship to the play by subverting the emperor. For Macilente and Asper such a measure was unthinkable. The concluding Act of *Poetaster* seems plodding not just because it is Jonson retreading *Every Man Out* and *Cynthia's Revels* but because Ovid has let a breath of fresh air into this little satiric pageant. Perhaps, like Mercutio, he pays a heavy price because he represents a force which threatens the essential nature of socially reconstructive drama.

This is not to say that all is well with Ovid. He has struck many as childish for his acceptance of the fools of the play and for his gushing over Julia:

> How! subscrib'd Julia! O, my life, my heaven!
> . . . .
> Musique of wit! Note for th' harmonious spheares!
> Celestiall accents, how you ravish me!
> (I, iii, 20, 22-23)

Clearly these lines cannot be taken seriously, although knowing that Ben Jonson wrote them seems to prejudice the case. It strikes me, however, as overwritten romance, not weak satire. Unlikely as it may seem, Jonson's commitment to Ovid in *Poetaster* is almost as if he had attempted a romance that failed him after four acts. From another point of view, the play is an early *Epicene* that never got off the ground; Ovid's irreverent wit and charm veer off into mush instead of into ways of exposing and subverting the authority which threatens them. If the play is a failure, perhaps it is because the external pressures of the Stage Quarrel stalled development of Jonson's artistic interests, or because he was not yet ready to write *Epicene* or *Volpone*. He could not yet face the implications of that kind of drama in terms of the authority on which he relied to accomplish his satiric vision, authority which he articulates in both Cynthia and Augustus. In *Poetaster*, the majestic vision begins to unravel as the monarch is shown to be myopic and harsh. At the same time, Jonson suggests that Horace is confused, torn between allegiance to his prince and to the private impulses which are unquestionably related to Ovid and his drive to throw off social restraint and indulge his imagination. Ovid is at once silly and, as Horace affirms in his final support of Caesar, a threat to the social values underpinning a commitment to satire. The split continues in *Sejanus* as Jonson invests heavily in both the primal, amoral struggle between Tiberius and Sejanus and the moral values represented by the Germanicans. It was not until he created Volpone that Jonson finally set the rigid authority patterns of the comical satires safely in his past.

TWO

Sejanus: The People's Beastly Rage

PERHAPS the most troubling of Jonson's plays is *Sejanus*. It is generally felt to be powerful and intriguing, but there is very little agreement about why it is powerful or, finally, what it means. Readers have found this play to be far clearer in terms of its author's presumed intentions than in terms of their own actual experience. Jonas Barish, for instance, offers this comment at the end of his introduction to the Yale edition of the play:

> Sejanus faces, as tragedy must, the worst potentialities of human nature, and by realizing them dramatically, acts to inhibit their further actualization in reality. It exploits the evil in the world so as to promote the good in its audiences.[1]

As an inference of Jonson's conscious intent this statement seems to me impeccable, but as an analysis of the play it cannot answer the charge of confusion brought by Barish himself earlier in the essay:

> *Sejanus* tries to argue us simultaneously into a belief that we are free, which we see not to be the case, and that the gods are near, which we see equally to be not the case. Jonson's personages believe themselves free, act as though free, accept responsibility for their acts, yet all the while are being ground to pieces in an engine not of their own making.[2]

In other words, there is a discrepancy between intended meaning and dramatic action, a confusion of dramatic perspective. Arthur Marotti concurs in this judgment, quoting Robert Ornstein's response to the play:

"As it is, it is neither a tragedy of civic decadence nor one of insatiable ambition. We are not allowed to pity and we are not moved to fear. Because Jonson does not clarify his tragic theme, the smoldering intensity of emotion that lies beneath the surface of *Sejanus* never bursts into flame." The question of unrealized intensity suggests that there is something wrong with Sejanus' audience-play dynamics, that Jonson failed or refused to create those emotional-intellectual effects which culminate in tragic catharsis.[3]

I think he failed because at the level of subconscious intent he refused; he simply could not give the play over to his audience.

In fact, *Sejanus* explains a great deal about Jonson's psychological investment in his work and about how that investment produced a tumultuous relationship between stage and gallery in the playhouse. At this point in his career, Jonson was beginning to feel the conflict generated by his determination to succeed both as a poet in the classical tradition, committed to learning, virtue, and commonwealth, and as a popular playwright entertaining a diverse audience. His theorizing about his work takes up this dichotomy, usually in terms of the Horatian prescription, *utile, dulci*, but any lasting and productive resolution was threatened from two directions: he found the role of poet, as he had idealized it, stifling and his playhouse audience revealed itself as a beastly group.

It is in *Sejanus* that Jonson admits publicly to the stress of the conflict and finally abandons his theatrical utopianism. Instead of moving toward a theatrical resolution that includes the spectators in the final vision of social harmony, as the earlier plays had done, *Sejanus* keeps its audience at a distance. Moreover, it self-consciously examines the assumptions that inform the early plays and the ways those assumptions determine the relationship between a playwright and his public. In *Poetaster*, Jonson treats with sympathy the pleasures that elsewhere in his work are shown to threaten social harmony and utility, and we are forced to consider several serious questions: to what extent are the utopias of Cynthia and Augustus confining? what are the real risks to the commonwealth of self-indulgence, particularly as it tends to sexual license? are those risks worth taking in the name of freedom and self-expression, or should one's social role be the sole source of pleasure? The issues have been joined, social responsibility versus self-indulgence, freedom versus license. Caught in the middle is the poet who, all of a sudden unsure of his alliances, faces the problem of establishing an audience and dealing with meanings that will not come clear anymore.

These are serious artistic issues for a playwright committed to socially significant drama, but in Jonson's case the issues are also intensely personal. The conflicts in the plays mirror his relationship with his audience, and the fact that, on one hand, the plays deal with the conflict more subtly and fully after *Sejanus* and, on the other hand, Jonson's approach to his spectators seems significantly more controlled after 1605 suggests that he was coming to terms with his extraordinary reserves of aggressive energy. Moreover, he was beginning to sort out the tangle of relationships intrinsic to the role of commercial playwright. The middle term in the relationship between Jonson and his audience, the currency of their interpersonal transactions, is theatrical meaning. Jonson wished to supply his spectators with ethical and moral meaning, and he took as the measure of his success their willingness to enact it in their lives.

The comical satires deal, for the most part, in clear, palpable meaning in harmony with all the other factors that determine the nature of theatrical experience; in other words, meaning and dramatic action are indistinguishable. As one might expect, however, when Jonson began to question the kinds of authority on which he had come to rely, the relationship between meaning and dramatic action became far more complex. *Sejanus* complicates response; the action of the play repeatedly denies the moral and ethical propositions that it apparently wishes to affirm rhetorically. We may be thrilled by the magnificence of Tiberius' absolute theatrical skill or comforted by the essential goodness of the Germanicans and their ability to perceive the working of evil—but either way Jonson slaps our wrists. The Germanicans are impotent and Tiberius is degenerate. In short, this is a terribly bleak play, not simply because it deals with human depravity but also because it manipulates its audience in uncomfortable ways, exciting responses in order to reject them and soliciting judgments that go unsupported by the dramatic action. It is in this sense that the play can be said to reject its audience.

Thus, *Sejanus* is a play about self-interested theater which itself becomes such a theater, casting its audience as "victims" in much the same way that first the Germanicans and then Sejanus become victims of a drama ultimately directed by Tiberius. This analogy suggests the identification of Tiberius with Jonson, although this seems improbable at first since Jonson surely understood Tiberius' depravity and meant to hold him up to us as a negative example. Yet, this is exactly the direction in which the play pushes us. Tiberius is the master of manipulated appearance, the quintessential dramatic satirist, providing his characters the means of revealing their foolish and grasping natures, even putting the words in their mouths, before sweeping them from the stage. And in terms of Jonson's changing sense of theater, the identification is not at all farfetched. I suspect that this change was in part the result of Jonson's recognition of the hostile and sexually aggressive side of satire and his acceptance for its own sake of the pleasure to be had in controlling and exposing his audience through his satire. In this sense, his decision to write plays like *Volpone, Epicene, The Alchemist,* and *Bartholomew Fair*, plays which do not deny the untoward aspect of satire as *Cynthia's Revels* does, represents Jonson's retirement into a kind of artistic perversity, his own island resort to match Tiberius' Capreae.

But it is the process of the play itself that offers us the best evidence of these connections. The struggle among Tiberius, Sejanus, and the Germanicans for the authority to establish as dramatic fact their individual perspectives is certainly significant in moral and ethical terms, but it also determines the way the play deals with its audience. The Germanicans provide the perspective that constitutes our means of moral valuation, functioning exactly like the satiric commentators of the comical satires. They are the conscience of the play, but a conscience without authority, because Jonson has cut them off from the social authority that would give their judgment the force of law. Seeing things clearly as they are but unwilling to do anything about the situation, they feel a complicity with the agents of evil. Their rhetorical nihilism, their sense that language has ceased to express truth and virtue in Rome, provides the play's central perspective. All but six of the nearly six hundred lines spoken in act 1 are delivered in the presence of the Germanicans and are, therefore, subject to their judgment. Silius, Sabinus, and Arruntius hold the stage until Sejanus' soliloquy which concludes act 1, and they serve as a primary audience for the stage action, explicating it for all of us in the "theater" audience and providing a dramatic framework which gives the action meaning.

Soon after his initial appearance, Titius Sabinus makes the following assertion about himself and his Germanican associates: "We are no guilty men, and then no great" (I, 12). The association of guilt with greatness expresses what Sabinus feels to be a fundamental truth about Roman society, and this is only one of several social and ethical propositions underpinning the first Germanican lament. Sabinus also claims that height and power in this world are to be had through slavery, "that proud height, to which/We did by slaverie, not by service, clime" (I, 10-11). By implication, then, freedom in Rome is impotence. What is common among these assertions is that they represent the startling recombination of social and ethical qualities which have been divorced from their familiar associations. Where in some ideal world greatness might be expected to accompany goodness, and guilt to be reflected in lowness, in Tiberian Rome these pairings have been broken and the elements reshuffled. This process of dismembering the social and ethical propositions by which a good society constitutes itself, and rejoining the fragments into propositions which describe the antithesis of any utopia, is the business of *Sejanus*. The characters continually provide assertions about the social fabric of their world which the dramatic process of the play then tests.

When Silius and Sabinus have finished their appalling depiction of Roman society, Arruntius supplies the historical perspective which makes their judgments meaningful:

> The men are not the same: 'tis we are base,
> Poore, and degenerate from th'exalted streine
> Of our great fathers. Where is now the soule
> Of god-like Cato? he, that durst be good,
> When Caesar durst be evill; and had power
> As not to live his slave, to dye his master.
> Or where the constant Brutus, that (being proofe
> Against all charme of benefits) did strike
> So brave a blow into the monsters heart
> That sought unkindly to captive his countrie?
> O, they are fled the light. Those mightie spirits
> Lye rak'd up, with their ashes, in their urnes,
> And not a sparke of their eternall fire
> Glowes in a present bosome.
>
> (I, 87-100)

The world of Cato, Cassius, and Brutus is a world where goodness and good men have power and can, therefore, effect virtuous action. The Germanicans have their own version of the Edenic myth: mankind has passed, evidently, from its prelapsarian ignorance of evil; through a postlapsarian, pre-Imperial state where active virtue and active evil maintain a precarious balance; and, finally, since the solidification of the empire, to an age in which goodness has been shackled. Silius describes the etiology of the social disease as a kind of vicious self-dissipation:

> Well, all is worthy of us, were it more,
> Who with our ryots, pride, and civil hate,
> Have so provok'd the justice of the gods.
> We, that (within these fourescore yeeres) were borne
> Free, equall lords of the triumphed world,
> And knew no masters, but affections,
> To which betraying first our liberties,
> We since became the slaves to one mans lusts;
> And now to many.
>
> (I, 56-64)

He insists that virtue has been subdued not by the frontal attack of the forces of evil but by treason, by the betrayal of the spirit to the passions. Julius Caesar, Augustus, and Tiberius, far from usurping power, took only what was offered them by free men. This amounts to an intriguing theory of Roman history—history as psychomachia, in which the fate of a society is only the mirror of the struggles within individual men.

Sejanus' first appearance permits the Germanicans to discover to us the nature of Tiberius' minion, his history, his ambitions, and the extent of his influence. When he reappears with Eudemus, shortly thereafter, he unwittingly supplies the proof of their assertions:

> The coarsest act
> Done to my service, I can so requite,
> As all the world shall stile it honorable:
> "Your idle, vertuous definitions
> "Keepe honor poore, and are as scorn'd as vaine:
> "Those deeds breathe honor, that do sucke in gaine.
>
> (I, 327-32)

We watch as Sejanus creates the courtier role which Sabinus had written for him at the opening of act 1. We see him in the act of perverting learning and medical art, values we understand as crucial to a good and healthy society, to voyeurism and pandering. Love, for Sejanus, is a political tool, and service, for Eudemus, is criminal complicity. The following scene between Sejanus and Tiberius continues to substantiate Germanican accusations. Cordus and Arruntius reveal the sophisticated mechanism of flattery which Sejanus and the emperor play out. In his first great speech, Tiberius offers convincing evidence of his rhetorical and theatrical gifts, his power over words and appearances which gives him power over men. He begins by verbally prostrating himself to the will of the Senate, and then, armed with his new-bought humility, he methodically controverts their wishes whenever he pleases. The Germanican audience makes certain that we miss none of the chicanery. When Tiberius leaves the stage, Sabinus, Silius, and Arruntius have been vindicated entirely by the dramatic content of the opening act.

When Drusus challenges Sejanus at the end of the act, however, Sejanus takes control of the play. Drusus proves himself an astute critic with a clear understanding of Sejanus' ambition:

> Is my father mad?
> Wearie of life, and rule, lords? thus to heave
> An idoll up with praise! make him his mate!
> His rivall in the empire!
>
> (I, 548-51)

His braving Sejanus in public is a great moment for Arruntius and the rest: their judgment of the civil plight of Rome has been substantiated, and Drusus' vision and courage promise to meet their high expectations. But Sejanus has the last word. Like Shakespeare's Richard III or Webster's Bosola, he steps up, when the others have gone, to speak a soliloquy which asserts his control over the plot of the play; in fact, he revises in this moment our entire relationship to the play. Up to this point we have experienced all of the dramatic action through the mediating vision of the Germanicans. When they leave the stage, they relinquish this theatrical authority for good.

Sejanus takes over, and as he does the dramatic authority passes from those who use theatricality to display the truth to those who use it to conceal the truth by making their own self-serving dramas. The Germanicans continue in their role, but because they have been surrounded by a new frame of reference supplied by Sejanus and his spies, because they have become his unwitting victims, they are pathetic.

It is difficult to overestimate the importance of this moment in the context of Jonson's entire career: the passing of the Germanicans is a failure of Jonson's satiric voice, at least as a tool of social reconstitution. Gone are the hopes invested in the comical satires—Jonson has chosen to abandon an entire approach to the theater and to expend his energy exploring the human impulse to control the world through self-interested theater. From this point on, the relationship between satire and social value is painfully strained. In *Sejanus*, the Germanicans never regain theatrical authority. In their sole appearance in the second act, Silius makes the connection between Drusus' death and his confronting Sejanus in the street, but we already have the information first-hand, and we also know that plans for action against Silius and Sabinus already have been drafted. Thus, the force of their satire has been crippled beyond repair.

As Sejanus takes power from the Germanicans, so Tiberius eventually takes it from Sejanus. The real emotional and theatrical heart of the play lies in the relationship between these two. The others become, finally, only fodder in the death struggle between emperor and minion. It is theatrical skill which is the means of power in this struggle. The prize is Rome and, perhaps even more important, the triumph of self-possession and the freedom from the theatrical coercion of others. To "take power from" has double meaning in this play: it refers, first, to taking control from another and, second, to the fact that once authority has shifted, the victim serves as a source of power for the victor, acting as a character in a drama which confirms the victor's sense of himself. To lose the struggle is to forfeit social and political self-determination and to face the logical extreme of that forfeiture, death.

For Sejanus the campaign has two facets. Because of his low station, he must make himself appear to be a suitable heir to the throne, a worthy "son" to Tiberius. Only then can he set about the second phase, his drive to unseat the emperor. He accomplishes the first objective by eliminating all of the natural heirs while simultaneously procuring the trust and affection of Tiberius. In effect, Sejanus becomes the emperor's son by taking over Drusus' wife, his servant, and his filial place in the father's regard. In addition, he comes to personify forces which disrupt natural social processes as he reconstructs from the chaos he creates a new, perverse social order. The Germanican description of Rome as a dismembered society acquires dramatic force in the hands of Sejanus. The intrigues which he enacts with Livia and Eudemus rupture the bond between sexuality and procreation which orders society and transmits social values between generations. Using self-serving and destructive sexuality, Sejanus breaks the bonds of family, of marriage, of masters and servants. He forges in their stead links binding sexual energy to sensual self-indulgence and barren political aggression. Social and moral order cease to be a Roman legacy, becoming instead a cosmic accident dependent solely on the will of the strongest man.

The talk of the conspirators is full of procreative energy, but Jonson makes it clear that the energy has been directed toward perverse and egocentric ends. Eudemus declares to Livia, "How are you blest in the fruition/Of this unequald man" (II, 54-55), and shortly thereafter Sejanus remarks, "A race of wicked acts/Shall flow out of my anger, and o're-spread/The worlds wide face" (II, 151-53). Here, as elsewhere in the play, anger, aggression, and evil are associated with sexual potency. The root of Sejanus' family tree, he brags, is evil, and he specifically describes a world in which a man's deeds are his children. He gleefully talks of "cuckolding" Tiberius and filling the royal family with his own bastard deeds. Later, in act 5, he considers his success:

>   I, that did helpe
> To fell the loftie Cedar of the world,
> Germanicus; that, at one stroke, cut downe
> Drusus, that upright Elme; wither'd his vine;
> Laid Silius, and Sabinus, two strong Okes,
> Flat on the earth; besides, those other shrubs,
> Cordus, and Sosia, Claudia Pulchra,
> Furnius, and Gallus, which I have grub'd up;
> And since, have set my axe so strong, and deepe
> Into the roote of spreading Agrippine;
> Lopt off, and scatter'd her proud branches.
>   (V, 241-51)

Scarcely concealed beneath all of this axe wielding, lopping, withering, and grubbing up is terrible sexual violence. When he addresses his soul in act 2, Sejanus assumes full paternal potency:

>   Tell proud Jove,
> Betweene his power, and thine, there is no oddes.
> 'Twas onely feare, first, in the world made gods.
>   (II, 160-62)

He has finally stripped away and cast off as "fears" all of the social, moral, and religious ideals with which man has surrounded the succession of generations. All that matters in Sejanus' world is his primal struggle with Tiberius.

In this struggle power is achieved through the understanding and command of theater. Here theatrical authority means self-possession, freedom from the threat of victimization in someone else's plot. Theatricality is also tied to sexual authority, the right and power to recreate oneself and remake the world in one's own image. In other words, theatrical authority means fatherhood. I think it is no exaggeration to suggest that *Sejanus* presents us with a crisis of fatherhood. Tiberian Rome is devoid of strong and virtuous men because, as Arruntius explains in act 1, the spirit of past Roman heroes has perished with them. Cato, Cassius, and Brutus, and now the Germanicans, have failed to sire potent sons. Silius makes this explicit when he corrects Arruntius' assessment of Germanicus:

> ARRUNTIUS. O, that man!
> If there were seedes of the old vertue left,
> They liv'd in him.
>
> SILIUS. He had the fruits, Arruntius,
> More then the seedes.
>
> (I, 118-21)

Heroic virtue in this world consists of the union of two qualities, the will to perform virtuous action and the authority to act, implying both courage and the wisdom to avoid the snares of others. Germanicus, by allowing himself to be trapped by Tiberius, proves that he lacks wisdom, and Tiberius, who has all of the requisite wisdom, lacks virtue. What Jonson has given us, then, is a world where heroism is unable to recreate itself, where virtue and fatherhood have been divorced. Within that world we are shown the clash of a vicious father and his equally vicious "son."

The crisis comes in act 5 when Tiberius demonstrates his superiority by setting in motion the drama which crushes Sejanus. The triumph of the emperor's skill is that he pulls the strings from a distance, disdaining confrontation. Tiberius is a master of passive manipulation, compelling others to do his bidding by virtue of his seeming incapacity or lack of interest. Although the appreciation is available to us only in hindsight, Tiberius offers a remarkable display of his theatrical genius early in act 2, during his first private interview with Sejanus. In an exchange of 160 lines, Tiberius speaks fewer than one-quarter of them, and yet his control of Sejanus is absolute. With question after question he leads his victim through a subtle interrogation, and Sejanus supplies all of the energy and information, as if he were running the show himself. Then, abruptly, Tiberius reins him in by claiming for himself all of what Sejanus has just laid before him:

> We can no longer
> Keepe on our masque to thee, our deare Sejanus;
> Thy thoughts are ours, in all, and we but proov'd
> Their voice, in our designes, which by assenting
> Hath more confirm'd us, then if heartning Jove
> Had, from his hundred statues, bid us strike,
> And at the stroke clickt all his marble thumb's.
>
> (II, 278-84)

Tiberius reveals himself here to be a sublime masker. He accords Sejanus the ultimate compliment by comparing him to Jove, but, in reality, he has reduced him to a ventriloquist's dummy, used by Tiberius to test his own voice. As is his manner, the emperor has expunged from his little drama any trace of the autonomy a playwright might offer an actor: Sejanus has spoken "their voice," the voice of Tiberius' own thoughts, and it is the thoughts which assent, not Sejanus. The comparison of Sejanus to the statuary of Jove is brilliantly apt. There is about as much chance of Sejanus acting on his own in this regard as there is of motion coming to marble. And when marble statues do come to life in act 5, it is Tiberius' breath that moves them.

Throughout this display Tiberius shows his hand neither to Sejanus nor to us; his principle of action is reaction, bleeding the energy of others to fuel his own schemes. When Sejanus, like Volpone, opens the final act of the play riding a crest of tumescence, we know already that Tiberius is in control. There is a strangeness about this final act that resists easy definition, but which seems, nevertheless, to affect crucially our understanding of the play. Barish speaks to the difficulty:

> When logical explanations reach their limit, Jonson will have no recourse to illogical ones. Though he speaks of the gods, he does not make us feel them lurking at the fringes of the action. He avoids creating the aura of wonder that tinges the woe in so much other tragedy. If the portents in Act V lack resonance compared to their counterparts in *Julius Caesar*, it is because one feels that Jon-

son does not believe in them any more than Sejanus does.
. . . Fortune, at base, is a metaphor, a desperate trope
whereby men shirk the consequences of their folly.[4]

The question is why Jonson, to this point in the play so rigorously insistent upon human agency, should turn to the supernatural in the final act. All of a sudden we are met with a deluge of supernatural phenomena, but their appearance does not fit with usual expectations of such devices. What Jonson had in mind is difficult to determine, particularly since his choices in this matter generally are felt to weaken and confuse the play. It is a much more reasonable prospect to consider what the introduction of the supernatural actually does to the play. On the negative side, Barish surely is correct that nothing Jonson does in the final act convinces us that we should believe in these agencies—or that he did himself. Arthur Marotti, on the other hand, supplies a good deal of what I think are the positive effects of this dose of Jove and Fortune:

> The omens of Act V . . . seem to be part of Tiberius' scheme, although, realistically speaking, he could have had nothing to do with them. . . . All these supposed accidents, which designate the stage in the *de casibus* pattern just before the inevitable fall, despite their almost comical profusion, fit Tiberius' design so well that he seems, in the light of what takes place in the second Senate scene, to stand behind the play as a kind of malicious deity manipulating both the actions of men and the preternatural happenings in the realm of Fortune. His art, at this point in the tragedy, most vividly mirrors Jonson's.[5]

In the early part of the play, supernatural agents are invoked primarily as a means of expressing rhetorically the authority of Sejanus and Tiberius. But, in act 5, the supernatural becomes a dramatic fact, and it sides entirely with Tiberius. Whether he intended it or not, Jonson has encouraged the identification of Tiberius with Jove. The emperor's absence in act 5 contributes greatly to his apotheosis: his physical self is absent, but his presence is felt everywhere. With Tiberius gone, Sejanus transposes his struggle with the emperor into a struggle with Jove and the gods by attributing to them the same power which we know, and he ultimately knows, resides with Tiberius. Macro reinforces the hyperbole by casting Sejanus as a Titan, "Come downe, Typhoeus," describing his ambition as the overthrow of Zeus:

> Phlegra, the field, where all the sonnes of earth
> Muster'd against the gods, did ne're acknowledge
> So proud, and huge a monster.
> (V, 685-87)

Tiberius' physical absence, then, results in his becoming bigger than life. He becomes the ultimate authority, invested with the power of Jove on Olympus.

It is significant that what initiates Tiberius' reassessment and consolidation of his position is Sejanus' request to marry Livia. Jonson calls no special attention to the episode, but Tiberius notes in his letter to the Senate that this request is one of the things that aroused his suspicion. Sejanus' wish to marry his mistress is a direct threat to Tiberius' position as patriarch of Rome. Sejanus makes one move too many in his effort to cripple the royal family, and Tiberius perceives the threat immediately. I can recall no more pregnant pause than the "H'mh" with which Tiberius greets the request. The role of father is defined by control of the family tree, and Tiberius will not relinquish it. Discreet love affairs pose no such threat because they lack social and legal legitimacy, but marriage is a social act in which sexuality joins social order and responsibility. This is the essence of Tiberius' response to Sejanus, a recondite warning that the letter fails to heed. The office of a good son is to pose no threat to the position and prerogatives of the father, and a wise son learns to conceal his aggressions. In essence, the quarrel over Livia is really over control of the Imperial family, and Caesar responds when he feels the threat to his patriarchal monopoly.

At stake in this struggle are self-possession, the role of imperial patriarch, and control of Rome. The play continually asserts the relationship among these elements, and one of the most important examples of the way the play pushes us toward understanding these relations is the "sexualization" of Rome, the association of Rome with female energy. There are many female agencies in the play, Livia, Agrippina, Augusta lurking behind her son, and the agencies of Fate and Fortune. Act 5 permits no woman to appear on stage, but there is a vague female presence throughout, the command of which becomes the measure of manhood between Sejanus and Tiberius. With the qualified exception of Apicata, there is no representation of "natural" womanhood in its traditional sense of beauty and nurturing love. Livia cuckolds and kills her husband, and her narcotic fascination with cosmetics is a sure sign in Jonson's theatrical cosmos of female degeneracy. Agrippina is no woman: she has become, in the default of effective males, the masculine principle of her household. Her execration constantly reminds us that there is no place for natural womanhood in her world.

Sejanus presents femininity as ruthless, aggressive, sexually capricious, and egocentric—and it so happens that this is exactly how Fortune is described in the final act, as Sejanus calls her, a giglot. The first important personification of Fortune is by Sejanus:

> I know not that one deity, but Fortune;
> To whom, I would throw up, in begging smoke,
> One grane of incense: or whose eare I'ld buy
> With thus much oyle. Her, I, indeed, adore;
> And keepe her gratefull image in my house,
> Some-times belonging to a Romane king,
> But, now call'd mine, as by the better stile:
> To her, I care not, if (for satisfying
> Your scrupulous phant'sies) I goe offer.
>
> (V, 81-89)

THE PEOPLE'S BEASTLY RAGE

Like Livia, she is to be courted with "masculine odors" and "night vestments." Like Rome, her statue belonged once to a Roman king and now to the man who thinks he controls the empire. The sacrifice in act 5 is a kind of symbolic marriage ceremony in which Sejanus seeks the hand of Fortune, represented by the flamen as our ur-mother:

> Great mother, Fortune, Queene of humane state,
> Rectresse of action, Arbitresse of fate,
> To whom all sway, all power, all empire bowes,
> Be present, and propitious to our vowes.
> (V, 178-81)

The emphasis on purity and ritual during the sacrifice makes a neat irony out of Sejanus' urgent pursuit of Livia and his feelings about women in general.

Fortune, coy goddess, averts her face, and Sejanus responds by asserting his dominance over her verbally, performing a rhetorical rape. His oratorical power recasts her as a fool and a strumpet, but his real power over her is gone. He is left, finally, to ponder his doom:

> These things begin
> To looke like dangers, now, worthy my fates.
> Fortune, I see thy worst: let doubtfull states,
> And things uncertaine hang upon thy will:
> Me surest death shall render certaine still.
> Yet, why is, now, my thought turn'd toward death?
> (V, 234-39)

He has confronted failure for the first time, and he describes his weakness in rhetorical terms as the inability to speak: "I faint now ere I touch my period." The irony is deepened when Macro, the agent of Sejanus' destruction, allows him to recapture momentarily his sexual victory over Fortune:

> Fortune, be mine againe; thou' hast satisfied
> For thy suspected loyaltie.
> . . . .
> By you, that fooles call gods,

SEJANUS

Hang all the skie with your prodigious signes,
Fill earth with monsters, drop the scorpion downe,
Out of the zodiack, or the fiercer lyon,
Shake off the loos'ned globe from her long henge,
Rowle all the world in darknesse, and let loose
Th'inraged windes to turne up groves and townes;
When I doe feare againe, let me be strooke
With forked fire, and unpittyed die:
Who feares, is worthy of calamitie.

(V, 366-99)

Sejanus' response to Macro, just preceding this encomium, underscores the sexual turn of his thought: "You take pleasure, Macro/Like a coy wench, in torturing your lover" (V, 360-61). There is a tradeoff here: when Sejanus feels he possesses Fortune he confidently rejects both fear and the gods; he rejects weakness, the role of being a son, because he supersedes the father Jove-Tiberius. When he loses Fortune, he loses his manhood.

Just as Fortune becomes an agency whose essence transcends the sum of events ascribed to her actions, Rome acquires a character which exceeds the sum of all the various people and institutions it comprises. In *Catiline*, Rome is clearly identified with motherhood, becoming a kind of *mater publica*. *Sejanus* never makes this relationship explicit, but the characters in the play speak about Rome as if it were a person, and usages such as "Caesar and his Rome" abound. In act 5, the "rude multitude" which lies close to the heart of Rome is represented as the embodiment of Fortune's power, subject to her caprice and to her incredibly willful violence. The letter from Capreae does not work on the rational faculties; it taps a source of power and unleashes a force which Tiberius, not Sejanus, finally controls. The control of this force is the essence of imperial command; this is what it is to have Rome as one's mistress, and only Tiberius knows the secret of arousing this mindless, orgasmic fury.

Livia, Rome, and Fortune eventually coalesce into a single pervasive sense of female power, and from the complex web of individuals which constitutes this play, there emerges a triad: Tiberius, whose association with Jove underscores his position as the ultimate patriarch; Fortune, the emperor's mistress, who masks herself as the civic anima of Rome; Sejanus, the contumacious son who, after deposing the rightful heirs of Rome, would depose his "father" and claim his mistress-mother. What Sejanus does not comprehend is the essential complicity between parents. This is a particularly bleak version of oedipal conflict. The child's attempt to assume his own manhood can be realized only at the expense of the father, and the father meets the threat by destroying the would-be usurper with the help of the mother. There is no accommodation, no compromise, no sense that the natural processes of human succession can work in this world. Tiberius makes the point brilliantly: "While I can live, I will prevent earths furie:" Ἐμοῦ θανόντος γαῖα μιχθήτω πυρί [When I am dead, let fire overwhelm the earth] (II, 329-30). This psychological drama equates potency and evil. After all, Sejanus is the only potent son left to Rome. To be virtuous is to be weak, to refuse to take action. Particularly frightening about Sejanus' case is that it is when he is so sure he has vanquished Tiberius, seeing him off to Capreae to indulge his polymorphous appetites, that the emperor reaches back violently to assert his power.

The ending of this play is very peculiar. After the messenger's depiction of the demise of Sejanus at the hands of the mob, the survivors offer a flurry of *de casibus* nostrums:

LEPIDUS. How fortune plies her sports, when shee
 begins
 To practise 'hem! pursues, continues, addes!
 Confounds, with varying her empassion'd moodes!
ARRUNTIUS. Do'st thou hope fortune to redeeme thy
 crimes?
 To make amends, for thy ill placed favours,
 With these strange punishments? Forbeare, you
 things,
 That stand upon the pinnacles of state,

SEJANUS

> To boast your slippery height; when you doe fall,
> You pash your selves in pieces, nere to rise:
> And he that lends you pitty, is not wise.
> TERENTIUS. Let this example moove th[e] 'insolent man,
> Not to grow proud, and carelesse of the gods:
> It is an odious wisedome, to blaspheme,
> Much more to slighten, or denie their powers.
> For, whom the morning saw so great, and high,
> Thus low, and little, 'fore the 'even doth lie.
>
> (V, 888-903)

But so overwhelming is the presence of Tiberius and Macro throughout the final act, and so clear the identification of the Emperor with Fortune, that such talk seems bizarrely at odds with our experience. Again the play refuses to enact the meaning it states discursively; Jonson's investment is elsewhere, primarily in his study of the relationship between Sejanus and Tiberius and, ultimately, between theater and authority. His personal investment in dramatic satire has evolved a remarkable complexity, reflected in his manifold relationship to Sejanus. His rejection of the Germanicans as a potent satiric force is a repudiation of his earlier work, that simple satire in which the lines of authority are clear and reliable; it is, moreover, a confession that, in allowing his satire to cut him off from his comic audience, he has left himself impotent, talking only to himself and his friends.

On the other hand, this play is tremendously powerful at times, alive in ways that *Cynthia's Revels* and *Poetaster* are not, and while Jonson is certainly committing himself to this vitality, he is clear about the cost in terms of his poetic ideals: if he found the impulse toward virtue and social order deadly dull and troublesomely antitheatrical, he found this new vitality inextricably allied with imposture, manipulation, aggression, and violence. I think his involvement with Tiberius is part fascination, part expiation: fascination with the kind of self-posturing that spurns all moral principle except what it incorporates disingenuously into its self-gratifying theatricality, expiation for his selfishness with principles that seemed to him to require selflessness. In the comical satires, he had portrayed himself to his audiences as a father, protecting their virtue, fending off impostors, preaching the value of commonwealth. Yet he was slowly coming to realize that his investment was in large measure personal, therefore sullied, and that competition for an audience involved at some level fraud and deception.

In a much less violent way, of course, *Sejanus* does to its audience what Tiberius does to Sejanus; that is, it offers us a part in a drama which appears to be one thing and turns out to be quite another. It manipulates the gap between experience and meaning in a way that frustrates and confuses, finally defeating our attempts to control our experience by refusing to let us take what we want, and what it seems to offer, clear and useful meaning. One might say that Jonson was involved at this moment in his career in making himself, like Tiberius, an absent father, and, ironically, it is his subsequent success at isolating himself from his audience, refusing to be a present, strong authority in his drama, that allowed him to win back the common audience with plays like *Volpone, The Alchemist,* and *Bartholomew Fair.* In none of these plays is he willing to assume the responsibility for providing clear and adequate dramatic solutions to the moral and ethical problems he creates; instead, he relishes the endless revision and complication of dramatic perspective. Yet these are immensely engaging plays, accessible to the widest range of spectators.

A significant portion of Jonson's artistic psyche also is tied up in Sejanus. Insofar as he represents filial aggression, Sejanus embodies Jonson's anxiety about taking on the authority of a poet and playwright. Every artist is in some measure a usurper, both in terms of his audience and in terms of the sources, traditions, and authorities with which he works. In a sense, he fashions his artistic self by taking from others in order to return the borrowings newly fashioned. But Jonson was obsessed with the taking, and his plays assert again and again that theatricality inevitably reduces humanity to oppressors and oppressed. Theatricality for Jonson guarantees conflict; it is just another form of aggression. One of the first observations to be made about what transpires on his stage is that to be an audience is to be a victim, for unless one has the power to create his own role in his own drama he will be made to play in someone else's.

Jonson experienced his attempts to establish himself with his audience as a series of battles in a holy war. He fastened on the polarities inherent in a diverse public audience, multiplying for himself both the emotional rewards of acceptance and the emotional risks of rejection, because he could not live on the middle ground. *Sejanus* suggests that this conflict is an expression of his extreme ambivalence about the roles of sons and fathers. For Jonson, oedipal conflict took a particularly grim, unforgiving form in which all of the son's attempts to acquire manhood come at the father's expense. In relation to his audience, Jonson was alternately a son, who seeks fatherly approval but is aware at some level that such approval is a sign of weakness, defect, and defeat, and a father, who senses that any challenge to his authority requires uncompromising aggression in response. In such a relationship, paternal acceptance and filial gratitude are chimeras—all that is real is the conflict itself.

The resolution offered by *Every Man Out of His Humor* and *Cynthia's Revels* is the mutual acceptance, on the part of poet and audience, of an enhanced adolescence: both the satiric poet and the objects of his satire accept subordination to the monarch because it allows them certain rewards, as pageant poet and dutiful subjects respectively, and it is significant that this resolution is made possible by a motherly queen. When males dominate Jonson's stage, as in *Poetaster* and all of the plays that follow, at least until *Bartholomew Fair*, this kind of conflict is never resolved entirely, and the relationships between men and women become extremely problematic.

There is a single moment of profound tragedy in this play, in the portrait of Apicata at the end of the messenger's tale.[6] Tiberius has called forth the fury of Rome, the wild, sadomasochistic frenzy which is as self-destructive and self-degrading to Rome as it is vengeful toward Sejanus. Rome destroys a part of herself, and when the dust has settled she is ashamed. Apicata is a poignant reflection of the public riot, committing a "world of fury" on herself. Then with such curses:

> As might affright the gods, and force the sunne
> Runne back-ward to the east, nay, make the old
> Deformed Chaos rise again, t'ore-whelme
> Them, us, and all the world) shee fills the aire;
> Upbraids the heavens with their partiall doomes,
> Defies their tyrannous powers, and demands,
> What shee, and those poore innocents have
>   transgress'd,
> That they must suffer such a share in vengeance.
>   (V, 867-74)

What she asks of the gods is meaning, meaning which the gods refuse her. This play is for all of us a world of "partial doomes," and her response is perhaps the only proper response of anyone seeking easy meaning in *Sejanus*, execration.

THREE

Volpone: "Fooles, They Are the Onely Nation Worth Mens Envy, or Admiration."

DAVID MCPHERSON'S essay, "Rough Beast Into Tame Fox: The Adaptations of *Volpone*," makes an important point about the history of Jonson's play in the hands of adapters: "There is a common element in the various adaptations down through the years: the main effect has always been the transformation of an extremely unconventional comedy into a more conventional one." He goes on to quote William Butler Yeats on Celia and Bonario, a comment worth repeating here: "They looked so pathetic, they were not even lovers."[1] As McPherson shows, the adapters of *Volpone*, beyond their efforts to rid the play of shocking language and sexually suggestive behavior, have sought to make it offer more in the way of conventional satisfactions such as heroes and happy endings. The adaptations have sought to soften what Yeats terms Jonson's "implacability," his refusal, in other words, to permit his play to please us fully in the ways we expect comedy to please.

Yeats's remark goes right to the heart of the matter. In another play, Bonario's rescue of Celia would have signaled the arrival of a hero to vanquish the villain and claim the damsel, but this play does not endorse any such conventional activity. In fact, Jonson explicity acknowledges his departure from "the strict rigour of comick law" in the epistle dedicating the play to Oxford and Cambridge:

> And though my catastrophe may, in the strict rigour of comick law, meet with censure . . . I desire the learned,

and charitable critick to have so much faith in me, to thinke it was done off industrie: For, with what ease I could have varied it, neerer his scale (but that I feare to boast my owne faculty) I could here insert. But my speciall ayme being to put the snaffle in their mouths, that crie out, we never punish vice in our enterludes, &c. I tooke the more liberty; though not without some lines of example, drawne even in the ancients themselves.

(Epistle, 109-18)

Jonson tells us that the ending of his play was dictated by the wish to meet the expectations of a certain segment of his audience, and that he was willing to act on this impulse even at the expense of other, seemingly more important, artistic considerations. This may wound whatever sense we have of dramatic compositions as organisms governed by their own internal laws, set in motion by creators who think of their work in terms of theme or artistic integrity, but it nevertheless reveals a great deal about Jonson's overall sense of his drama. Questions of form and meaning were for him inevitably questions of audience response. He intended the stage to reflect the gallery, not just in the obvious and relatively simple ways that comical satire displays the deficiencies of its spectators or morality plays instruct, but also in more subtle and sophisticated ways.

Volpone is one more attempt to come to terms with an audience, and what Jonson says about the play in the Dedicatory Epistle is only half the truth. The verdict of the avocatori certainly punishes vice, and in so doing it may well have applied the snaffle to certain contentious spectators, but, in relation to the rest of the play, it exists in a strangely diminished light. More is involved than Jonson's tacking on an ending that does not quite fit: the rest of the play actively rejects the conclusion as the human body rejects foreign tissue. Its characters attempt to mitigate the impact of the ending, to qualify whatever meaning it holds for us. In short, *Volpone* calls attention to itself not simply because it meets one set of conventional standards instead of another but because it employs conventions generally in oblique ways in a sustained effort to manipulate its audience. At this point in Jonson's career, he was writing plays that sustain only with difficulty the principles of morality and justice to which he was publicly committed.

Jonson's two previous plays, *Poetaster* and *Sejanus*, digress from the clear and certain world of *Cynthia's Revels* where satire, theater, morality, and judgment all flow from and contribute to Cynthia's majestic authority. Jonson's sympathy with Ovid in *Poetaster* and his fascination with the struggle between Sejanus and Tiberius in *Sejanus* interfere with his ability to meet his commitment to the values of Gargaphie. He seems to have grown progressively more involved with the nether side of comical satire, the self-conscious use of language and theatricality as means of self-definition and self-gratification, and, as one might expect, he slowly divorced his drama from the impulse to order the world for the sake of humane values. Undoubtedly the reasons for the shift are complex. *Poetaster* suggests that in part they were personal, that the role Jonson had made for himself as Crites to Cynthia's Elizabeth was wearing thin because, in addition to the fact that Elizabeth had refused to go along with the scheme, the role was stifling. Alongside Ovid's intense, lyrical self-involvement, Horace seems tired and nervous, trapped by a social role he no longer relishes. Jonson's vision of a commonwealth protected and nurtured by satiric theater had not been realized. Furthermore, his experience in the playhouse had revealed the audience to be an intractable, unregenerate mass, entirely unconcerned with his program for profit and pleasure. Disposed by nature to regard petty self-interestedness as the ruling passion of mankind, and convinced by experience that he could do little about it, Jonson sought to redefine his concept of recreation in order to accomodate his audience. For another playwright this might have meant throwing himself into lighthearted, lightheaded drama, but for Jonson the change meant examining his relationship to his

"THE ONELY NATION WORTH MENS ENVY"

spectators even as he altered it. And, finally, it meant developing the means to defend himself against the assaults of his spectators, even as he sought to entertain them.

In *Volpone*, characters seek other characters primarily to indulge the most primitive self-gratifying impulses, and the play defines its major characters not in relation to social values but in terms of what they want for themselves. Volpone's first soliloquy is a remarkable speech, revealing both the basis of his actions and the nature of the theater he creates:

> What should I doe,
> But cocker up my *genius*, and live free
> To all delights, my fortune calls me to?
> I have no wife, no parent, child, allie,
> To give my substance to; but whom I make,
> Must be my heire: and this makes men observe me.
> This drawes new clients, daily, to my house,
> Women, and men, of every sexe, and age,
> That bring me presents, send me plate, coyne, jewels,
> With hope, that when I die, (which they expect
> Each greedy minute) it shall then returne,
> Ten-fold, upon them; whil'st some, covetous
> Above the rest, seeke to engrosse me, whole,
> And counter-worke, the one, unto the other,
> Contend in gifts, as they would seeme, in love:
> All which I suffer, playing with their hopes,
> And am content to coyne 'hem into profit,
> And looke upon their kindnesse, and take more,
> And looke on that; still bearing them in hand,
> Letting the cherry knock against their lips,
> And, draw it, by their mouths, and back againe. How now!
> (I, i, 70-90)

This act of self-substantiation reflects the immense, exhilarating sense of self celebrated by Renaissance philosophers like Vives and Pico. Volpone presents himself as the quintessential ego, free of ensnaring relationships and possessing fully his "substance." By substance he means, most immediately, his estate, but the boast is all the more powerful for the implied sense of substance as "self." Giving one's substance, in both senses, is what marriage, fatherhood, and friendship require, but Volpone is a sort of ur-adolescent, full of energy, free of obligation. The word "make," set at the end of the fifth line, has a particularly eerie ring to it. Though Volpone exults in the role of creator, we understand his "making," his bestowal of substance, as procreation devoid of sexuality, affection, and natural bonds. He is a very peculiar father, recreating himself by turning old men into his foolish children. And in this play, paternal authority becomes theatrical authority explicitly:

> But whom I make,
> Must be my heire: and this makes men observe me.
> This drawes new clients, daily, to my house."

In a sense, we all go to the playhouse seeking to be made heirs to a playwright's substance, but Volpone's theater emphasizes only the self-interested aspect of theatricality. The sense of "make" as "create" or "designate," in line five, gives way in the following line to the sense of "compel," suggesting a link between theatrical creation and coercion, and the sense of "make" as "cheat" is always close at hand in this play. Volpone causes his spectators to display their foolishness not to reform them, as Jonson's comical satires had done, but to entertain himself and to make himself rich.

If we look more closely at Volpone's speech, however, the existence he describes as "living free" seems anything but free. He attracts clients who are greedy and covetous, who wish him dead and seek to engross him whole. Over the love of spouse, friend, and child, he has chosen relationships characterized by false displays of such love, but these relationships allow him a measure of control. The means to this control is a series of scenes that reverse theatrical roles: Volpone and Mosca act in a way that allows them to become spectators, while their spectators, the parade of gulls, are made to enact roles that reveal them as fools and victims. Yet for all his delight, Volpone is trapped by his audience; the drive to create is fed by the conviction that to lose control is to lose one's entire self. Volpone translates the "joy, in children, parents, friends," to a grotesque form of solipsistic recreation, a parodic version of true joy, because life for him is a matter of control. In theatrical terms, it is a matter of one's either writing his own script or being forced to enact someone else's. The implications for Jonson's own theater are important. The greedy and covetous spectator bent on engrossing the playwright was a real threat to Jonson as early as *Every Man Out of His Humor*, in which a lengthy and formidable induction confronts the problem of audience response. The threat grew until, in the Apologetical Dialogue appended to *Poetaster*, Jonson angrily rejected his comic audience altogether. Volpone creates a theater to enthrall, in both senses of the word, an audience whose interests are meanly self-gratifying. He victimizes his spectators by stimulating, but refusing to gratify, their expectations, offering his substance but never relinquishing it. And at the same time as the drama deflects the threatening spectator, it provides the energy to sustain the creator's self-image. The analogy between Jonson and his spectators and Volpone and his gulls is one to be approached carefully, but I think there is good reason to believe that at this moment in his career Jonson shared with his magnificent creature an interest in the theater as a place to manipulate foolish and ignorant spectators, "playing with their hopes . . . content to coyne 'hem into profit."

Any successful professional artist coins the hopes of his clients into profit, but Jonson is one of the few who worried in public over the possibility that this activity is fundamentally a form of fraud. His concern was two-fold: first, he sought to live off the theater in a way which had been, before his time, impossible. Only in the latter years of the sixteenth century had "cockering up one's genius" offered a life free from direct patronage, and, while only one man in Jonson's lifetime ever really achieved social rank and financial independence writing for the playhouse, Jonson certainly nurtured the dream.

But this circumstance alone will not account for the association of theater with fraud. The second of Jonson's concerns, and one which was shared by Elizabethan and Jacobean culture generally, was that the playwright attempts to peddle something essentially worthless. In his essay, "Jonson and the Loathed Stage," Jonas Barish suggests that Jonson felt real anxiety about the insubstantiality of theatrical shows:

> One ground, evidently, for Jonson's distrust of both play and masque is the inherent impermanence of both forms. Jonson belongs in a Christian-Platonic-Stoic tradition that finds value embodied in what is immutable and unchanging, and tends to dismiss as unreal whatever is past and passing and to come. What endures, for him, has substance; what changes reveals itself thereby as illusory.[2]

Along the same line, but referring specifically to *Volpone*, Stephen Greenblatt contrasts Jonson the moralist, as he depicts himself in the Dedicatory Epistle, with Jonson the skeptic, creator of Volpone's Scoto. Of the mountebank scene he asks:

> Is this not derisive laughter at those sixteenth and seventeenth century apologists for the drama who never tire of telling us that our tuppenny admission is the best investment we could ever make, that plays cure all our moral hernias? Is this not the disturbing self-mockery of the man who in the Dedicatory Epistle to *Volpone*—an epistle addressed to those greatest of gulls, the universities of Oxford and Cambridge—wrote with a straight face of the "impossibility of any mans being the good Poet, without first being a good man"?[3]

Greenblatt offers an extremely valuable insight into the complex relationship among Jonson, his play, and his sense of himself as a professional dramatist, but self-mockery is only one aspect of Jonson's self-dramatization in *Volpone*. A playwright unable to affirm wholeheartedly theater's value as a substantial and significant social activity faces a number of disturbing questions: how does he justify his work? in what ways can it be said to be useful? who is to decide such matters? Once he begins to question the validity of the readymade systems of judgment embodied in tradition, morality, and literary theory, he has taken a long, dizzying step toward conceding to his audience the authority to judge his work. Or at least, by casting aside the buffering effects supplied by such systems, insofar as they represent ground shared by artist and audience, he risks escalating the sense of confrontation between stage and gallery. And if he finds, as Jonson did, that he is playing to an audience of fools, what then?

These are the problems Jonson began to face up to in *Volpone*. If this is a play threatened from one direction by the silence denoting failure of plot and dialogue, as Volpone himself is threatened by paralysis, it is threatened from another direction by the fact that this theater is powerfully partisan. In other words, it is not simply that theater might be revealed as nothing, but that it might be revealed as nothing but self-gratification of the meanest sort. Because its actors make only the most minimal gestures toward sublimating their interests, the whole motion is constantly on the verge of collapse. What makes this collapse potentially so unpleasant is that it might bring the various parties face to face with nothing to disguise their hostility toward one another. Here dramatic action conceals aggression, allowing the satisfaction of desires that cannot be admitted openly. This play and the ones that follow it, particularly *Epicene*, *The Alchemist*, and *Bartholomew Fair*, clearly emphasize the confrontational aspect of theater; they ask repeatedly how authority is established in a theater, or in a culture, where traditional authority has been subverted.

Volpone depicts this confrontation in many ways, but the most important is the relationship between Volpone and Mosca. They embody two opposing aspects of theater: Volpone, theater as expression of self and prosecution of self-interest; Mosca, theater as self-annihilation, the selfless enactment of roles created by others. In the opening scene of the play, Volpone accomplishes his frenetic self-projection, while the second scene, even as it entertains Volpone, allows Mosca to introduce his own perspective. As if to call our attention to the contrast, Jonson sets the scenes off against each other very clearly. Nano's prologue to the interlude speaks much more directly to the concerns of the playhouse audience than to the concerns of the stage audience:

> Now, roome, for fresh gamsters, who doe will you to know,
> They doe bring you neither play, nor Universitie show;
> And therefore doe intreat you, that whatsoever they reherse,
> May not fare a whit the worse, for the false pase of the verse.
>
> (I, ii, 1-4)

We have watched only one scene before Nano, Androgyno, and Castrone enter, and in that scene Volpone and Mosca open what appears to be a conventional play written in precise and elegant verse. As the second scene begins, *we* consider Volpone's fools "fresh gamsters," and it is we who have been concerned with the conventions of stage plays and university shows, we who have noted the "pase of the verse." None of these things is the concern of a Venetian magnifico in his bed seeking "sport." Greenblatt calls *Volpone* a play with a "false ending," but it has a false beginning as well, or rather a second beginning that suggests that this play is extraordinarily self-conscious about its action. Even at this early point, the play presents itself to us in terms of theatrical conventions. Certainly Jonson is a great deal more sophisticated here than he was when he sat Mitis and Cordatus on the stage to talk to us about plays during *Every Man Out*, but he is still up to the same old tricks.

Volpone's debt to Erasmus is considerable,[4] and nowhere

does it recall *The Praise of Folly* more clearly than in the fools' song which opens the interlude:

> Fooles, they are the onely nation
> Worth mens envy, or admiration;
> Free from care, or sorrow-taking,
> Selves, and others merry-making:
> All they speake, or doe, is sterling.
>
> (I, ii, 66-70)

Jonson must have known this passage from Erasmus:

> There are two great obstacles to developing a knowledge of affairs—shame, which throws a smoke over the understanding, and fear, which, once danger has been sighted, dissuades from going through with an exploit. Folly, with a grand gesture, frees us from both. Never to feel shame, to dare anything—few mortals know to what further blessings these will carry us.[5]

The issue in both passages is freedom from the influences to which the human psyche is normally subject, and each asserts that it is the fool, of all men, who is blessed with such freedom. Androgyno's foolish catechism stresses the theatrical aspect of transmigration of souls. The soul of Pythagoras is a vital force confined by a series of bodies to specific roles. Because this soul retains the capacity to observe itself, to remain a spectator regardless of the nature of its host, we are allowed the ironic perspective we get through Androgyno. Pythagoras' soul asserts that the fool is its chosen role, and for self-interested theater this point is significant. In a world of knaves and gulls, victims and victors, perhaps the best way to succeed is to put the two roles together, achieving the ultimate triumph by playing the ultimate victim, in other words, the fool. This is a serious theory of theater, and, recast in other terms, a serious theory of religious life. It had been on Jonson's mind for a while: his portrait of Tiberius, in *Sejanus*, suggests that it is the emperor's seeming naivete and incapacity as a ruler, his carefully cultivated "foolishness," that allows him the perspective from which to understand and eventually crush Sejanus.

It is in the opening scene of act 3 that Mosca explicitly sets himself up against his patron as the true Fool of the play. Volpone purchases his freedom by enslaving others in his drama; Mosca chooses instead to enslave himself. He distinguishes his own from Volpone's ruling passion, "living free," with a thesis that the play tests repeatedly: "All the wise world is little else, in nature,/But Parasites, or Sub-parasites." To Mosca freedom is negation of self, the scrupulous rejection of self-interest and the refinement of self into an anti-self which takes its nature from the will of others. He rejects need, the force which technically defines "parasite," allowing his role to be sustaining in itself. Gut and groin mean nothing to the true parasite because the self has been absorbed into the performance. His play on the word "parts" makes the point nicely: "I Feare, I shall begin to grow in love/With my deare selfe, and my most prosp'rous parts,/They doe so spring and burgeon." Flesh and blood cannot be distinguished from the dramatic role. This is unmistakably the same spirit that inspired the fools' entertainment in act 1; indeed, parasites and souls, from Mosca's perspective, have much in common: "Your Parasite/Is a most precious thing, dropt from above,/Not bred 'mong'st clods, and clot-poules, here on earth." He goes so far as to disembody the parasite, endowing him with the plasticity, the consciousness, and the freedom from human fetters with which we credit the soul:

> But your fine, elegant rascall, that can rise,
> And stoope (almost together) like an arrow;
> Shoot through the aire, as nimbly as a starre;
> Turne short, as doth a swallow; and be here,
> And there, and here, and yonder, all at once;
> Present to any humour, all occasion;
> And change a visor, swifter, then a thought!
> This is the creature, had the art borne with him;
> Toiles not to learne it, but doth practise it

> Out of most excellent nature: and such sparkes,
> Are the true Parasites, others but their Zani's.
>
> (III, i, 23-33)

Mosca and Volpone stand opposite one another, heroic self-abnegation against heroic self-projection. By act 3, however, both are in trouble. Volpone has already begun to overstep the limits of his power in his quest for Celia, and Mosca, even as he relishes his success, has grown impatient with his role. His soliloquy is exultant, but what he says with tongue in cheek, when taken seriously, describes his great vulnerability:

> I Feare, I shall begin to grow in love
> With my deare selfe
> . . . .
>   I can feele
> A whimsey i' my bloud: (I know not how)
> Successe hath made me wanton.
>
> (III, i, 1-5)

This self-love is terribly destructive; it generates need, and need generates self-interested action and conflict. As the peculiar deadness of the opening scene in act 5 reveals, need traps Volpone in his role;[6] success only threatens because it requires more self-assertive playing. Mosca's acting has much the same effect: it stirs his blood, it brings him alive by suggesting the possibility of a self existing beyond his role. It is this "whimsey" in Mosca's blood that burgeons into the idea that he can replace his patron. As Volpone seems to lose himself in his role, Mosca seems to find himself, but in discovering this self he risks losing it. He abandons his role as the true parasite the moment he begins to value his own actions outside the context of their relationship to his patron.

Jonson has brought into direct conflict two aspects of theatricality and shown that while both are absolutely necessary for the creation of our experience in the theater, in their extreme forms they are a threat to the very theater they create.

We see that although theatricality is everywhere, theater is the rare and fragile, momentary conjunction of self-interestedness and self-negation. Volpone without Mosca is a heroic role with no context, no play to act in. Mosca without Volpone is a play without its leading actor. Jonson's theater, as precarious as Volpone's, tends to be forever involved in fending off the things which might destroy theater, self-interestedness, inertia, the fundamentally "atheatrical" things in life, and it does so frequently by trying to encompass them. Just as Volpone asserts his vitality and control by feigning sickness and impotence, Jonson's drama acquires its greatest power in plays that act out the threats to drama.

This commitment to theater, which expressed itself more often than not as an obsession with the threats posed by the theater to itself, frequently left Jonson in strange company. One cannot read Gosson's *Schoole of Abuse* with Jonson in mind without experiencing a peculiar vertigo at certain points when Gosson anticipates Jonson remarkably. Here is a passage on womanizing in the theater:

> In our assemblies at playes in London; you shall see suche heaving and shooving, suche ytching and shouldering to sytte by women; such care for their garments that they be not trode on; suche eyes to their lappes that no chippes lighte in them; such pillowes to their backes that they take no hurt; suche masking in their eares, I know not what; suche geving them pippins to passe the time; suche playing at foote saunt without cardes; such ticking, such toying, such smiling, such winking, and such manning them home when the sportes are ended, that it is a right comedie to marke their behaviour.[7]

This sounds like Jonson taking on his spectators in a prologue, but what Gosson perceived as a threat to public order and private morality Jonson perceived as a threat to the theater. Ironically, in view of our present scorn for Gosson, it was he, not Jonson, whose grip on actuality was firmer. Jonson spent a great deal of time defending a theater which existed only in his mind, while Gosson attacked one which existed in the playhouse. What Gosson saw was the Elizabethan theater, while Jonson sought without success to establish his theater of the soul. His defense against the subversive elements was to parade them on his stage in order to neutralize them, but the defense of theater became an endless, self-generating project. Each defense made another, more formidable defense imperative, until Jonson became more interested in the conflict itself than in the ideal he was defending. Whereas the early plays assert that substance and theatricality can be one, that the substance of Jonson's dreams can be realized in the theater, the later plays describe the divergence between substance and theatricality that Gosson understood all along. But unlike the Puritans, Jonson taught himself to accept the unfortunate aspects of the theater.

Volpone suggests that "substance," in all of its various meanings, and theatricality are not only antithetical but mutually threatening as well. Mosca in his prime has no substance, and this lack allows him to be purely theatrical. To those with substance, moral or financial, theater is very destructive. Celia and Bonario, but for a turn of events entirely outside their control, would have been locked up; the others, Voltore, Corvino, Corbaccio, and Volpone, all lose the substance they have. The concept that relates substance and theatricality for Jonson is possession. In its simplest sense, "possess" means "to have or own," but there is a great deal in this play about spiritual possession, as when the devil, "In shape of a blew toad, with battes wings," visits Voltore in the courtroom. The distinction between the two senses of the word can be made in theatrical terms. The first sense has at its base self-possession, the capacity to control oneself by acting self-consciously in a play of one's own making. When Volpone, anticipating Voltore's arrival in act 1, declares, "I long to have possession/Of my new present," we understand that this possession is a condition of his own self-possession, and that the gulls, who have no intention of surrendering their gifts, have already done so by virtue of their inability to see the larger picture of Volpone's hoax. The means to possession in this play is "purchase," and purchase becomes synonymous with playing. Volpone's dramas purchase his clients, their possessions, and his own sense of himself.

The second sense of possession is to be possessed, to be made to act unwittingly in another's play. Again Mosca makes the point nicely: after Corvino, using the terms of the theater, begs Mosca to explain the offering of Celia to Volpone as Corvino's own husbandly idea, "sweare it was,/On the first hearing (as thou maist doe, truely)/Mine owne free motion," Mosca responds, "I'le so possesse him with it, that the rest/ Of his starv'd clients shall be banisht, all" (II, vi, 93-97). Volpone will be possessed by the idea, and this will render him Mosca and Corvino's object. Voltore's courtroom possession literalizes the metaphor, with Corvino again the unwitting source of wisdom: "Grave fathers, he is possest; againe, I say,/ Possest: nay, if there be possession,/And obsession, he has both" (V, xii, 8-10). Finally, all of these meanings are neatly, if sternly, tied together by the avocatori: "These possesse wealth, as sicke men possesse fevers,/Which, trulyer, may be said to possesse them" (V, xii, 101-2).

This theater is set in motion by purchase, and primary among the possessions sought is self-possession. All of the brilliant acting is reduced to the level of transaction, and playing is valued for what it can purchase. Yet these are exactly the terms in which Jonson deals with his audiences in the prologues, epistles, and epilogues to his plays. He offers us pleasure and profit, wholesome remedies, fair correctives, mirrors, matter, and square meals, but we are never allowed to forget the cost to him in poverty, abuse, and long, late hours. In *Volpone*, Jonson seems to parody this inability to set his work beyond the costs of its begetting and the profits of its sale. At times, like Mosca, he must have considered that his role, in relation to his audience, was to "give 'em wordes;/Powre oyle into their eares: and send them hence." Mosca's encomium on lawyers in act 1 recalls simpler days of Jonson's career, when Asper made this boast:

"THE ONELY NATION WORTH MENS ENVY"

> And I will mixe with you in industrie
> To please, but whom? attentive auditors,
> Such as will joyne their profit with their pleasure,
> And come to feed their understanding parts:
> For these, Ile prodigally spend my selfe,
> And speake away my spirit into ayre;
> For these, Ile melt my braine into invention,
> Coine new conceits, and hang my richest words
> As polisht jewels in their bounteous eares.
> *(Every Man Out,* Induction, 200-208)

Jonson's feelings about Asper are relatively uncomplicated alongside the mixture of scorn for lawyers and bitter, self-implicating sarcasm with which he invested Mosca's speech:

> I, oft, have heard him [Volpone] say, how he admir'd
> Men of your large profession, that could speake
> To every cause, and things mere contraries,
> Till they were hoarse againe, yet all be law;
> That, with most quick agilitie, could turne,
> And re-turne; make knots, and undoe them;
> Give forked counsell; take provoking gold
> On either hand, and put it up: these men,
> He knew, would thrive, with their humilitie.
> And (for his part) he thought, he should be blest
> To have his heire of such a suffering spirit,
> So wise, so grave, of so perplex'd a tongue,
> And loud withall, that would not wag, nor scarce
> Lie still, without a fee; when every word
> Your worship but lets fall, is a cecchine!
> (I, iii, 52-66)

The image is the same in both speeches, the professional man of words, the manipulator of language, coining his spirit, turning words to gold. Jonson, like Scoto, forever disclaims his self-interestedness, "for I have nothing, little or nothing to sell," yet he is obsessed with matters of purchase and possession.

VOLPONE

Volpone is not just an image or a series of images of a playwright's relationship to his audience, however; it is itself an expression of that relationship. Each time we see the play in performance or read it at home, we enact the relationship Jonson meant to establish with his spectators. We give our substance to multiply his substance upon ourselves, literally, when we pay our admission in hope of taking on his wisdom and genius. In this theater, however, pleasure and profit come at a price. In one sense we come, like Corbaccio and the other gulls, seeking some momentary relief from our infirmities:

> Nay, here was one,
> Is now gone home, that wishes to live longer!
> Feeles not his gout, nor palsie, faines himselfe
> Yonger, by scores of yeeres, flatters his age,
> With confident belying it, hopes he may
> With charmes, like Aeson, have his youth restor'd:
> And with these thoughts so battens, as if fate
> Would be as easily cheated on, as he,
> And all turnes aire!
> (I, iv, 151-59)

Volpone's speech, by minimizing the relationship between the confidence man and his victim, puts the risk to Corbaccio in relatively benign terms, as if the old man enacts an illusion entirely of his own making. Volpone excludes himself from his description of the cheat, as a playwright might exclude himself from a description of the effect of his work on an audience. A good con, like a good play, turns the spectator's attention inward, presenting itself to him as an entirely self-reflexive experience. For the cheater this achievement is his guarantee against exposure; for the playwright it is an esthetic value, his gift to his audience. Jonson, of course, tangles the two roles, mixing his gifts with his swindles. The most intriguing instance of this practice in *Volpone* is the attack on Celia. Yeats's complaint only scratches the surface of what is a profoundly disturbing aspect of this play—its determination to turn Celia into a whore, and to do so, moreover, with the complicity of its audience. Jonson structures our response to the attempted rape as a choice between two radically polarized extremes, so that either response involves some penalty to the spectator. Having solicited our admiration for Volpone's imaginative energy and theatrical skill, the play confronts us with a set of values hitherto excluded from our ken. In other words, Celia's presence is an intrusion, a threat to our enjoyment of the play, enjoyment which depends in large measure on our concurrence in values she reveals to be self-indulgent and vicious.

Occurring in the middle of act 3, the rape scene lies at the center of the play. It provides the first tug in a series that finally pulls the plot away from Volpone. Even by Jacobean standards it is, I think, a distressing scene. For one thing, it records a substantial shift in dramatic perspective. Up to this point our admiration for Volpone has come largely from his comic exploitation of Corvino, Voltore, and Corbaccio, and there has been little in the play to qualify this admiration. Celia not only imposes a limit, she puts Volpone in the grotesque company of his own gulls. For the first time in the play he wants something as badly as they want his gold, and when he fails to sway Celia in his chamber, he reenacts for us the ugly wrangling we have just witnessed between Celia and Corvino. The lyric assurance of his attempted seduction, "for thy love,/In varying figures, I would have contended/ With the blue Proteus, or the horned Floud" (III, vii, 151-53), quickly gives way to rage:

> Thinke me cold,
> Frosen, and impotent, and so report me?
> That I had Nestor's hernia, thou wouldst thinke.
> I doe degenerate, and abuse my nation,
> To play with opportunity, thus long:
> I should have done the act, and then have parlee'd.
> (III, vii, 260-65)

And so Volpone surrenders the margin of theatrical control that sets him apart from the gulls. We can maintain our sympathy for him only by dismissing Celia as silly,[8] but, while she is no Duchess of Malfi, she makes her case as eloquently as her limited position in the play allows. Celia comes from a world entirely apart from the world of Volpone, Mosca, and the gulls; her virtue reflects poorly on them all, reminding us for a moment that Volpone is as vile as his besotted suitors. Whether Jonson consciously intended it to be or not, Volpone's attack on Celia is a vertiginous moment for its audience. At the very least the confusion of values seems to be an attempt to put some distance between stage and spectator; at most, one might construe the scene as an act of real aggression, however subtle, however ephemeral. In Volpone's desperate need to embrace Celia, whose values pose a very serious threat to his theater, one glimpses Ben Jonson's need to encompass the threats to his own theater, on one hand the moral seriousness of his Puritan critics, on the other the potentially destructive sexuality that he placed very close to the source of human recreative energy, at least within himself.[9]

Another way to describe Jonson's psychological investment in his character Volpone is in terms of the idea of identity advanced by the play. Whereas identity in the comical satires depends on a self developed in relation to secure, positive social values, in *Volpone* identity is a function of theatricality, the repeated enactment of manipulative drama. Those who see themselves as centered individuals in this play are finally ridiculed. To succeed here, to actually define oneself, one must compel others to play roles in a drama of one's own making, without their knowing it. Thus, identity is linked to the aggressive projection of one's own fantasies onto others, and the implications of this are intriguing in light of Jonson's professed beliefs regarding the satirist's role in society.

In his Yale edition of the play, Alvin Kernan draws the analogy between Scoto of Mantua, as Volpone plays him in the mountebank scene, and Ben Jonson as a struggling playwright working for London's commercial theater.[10] The argument is a striking one, and I think Kernan's reluctance to push it to its logical end testifies to its disturbing potential. He concludes that Jonson's investment in the metaphor is purely ironic and that satiric theater finally opposes real social medicine to Scoto's snake oil. My own sense is that Scoto is Jonson's oblique confession to his audience that he had recognized both the powerful self-interestedness of satire and the fact that for him the excitement of performance was inextricable from self-loathing. The mountebank scene appeals to the audience of *Volpone* to take seriously the relationship between the author and his work, a relationship worked out just beneath the surface of the play's action.

The attempt on Celia's virtue is perhaps the most vivid example of the fantasy material alive in this play, but it is only one facet of an extremely convoluted scheme. Jonson has come a long way from Cynthia and Arete: here the virtuous female is imagined to be sexual as well, a factor which complicates the entire father-son, wife-mother dynamic. Volpone acquires paternal authority, that is, the power to create heirs, by victimizing a group of old men. Although he is in fact relatively young and vigorous, he plays the aged patriarch, allowing them to imagine themselves young and vigorous. Though Volpone bilks his gulls of their money, the ultimate act of oedipal conquest would have been his seduction of Celia, had he succeeded. But though he fails to satisfy his desire physically, he satisfies the aggressive component of that desire in another way, by surrogate, through his attorney.[11] In the first courtroom scene, Voltore establishes Celia as an adulteress, rhetorically:

>   This lewd woman
> (That wants no artificiall lookes, or teares,
> To helpe the visor, she has now put on)
> Hath long beene knowne a close adulteresse,
> To that lascivious youth there; not suspected,
> I say, but knowne; and taken, in the act;
> With him.
>   (IV, v, 34-40)

This scene accents two aspects of the sexual drama: first, the strong aggressive component; second, with Bonario's implication in the "plot" against Corbaccio and Corvino, the completion of a fascinating oedipal drama. Again Voltore outdoes himself:

> That parricide,
> (I cannot stile him better) by confederacy
> Preparing this his paramour to be there,
> Entred Volpone's house (who was the man
> Your father-hoods must understand, design'd
> For the inheritance) there, sought his father:
> But, with what purpose sought he him, my lords?
> (I tremble to pronounce it, that a sonne
> Unto a father, and to such a father
> Should have so foule, felonius intent)
> It was, to murder him. When, being prevented
> By his more happy absence, what then did he?
> Not check his wicked thoughts; no, now new deeds:
> (Mischiefe doth ever end, where it begins).
> An act of horror, fathers! he drag'd forth
> The aged gentleman, that had there lien, bed-red
> Three yeeres, and more, out off his innocent couch,
> Naked, upon the floore, there left him; wounded
> His servant in the face; and, with this strumpet,
> The stale to his forg'd practise, who was glad
> To be so active, (I shall here desire
> Your father-hoods to note but my collections,
> As most remarkable) thought, at once, to stop
> His fathers ends.
> (IV, v, 66-89)

Bonario is made to take Volpone's place as the aggressor; he is accused of both oedipal crimes, adultery and parricide. Granted Celia is not his mother, but the courtroom scene clearly structures the conflict as a generational one, Volpone and his three gulls arrayed against the children.

This psychological tangle is typically Jonsonian, his characteristically bleak version of oedipal confrontation. Voltore creates a scene of filial aggression and marital betrayal which is really the opposite, a father who disinherits an honorable son and a husband who proffers the sexual favors of his innocent wife, both for purely selfish reasons. And Volpone is the axis about which the drama revolves, right at the center of the maelstrom but absent from the conflict. He cooks up the scheme and sets it in motion, but he is not involved in it. For much of the scene he is not in the courtroom at all; later he is carried in on a stretcher "as impotent." His pitting fathers against sons and husbands against wives allows him to play out an oedipal fantasy without risking himself. Thus, the play enacts the fantasy of a son-wife alliance against the father-husbands, a fantasy in which Jonson himself had a great deal invested. On the surface it appears that the fantasy is acted out just so it can be rejected, as if Jonson meant to assert here, as he does in *Poetaster* and *Sejanus*, that filial aggression is always doomed to fail. But in this play there is a larger context that qualifies this conclusion, namely Volpone's ulterior plot. The defeat of Celia and Bonario's "plot" is Volpone's victory, temporary though it may be. He plays the role of the passive patriarchal victim, while he is in fact the successful filial aggressor.

There are three closely related issues that bear upon the psychological structure of the play: the Wouldbe subplot, the homosexuality implicit in the play, and the fact that Volpone "has his way" with Celia in a specifically nonsexual way, through words and money. The thread of homosexuality that runs through *Sejanus*, *Volpone*, and *Epicene* takes an intriguing twist in the course of the three plays. In *Sejanus*, Jonson uses homosexuality as a charge against Sejanus. When Arruntius refers to him as Apicius' "pathick" there is no doubt that this is a sign of Sejanus' degeneracy. By the time we reach *Epicene*, however, homosexuality is presented as the acceptable behavior of a young man about town. There is a sense of completeness in Truewit's teasing evalution of Clerimont: "Why, here's the man that can melt away his time, and never feeles it! what, betweene his mistris abroad, and his engle at home, high fare, soft lodging, fine clothes, and his fiddle; hee thinkes the houres ha' no wings, or the day no post-horse" (I, i, 23-27). *Volpone* is pivotal in the transition. Mosca's interlude presents Androgyno, the hermaphrodite, as the paragon of human life. Interrogated by the dwarf Nano, Androgyno shrugs off the sexual aspect of his life, but the playful treatment keeps the issue before us:

> NANO. Now 'pray thee, sweet Soule, in all thy variation,
>   Which body would'st thou choose, to take up thy
>   station?
> ANDROGYNO. Troth, this I am in, even here would I
>   tarry.
> NANO. 'Cause here, the delight of each sexe thou canst
>   vary?
> ANDROGYNO. Alas, those pleasures be stale, and
>   forsaken;
>   No, 'tis your Foole, wherewith I am so taken.
>   (I, ii, 51-56)

The issue surfaces again in the subplot, though in a far less obvious fashion. One of the structural parallels between main plot and subplot is that Sir Politic's paternal or at least avuncular investment in Peregrine, like the investment Corvino, Voltore, and Corbaccio make in Volpone, is repaid in a gulling. Like Volpone, Peregrine is a master of satiric exposure, which allows him to pull off another Jonsonian oedipal reversal. But the most obvious link between the two plots is Lady Wouldbe, the only character to play a major part in both. The specific impulse that steers her from plot to plot is the suspicion, planted in her head by Mosca, that her husband has been philandering. Eventually she encounters Sir Pol and Peregrine on the street and accuses the latter of being a courtesan in male clothing. When she fails to make headway with her charge, she widens the scope to accuse him of being a hermaphrodite, comparing him to Sporus, a boy favorite of Nero "who," to quote Herford and Simpson, "made him a eunuch, dressed him as a woman, and publicly went through the form of marriage with him in A.D. 67."[12] Here again is sexual confusion which recalls Volpone's menagerie of Androgyno and Castrone. Lady Wouldbe's final contribution is a courtroom appearance in which she joins the clamor against Celia, "Out, thou chameleon harlot; now, thine eies/Vie teares with the hyaena" (IV, vi, 2-3).

Thus, Lady Wouldbe provides a strong link between the two plots, but she also fills in a missing piece of the psychological puzzle: the seductive, aggressive, and betraying wife. She is Celia's opposite, proffering her sexual favors to Volpone, Peregrine, and perhaps Mosca. Though there is nothing to identify her as explicitly maternal, there is the curious detail of the cap her ladyship knits for Volpone. Finally, she is the prototype of *Epicene*'s Collegiate women, who refuse to bear children and pride themselves in their adultery. In *Volpone*, moreover, there is a hint that becomes a full-fledged theme in *Epicene*: that homosexuality, autoeroticism, and hermaphroditism are defenses against sexually aggressive women and the threat of betrayal. After all, Sir Pol and Peregrine establish their companionship, innocent as it is, because Lady Wouldbe is off learning "of tyres, and fashions, and behaviour/Among the courtizans" (II, i, 28-29).

What emerges in *Volpone* is a world of sexual and psychological polarization, a world which denies acceptance and accommodation. In an odd way, Celia and Lady Wouldbe have much in common: one is lovely and unattainable, the other promiscuous and, from Volpone's vantage, repulsive. In short, neither offers the possibility of heterosexual satisfaction. The play repeatedly denies that such satisfaction is possible, embracing both extremes of the preplexing Freudian dichotomy: in Corvino and Lady Wouldbe, the anxiety that all women are by nature unfaithful; in Volpone, the intense need to prove them so.[13] This play deflects sexuality into the explicitly nonsexual, male-to-male game that Volpone plays with his victims. The point that Androgyno makes is that hermaphroditism and castration are finally identical; as Nano puts it, in response to Androgyno's comment about stale pleasures:

> This learned opinion we celebrate will,
> Fellow eunuch (as behooves us) with all our wit, and art,
> To dignifie that, whereof our selves are so great, and
> speciall a part.
>
> (I, ii, 60-62).

Sexual potency is expressed in words and gold coin, and in this realm Volpone is truly androgynous, as his opening speech reveals:

> Good morning to the day; and, next, my gold:
> Open the shrine, that I may see my saint.
> Haile the worlds soule, and mine. More glad then is
> The teeming earth, to see the long'd-for sunne
> Peepe through the hornes of the celestiall ram,
> Am I, to view thy splendor, darkening his.
>
> (I, i, 1-6)

Volpone identifies himself with female earth, impregnated by the vernal sun; later in the play he uses the gold to generate heirs for himself, to establish his male potency, and, through Voltore, to verbally rape Celia. Thus, both gold and words are generative and degenerate, inspiring and degrading, and at some level this play equates semen and shit.

These relationships, subliminal though they may be, lie at the heart of Jonson's relationship to his audience, as it is articulated through the plays. In *Volpone*, Jonson faces the fact that part of his investment in satiric comedy is sexual and aggressive. He is clearly ambivalent about the perception, at once reveling in it and shunning it, and he forces us to repeat, to reenact this ambivalence in our own response to the play. We go to the theater to have our expectations flattered, our sense of ourselves massaged—or, to use Scoto's term, "fricaced"—and as a play proceeds, we invest ourselves more and more heavily. Unlike most plays, in which the question of value is never addressed openly, *Volpone* asks us to consider if we have been cheated. Here is a play that will not readily yield the substance that we expect and that Jonson offers in the Dedicatory Epistle, yet it forces us to the uncomfortable task of evaluating our experience in the theater. Volpone concludes the play by suggesting his dependence on our favor, but the context of his remarks reminds us how dependent he has made us on him:

> The seasoning of a play is the applause.
> Now, though the Fox be punish'd by the lawes,
> He, yet, doth hope there is no suffring due,
> For any fact, which he hath done 'gainst you;
> If there be, censure him: here he, doubtfull, stands.
> If not, fare jovially, and clap your hands.
> (Epilogue, 1-6)

This is no standard, *pro forma* epilogue. Such epilogues profess humility, excuse a play's shortcomings, and solicit applause at the completion of the theatrical motion. In other words, they minimize the judgmental aspect of our experience. Volpone does all he can to stress the significance of our judgment. He explicitly extends the invitation to censure him, and he clearly resists conventional humility when he declares, "He, yet, doth hope there is no suffring due,/For any fact, which he hath done 'gainst you." Far from being bowed, he almost dares us to censure: the issue at hand is not whether any "fact" has been done against us, but whether any suffering is still due.

Volpone's doubt stirs an interesting echo from Jonson's past, in the prologue to *Cynthia's Revels*:

> If gracious silence, sweet attention,
> Quicke sight, and quicker apprehension,
> (The lights of judgments throne) shine any where;
> Our doubtfull authour hopes this is their sphere.
> (Prologue, 1-4)

As Peter Carlson points out in his essay "Judging Spectators," Jonson's doubt is a function of his apprehension about the fate of his work in the hands of the multitude: "In the hopes of 'our doubtfull authour' we come to a pivotal and particularly cutting equivocation. This author doubts that he can be fairly judged in the theater, and responding to his audience on an intensely personal level, views them as potential aggressors, if not open antagonists."[14] Volpone is far more sure of himself; his doubt stems from a specific recognition of what the play has attempted in relation to its audience. To the extent that it has vexed us, Volpone justly acknowledges the ground for censure. Moreover, the epilogue's peculiar use of the feast metaphor adds emphasis to this judgmental aspect. Seasoning is applied before a meal, yet here, at the conclusion of the play, our applause is solicited as seasoning, and we are invited to "fare jovially." The suggestion, surprisingly, is that our experience of the play is just about to begin. Certainly this is Jonson again qualifying the importance of our immediate experience in the playhouse, that is, our participation in the performance, by telling us that the meaning of the play extends beyond the stage and subsequent to the performance, as we begin to analyze and judge.

Nor should the epilogue come as a surprise to us. The pressure to regard *Volpone* in a context removed from immediate involvement in the performance begins much earlier, with Nano calling our attention to the conventional aspects of the play. The entire force of the play suggests Jonson's reluctance to affirm theater either as entertainment or as social medicine. Other aspects of the play, like the subplot, push us toward abstract considerations. Shortly after his discovery of Sir Pol, Peregrine turns aside to the audience:

> O, this Knight
> (Were he well knowne) would be a precious thing
> To fit our English stage: He that should write
> But such a fellow, should be thought to faine
> Extremely, if not maliciously.
>   (II, i, 56-60)

Here Peregrine calls our attention directly to the fact that this is a play written by Ben Jonson (and viewed by the typical Jonsonian audience, most likely), and he asks us to place the play and Sir Pol and Volpone in the evolution of both Jonson's career and the history of the English stage.

Peregrine's aside is not just a joke about the fact that Sir Pol *is* a character in someone's play, but also about Sir Pol's being an anachronism in this Jonson play. Sir Pol is right out of the humor plays and the comical satires, and our sense that the Wouldbe subplot parodies the intrigue of the main plot is a measure of how far Jonson has come from *Poetaster*. Sir Pol is simply out-of-date, not only because Jonson has turned from English folly to Italian vice, but also because he has turned to a kind of theater which is far more cautious about its ability to resolve comic and satiric problems. Peregrine puts Sir Pol through his paces as Horace or Macilente would have done, and, true to form, the resolution of this plot makes a symbolic point as well as accomplishing the necessary reformation, as Jonas Barish explains:

> Sir Politic, thus, so inquisitive about prodigies, has finally become one himself, a specimen fit to be housed among the freaks of Smithfield or amid the half-natural, half-artificial curiosities of Fleet Street. With the knowledge that he is destined to become a victim of the kind of curiosity he himself has exhibited, his disillusionment is complete and his chastisement effected. He and Lady Would-be, the only survivors, in this play, of Jonson's earlier humour characters, are now "out of their humour," purged of their imitative folly by the strong medicine of ridicule.[15]

We are witnessing vintage Jonson, and we are not allowed to forget it. At the conclusion of the subplot, Jonson again calls us back to the world of English entertainment with the reference to Fleet Street and Smithfield, but the prodigious world of English humors is not Volpone's, as his unhappy association with Lady Wouldbe demonstrates. Volpone has more serious business in mind than serving as a straight man for her follies.

That more serious business, in terms of the entire play, is a theater in which the easy, old, and conventional means of comic resolution are ineffective. Jonson has scrapped his earlier reformatory notions and begun to use theater as a way of dealing subtly and realistically with conflict between stage and audience. As if we are watching through a kaleidoscope, our initial response to Volpone and Mosca undergoes a series of revisions: the fools' entertainment is one; Sir Pol's introduction, through a parodic version of Volpone's own opening speech, is another; Mosca's soliloquy is a third, and so on. Celia and Bonario provide us yet another perspective, one which brings before us some disquieting moral issues. Like Sir Pol, neither Celia nor Bonario really belongs in the play; they are refugees from romance melodrama such as *A Woman Killed with Kindness*.

The interplay of the "false ending" with the true ending of *Volpone* is yet another perspective through which we view the play and its "hero." As it approaches its conclusion, the play becomes increasingly self-conscious about its own theatricality. What brings Volpone back to life after act 4 is the thought of vexing his victims. Unsatisfied with their material possessions, he wants their souls; he wants them to *know* they have been gulled and to suffer for it. To accomplish this, he surrenders his cautiously guarded theatrical authority and steps out of the play and closer to the audience. Act 5 is one of the places in Jonson's work where the anxieties of being a spectator are depicted most clearly. It demonstrates one of the primary tenets of Jonson's theatrical creed: to be a spectator is to be the potential victim of someone else's self-gratifying designs. The defect in Volpone's invalid role, namely the fact that it requires passivity, allows Mosca to abuse him from the beginning. Mosca incorporates into his own role as advocate for the gulls the opportunity to vent a good deal of aggression toward his patron. With Corbaccio, he lovingly depicts the degeneration of Volpone's body:

CORBACCIO. How do's his Apoplexe?
   Is that strong on him, still?
MOSCA.   Most violent.
   His speech is broken, and his eyes are set,
   His face drawne longer, then t'was wont—
CORBACCIO.   How? how?
   Stronger, then he was wont?
MOSCA.   No, sir: his face
   Drawne longer, then t'was wont.
CORBACCIO.   O, good.
MOSCA.   His mouth
   Is ever gaping, and his eye-lids hang.
CORBACCIO.   Good.
MOSCA. A freezing numnesse stiffens all his joynts,
   And makes the colour of his flesh like lead.
CORBACCIO.   'Tis good.
MOSCA. His pulse beats slow, and dull.
CORBACCIO.   Good symptomes, still.
MOSCA. And, from his brain—
CORBACCIO.   Ha? how? not from his brain?
MOSCA. Yes, sir, and from his brain—
CORBACCIO.   I conceive you, good.
MOSCA. Flowes a cold sweat, with a continuall rhewme,
   Forth the resolved corners of his eyes.
CORBACCIO. Is't possible? yet I am better, ha!
   How do's he, with the swimming of his head?
MOSCA. O, sir, 'tis past the scotomy; he, now,
   Hath lost his feeling, and hath left to snort:
   You hardly can perceive him, that he breathes.
                    (I, iv, 36-54)

Mosca returns to this activity at least twice more, both when he insists on reminding Volpone in act 5 how he sweated on his pallet before the avocatori and when he embellishes Volpone's instructions for handling questions about the patron's "corpse" when he feigns death:

99

> MOSCA. But, what, sir, if they aske
> After the body? VOLPONE. Say, it was corrupted.
> MOSCA. I'le say, it stunke, sir; and was faine t'have it
> Coffin'd up instantly, and sent away.
>
> (V, ii, 76-79)

Perhaps the best joke at Volpone's expense, however, is Mosca's response to Corvino's question, "Has he children?":

> Bastards
> Some dozen, or more, that he begot on beggers,
> Gipseys, and Jewes, and black-moores, when he was
>   drunke.
> Knew you not that, sir? 'This the common fable,
> The Dwarfe, the Foole, the Eunuch are all his;
> H' is the true father of his family,
> In all, save me: but he has giv'n 'hem nothing.
>
> (I, v, 43-49)

This is quite a swipe at both Volpone's taste in women and his procreative talents, and the line, "H' is the true father of his family," has a sting to it. Next, Mosca shouts in his patron's ear, a painful thing for a man only feigning deafness to endure, and the message he delivers is one we understand him to mean wholeheartedly by the time we reach act 5:

> The poxe approch, and adde to your diseases,
> If it would send you hence the sooner, sir.
> For, your incontinence, it hath deserv'd it
> Throughly, and throughly, and the plague to boot.
>   . . . would you would once close
> Those filthy eyes of yours, that flow with slime,
> Like two frog-pits; and those same hanging cheeks,
> Cover'd with hide, in stead of skin . . .
> That looke like frozen dish-clouts, set on ends.
>
> (I, v, 52-60)

The final action in this sequence is Mosca's "attempt" to stifle Volpone with a pillow, another real wish playfully acted out, surely to Volpone's discomfort.

Volpone, however, sees no foreshadowing of Mosca's ambition, and in the final act he surrenders his role of magnifico to the parasite. In doing so, he moves away from center stage to the periphery of the action and out toward us, the audience. Never one to resist an audience aside, Volpone now absents himself entirely from the stage action in scene 3. He is nearly out of the play, nearly a member of the audience as he calls the action for us, play-by-play. When he does reenter the play, it is in the menial role of a sergeant so that he might continue vexing the gulls. He has not just changed costumes; indeed, he has revised his entire relationship to the stage.

The overall effect of this revision is to distance us from the stage action, just as it distances Volpone. Whereas consensus seems to be that *Volpone* is a moral play by virtue of its effective application of "poetic justice," what I find striking about this play is the length to which it goes to mitigate the force of such justice. The climax of the play is a remarkably protracted affair, extending through one and one-half acts and featuring several false resolutions. It demonstrates nothing about the inevitability of comic justice.[16] Until the very last moment of the play, the entire plot might have been saved had Mosca and Volpone been able to reach a settlement. Volpone *wills* the ending as an alternative preferable to being gulled by Mosca; the artifice remains to the end impenetrable from the outside, an amazing tribute to human credulity and deceit.

Other things also mitigate the effects of the comic resolution. In the final act, both Mosca and Volpone move the action onto an allegorical level, allowing them a perspective which is normally only the audience's and which, consequently, undermines any emotional resolution. Mosca terms his plot to cozen his patron "the Foxe-trap," and announces:

> My Foxe
> Is out on his hole, and, ere he shall re-enter,
> I'le make him languish, in his borrow'd case.
> (V, v, 6-8)

Volpone constantly refers to himself now as "the fox." When he reaches the end of his hoax with the declaration, "The Foxe shall, here, uncase," he understands the action not as an unmasking by which he reveals his true self or abandons himself to the court but as a conscious choice to adopt another self-serving role that allows him to recover his position relative to Mosca. And he succeeds. His final words to Mosca via the avocatori are an assertion of his triumph, and they have their effect:

> VOLPONE. I thanke you, for him.
> MOSCA. Bane to thy woolvish nature.
> (V, xii, 115)

The punishment meted to Volpone is severe and appropriate, but again he does everything he can to keep it in the anesthetic realm of convention and allegory. After his uncasing he names all of the players in his drama, as if to assert, and correctly so, that it is he who has given them their roles, and, in doing so, created and controlled them. In other words, his self-definition, "I am Volpone," is in terms of his role as playwright, and, if he turns the play over to the court at this point, it is only to urge them to the *pro forma* conclusion of the play he has written. Of course we must have comic justice, so let's get on with it:

> And reverend fathers, since we all can hope
> Nought, but a sentence, let's not now despaire it.
> You here me briefe.
> (V, xii, 92-94)

It is clear that Volpone has removed himself from the play in terms of any personal involvement. His final assessment of his fate, "This is call'd mortifying of a Foxe" (V, xii, 125), offers us a beast fable in which he is but acting one of the beasts.

How, then, are we to judge *Volpone*? With a flurry of unusual dramatic perspectives, Jonson has gone to considerable length to deny us the full emotional force of his conclusion.

Acts 4 and 5 are tributes to his own boast in the Dedicatory Epistle, "With what ease I could have varied it." The ending of the play is a matter of Jonson's caprice, at least in relation to the world of dramatic convention. Our final meeting with Volpone in the epilogue underscores the strangeness of this play: as the malefactors stand before the bar contemplating their sentences, Volpone simply walks out of the play and addresses us. It is not an unusual occurrence on the Elizabethan and Jacobean stage for a major actor to deliver an epilogue, but here there is a difference. This is the final undercutting of the moral significance of this play, the final step in Volpone's transformation to a spectator of the play in which he began as an actor. Now when he confronts us, with the play behind him, there is a peculiar intimacy which includes us immediately in the play's examination of the relationship between actor and spectator. Whereas up to this point we have watched the play, the epilogue requires us to act as judges while Volpone and Jonson watch. And they mean us to feel all of the anxiety they have shown to be a part of acting in someone else's play. We are made to ask ourselves whether, even as we have enjoyed watching men cheat other men, we ourselves have been cheated.

Of course *Volpone* does not cheat its audiences. If it plays loosely with our sympathies and expectations, it rewards us handsomely in other ways. What is remarkable is Jonson's willingness to display publicly his anxieties about the theater and to use the stage to formulate the problems inherent in his relationship to his audience. In the course of this play, he entirely revises his approach to the theater. Applying to the drama the terms in which Stephen Orgel describes the masques, one might say that the comical satires seek to bridge the barriers between stage and gallery.[17] Jonson creates roles for his spectators to enact, hoping to bring forth a grand commonwealth of informed and self-consciously worthy individuals. *Volpone*, on the other hand, erects, or at least fortifies, those barriers. The stage has become the center of artistic control and self-possession; the gallery is a threat to this con-

VOLPONE

trol, to be repelled or taken by stratagem. The further Volpone strays from this stage, whether it is his great bed or his bank in the piazza, the more he sacrifices of his theatrical authority, and as the play concludes he surrenders it altogether. His final position, halfway between audience and stage, is a measure of his genius and his ability to transcend the limits of dramatic perspective, but it is also a sign of his becoming a victim of the play he once controlled. He is the bridge between two worlds, a member of neither.

Even our applause, which we give freely to this splendid play, becomes an equivocal gesture. For the audience's part, applause signifies acceptance of the play, the playwright, and the players; in this moment the barriers come down. But here we have a playwright reluctant to be accepted. Though he urges us to understand and judge his work in a context beyond our immediate amusement, he makes it difficult for us to do so with any confidence. After all, as the spectator assesses the meaning and value of a play for himself, he begins to control his experience and make it his own in a significant way. Jonson seems to have understood the implications of this process for his own proprietary interests in his work, and, wary of the consequences of abandoning his work to his audience, he gave us a play that emphasizes the problematic nature of judgment and the fact that stage and gallery, at some point, stand resolutely apart.

FOUR

Epicene: "I'le Doe Good To No Man Against His Will."

IN CERTAIN ways, *Epicene* seems out of step on the path from the comical satires to *Bartholomew Fair*. It comes between *Volpone* and *The Alchemist*, plays whose comic worlds stand outside the law, setting theatrical genius against morality and social order. *Epicene*'s is no outlaw world, however, and the conflict between social values and private urges, the conflict that threatens Volpone's chamber and Subtle's laboratory, remains in this play a bit of scenery in the background. *Epicene* tricks its spectators by revealing its heroine as a boy, but this stroke is lighthearted and mechanical, sleight of hand compared to the "trick" by which Lovewit dominates the end of *The Alchemist*, or to Face's oblique suggestion in his epilogue that theater seeks to exploit its audiences, or to the harsh collision between law and license in *Volpone*, about which Northrop Frye justly grumbles, "One feels perhaps that the audience's sense of the moral norm does not need so much hard labor."[1] In short, here Jonson seems more at ease with his material and with his audience than in any play since *Every Man Out of His Humor*.

On the basis of the prologue alone, one might suspect that *Epicene* is unusual. Given Jonson's self-consciousness about poetic tradition and his penchant for documentation both to defend his work and to provide a context for it, this prologue is a true departure from his normal practice. The tradition with which he aligns himself is popular, not learned:

> Truth sayes, of old, the art of making plaies
> Was to content the people; & their praise
> Was to the Poet money, wine, and bayes.
> (Prologue, 1-3)

EPICENE

Here Jonson interposes no Horace, Cicero, or Juvenal between his work and the audience, and the term "making plaies" seems to be an attempt to remove from the activity of the playwright the mystery, the intense self-involvement, and the adherence to precept and tradition which Jonson accents, for instance, in the induction to *Every Man Out*. Gone, too, is his eagerness to describe the stage in abstract terms which minimize or discount entirely the immediate response of the theater audience. The stage is now a table full of various delights set out to please the guests, and the act of attending a play is characterized as feasting. Instead of setting the poet against the beast multitude, or alluding vaguely to a distinction between the judicious portion of the audience and the "rest," this prologue deals with its audience in a particular and non-satiric fashion:

> The Poet prayes you then, with better thought
> To sit; and, when his cates are all in brought,
> Though there be none far fet, there will deare-bought
> Be fit for ladies: some for lords, knights, squires,
> Some for your waiting wench, and citie-wires,
> Some for your men, and daughters of white-Friars.
> (Prologue, 19-24)

Jonson welcomes everyone, and while he recognizes the distinctions to be made on the basis of social standing, there is no attempt to actively discriminate.

So it is, generally, with the play itself. The action has been scrubbed nearly clean of moral seriousness. The characters play for smaller stakes than either Volpone or Sejanus, and the penalties and tortures are appropriately softened. We never have the sense that, had the plot worked out differently, the world of the play would have been materially altered. What is intriguing, however, is that this is not quite a playful play. It is full of the traces of Jonson's attempts to make it playful, but there is abundant evidence to suggest that the guise of playfulness cost him heavily. *Epicene* embodies not the free, effervescent impulse to entertain but a powerful imagination bent to the task of entertaining, an imagination that cannot quite clear from its ken all of the reasons and inhibitions against entertainment.[2] The second prologue of the play, "occasion'd by some persons impertinent exception," Jonson's response, in other words, to hostile reaction to the play, makes it clear that the initial offer of *Epicene* to the public was conditional upon their unqualified acceptance of it. The arguments and authority of Horace and Juvenal quickly reappear when the audience refuses to keep its side of the bargain:

> The ends of all, who for the Scene doe write,
> Are, or should be, to profit, and delight.
> And still't hath beene the praise of all best times,
> So persons were not touch'd, to taxe the crimes.
> Then, in this play, which we present to night,
> And make the object of your eare, and sight,
> On forfeit of your selves, thinke nothing true:
> Lest so you make the maker to judge you.
>   (Prologue II, 1-8)

We are back to Horace's *utile et dulci* prescription, to satiric drama that serves as a tool by which social ends are administered, and to a theater in which judgment is the primary issue. The response of the spectator reveals his moral character and serves as the basis for the poet's judgment of the entire audience. Indeed, we are back to the world of the comical satires.

The play itself, however, goes further than any of Jonson's previous plays toward reconciling two elements of recreation that he often felt to be seriously at odds: profit, with its concomitants, morality, learning, and social order, and pleasure, the immediate, visceral, and self-gratifying response to experience, which Jonson suspected as a narcotic, the agent of consuming self-indulgence and social chaos. *Epicene* attempts to deal with the disparity between profit and pleasure with new sophistication; instead of denying it or stressing one extreme over the other, Jonson painstakingly seeks a resolution. For the first time, the recreative potential of satire is really liberated, both from the demands of profit, which require ethical and moral discriminations, and from their opposite, the antisocial, amoral needs of the self-seeking individual. The choice is no longer the simple one between satire that serves community and satire that threatens it. This resolution rests on Jonson's handling of three issues that are central to the development of his drama: first, exorcising, or fettering at least, the spirit of censorious authority; second, accepting as part of full human recreation noise, discord, extreme selfishness, foolishness, and blasphemy; third, facing a problem he had suppressed, more or less, in his earlier plays, female sexuality. It is Morose who embodies the first, Truewit the second, the Collegiate women the third.

In his opening speech, after announcing that "all discourses, but mine owne, afflict me, they seeme harsh, impertinent, and irksome," Morose considers the practice of mute service:

> The Turke, in this divine discipline, is admirable, exceeding all the potentates of the earth; still waited on by mutes; and all his commands so executed; yea, even in the warre (as I have heard) and in his marches, most of his charges, and directions, given by signes, and with silence: an exquisite art! and I am heartily asham'd, and angrie often-times, that the Princes of Christendome, should suffer a Barbarian, to transcend 'hem in so high a point of felicitie. I will practise it, hereafter.
> (II, i, 29-38)

He is neither prince nor potentate—indeed Jonson gets considerable mileage out of Morose's social and sexual impotence. Nonetheless, this foolish old man, who sits out his wedding reception "over a crosse-beam o' the roof, like him o' the sadlers horse in Fleetstreet, up-right," is what remains of such majesty as that displayed by Cynthia, Augustus, Tiberius, and Volpone in the earlier plays. Morose is a parody, the ridiculous extreme of the impulse to remake the world in one's own image and to use language and theater exclusively to articulate one's own vision. In the case of *Cynthia's Revels*, in which this impulse is tied both to a sense of morality and social responsibility and to impeccable powers of judgment, the result is the utopian world of Gargaphie. Where judgment fails but essential morality remains, the result is Jonson's version of Augustan Rome, which excludes the great poet Ovid. Where morality fails and judgment remains impeccable, we have the horrors of Tiberian Rome portrayed in *Sejanus*. A crucial aspect of Jonson's consideration of each of these cultures is the relationship between majesty and theater. Satiric theater and the masque, in the hands of Crites, become extensions of Cynthia's power and means of enacting and defending her social vision. In *Poetaster*, however, the young Ovid is expelled from Rome for his role in the masque of Jupiter and the gods, and later we see that Augustus endorses but one theater, his imperial chamber, where Horace and Vergil glorify the Empire. The struggle between Sejanus and the Germanicans and the subsequent struggle between Sejanus and Tiberius are depicted as theatrical manipulation, which reaches its culmination in Tiberius' great stroke, the letter to the Senate which guarantees the destruction of his rival.

In *Volpone*, the interest in theater, poetry, and the self-conscious use of language has taken refuge in the private world of a Venetian magnifico. Majesty has been divorced from theater—except for the majesty with which Volpone endows his existence through sheer imaginative energy. In other words, theater and self-conscious rhetoric are means of self-definition in a world that lacks real majesty: we have entered the world of middle-class authority, the world of *Epicene* and Morose, who, lacking Volpone's imagination, becomes the pitiful remnant of the once majestic impulse to order and control the world for the sake of humane values. Morose's complaint against the Christian princes is that they have foregone the practice of requiring silence of their subjects. To him the highest expression of majesty is military maneuvers by pantomime, and he reduces the power and beauty of language to the solipsistic appreciation of the sound of his own voice. But for his unremitting foolishness, Morose's nostalgic recollection of his father might have been touching—as it stands, however, it is only pathetic:[3]

> My father, in my education, was wont to advise mee, that I should alwayes collect, and contayne my mind, not suffring it to flow loosely; that I should looke to what things were necessary to the carriage of my life, and what not: embracing the one, and eschewing the other. In short, that I should endeare my selfe to rest, and avoid turmoile.
>
> (V, iii, 48-54)

If Morose's house, like Volpone's, can be considered his theater or even his sphere of magisterial influence, then this is a stage devoid of mirth, noise, speech, flirtation, everything except the figure of its repressive owner.

One would be hard pressed to add substantially to Jonas Barish's analysis of Truewit as the embodiment of Jonson's spirit of acceptance, but there are two points about Truewit worth stressing. First, he is one of Jonson's great satirists; the force of his satire, however, is neither didactic like Horace's and Macilente's nor entirely self-serving like Volpone's, but rather a mixture of the two dominated by the desire to entertain. Even as he tortures Morose with his diatribe against marriage in act 2, hoping to further his friend Dauphine's plot and to have some fun at the expense of an old fool, he makes us feel that he is performing for us. Second, Truewit is Jonson's second attempt to come to terms with the values of Ovid and his libertine society. The first attempt, in *Poetaster*, had resulted in Jonson's rejection of the poet, and that play is marred by his inability to resolve the disparity between his obvious attraction to Ovid and his equally obvious wish to affirm Augustus' judgment. Only when Augustus is reduced to Morose does the Ovidian spirit flourish. In the absence of that overwhelming authority, which tends to lump together as subversive everything that does not fully comply with its own values, Truewit can distance himself from his world in a way which Ovid cannot. In *Poetaster*, there is no easy way to distinguish the gifted young poets from their silly associates, Crispinus, Albius, and Chloe. But Truewit lives among fools, using his wit and his penchant for jest to keep his distance from them, and he is permitted this role because there is no larger authority in the play to force him to make serious choices. The reemergence of Ovid as Truewit, underscored by Truewit's defense of Ovid and his paraphrase, in act 1, of Ovid's work, parallels Jonson's own development as a playwright. *Epicene* was possible only because he had rejected the kind of drama that implies a clearly authoritarian relationship between playwright and audience. He had set aside the burden of paternal authority he had borne through the comical satires, although it was difficult for him to leave it alone.

Related to this development, and another measure of Jonson's achievement in *Epicene* is the play's great sexual vitality. Made to represent impotence and sterility, Morose pays the price of Jonson's admission that the agents of majesty, harmony, morality, and judgment inevitably choke off essential human playfulness, of which sexuality is undeniably a part.[4] The rest of the play is unabashedly free about sexual things. As Edward Partridge explains in *The Broken Compass*, it is epicene in every way, blurring all of the conventional lines between masculinity and femininity.[5] For the moment, easygoing androgyny is preferable to a chaste Cynthia or a sterile Morose.

Considered in light of the psychological themes developed in Jonson's work, the sexual energy of *Epicene* is even more striking. Jonson returns again and again in his plays to the issue of filial aggression and the enmity between son and father stirred by the attempts of the former to take on the manhood of the latter. The parties to the conflict in his plays usually are not natural fathers and sons but, instead, characters who define their existence in terms of certain kinds of authority and spend their time seeking to acquire or maintain that authority. In either case, it is a process requiring significant cost, physically, emotionally, or financially, to those involved in the struggle. This authority might be paternal, maternal, or both, and the seeker stands roughly in the relation of son to parent. In the first two comical satires, *Every Man Out* and *Cynthia's Revels*, the theme is relatively simple. Crites and (at the end of *Every Man Out*) Macilente are cast as good sons who protect the interests of a maternal queen by fending off threats to her authority. Their reward is sharing in that authority and, in serving as court poets, assuming the role of leading males in the dramas. But one condition of the satirist's elevation to a position of note and influence is his willingness to forego his sexual interests.[6] Sexuality, in this Platonic world, is characteristic of the objects of satire. The chastity and high-mindedness of the satirist, coupled with his role as protector, allow him to vent a great deal of hostile energy on the world without arousing suspicion of personal motives. And one suspects, particularly in light of the later plays, that this is energy which otherwise might have been directed into a violent struggle for supremacy.

When the primary power in Jonson's plays ceases to be exclusively female, violence escalates and alliances suddenly grow more complex. Not only do plays like *Poetaster*, *Sejanus*, and *Volpone* create serious ambivalence toward various authorities, they also admit sexual issues and frustrate the clear and safe discharge of hostility onto fools and knaves. The role of obedient son is progressively endangered, until *Sejanus* makes it extinct. In *Poetaster*, Ovid and Horace vie for the poetic honors, but Horace's victory leaves a bitter taste, for him as well as for us. When Augustus brings the full weight of his imperial authority to bear on the dalliance between Ovid and his daughter, we suspect that personal and social business have been confused. The fact that Jonson suppressed, or chose to ignore, the report, which he undoubtedly knew from Suetonius, that Augustus engaged in precisely the same blasphemous masquing as Ovid and his friends do in the play, and, moreover, that Jonson makes this masque the reason for Ovid's exile when there is no historical certainty to back him up is a fascinating way of visiting on the "son" the sins of the "father."[7] In other words, it is the sexual aggression of the would-be son that calls forth the wrath of the father. If this line of argument seems speculative, one need only consider that Jonson's very next play, *Sejanus*, presents another Roman emperor whose sexual sins are no secret and who engages in a lethal struggle with a far more vile and threatening aggressor than Ovid. Jonson has clarified and intensified the theme of filial aggression, and sexuality is a fundamental aspect of the conflict.

In Jonson's peculiar oedipal drama, begun with Macilente and acted in turn by Crites, Ovid, and Sejanus, only one of the "heroes" finally reaches a strange and precarious manhood, Volpone; one might even say that Volpone is the father of the bizarre group of "heirs" he makes for himself through his ruse. But Celia brings with her into the play a world of authority beyond Volpone's, denying him what he wants most and reminding us that achievements in this kind of drama are provisional at best. Celia and Lady Wouldbe represent the sexual aspect of qualified authority: both "belong" to other men who are foolish paternal types, but, whereas in a conventional comic world the possession of the father's woman represents a triumph, here no such triumph is possible. The available female is unappealing and the appealing female is unavailable. This situation skews the process of normal oedipal development, in which maturity distinguishes the mother from the wife, the unavailable mother ceases to be the object of interest, and the wife is both available and appealing. *Volpone* confirms the suspicion that Jonson's dramatic world will not make available to its heroes beauty, virtue, and sexual satisfaction.

Epicene maintains this sense of qualified satisfactions, but, in addition, it seeks to mitigate the male-to-male violence that characterizes the struggle for mature manhood in Jonson's world. Clearly hostility still exists on both sides, but, perhaps because the play is relatively free and open about the issues, the violence is muted. Jonson accomplishes this in part by reducing Morose and the authority he represents to comic proportions. Moreover, he distributes the role of usurper among the three friends, Dauphine, Clerimont, and Truewit. Dauphine is the real aggressor, but, though he engineers the main plot, he is overshadowed by the theatrical virtuosity of his friend Truewit, who is far more overtly and cruelly aggressive toward Morose than the nephew is. This split contributes substantially to the overall success of the play in divorcing satire and jest from serious aggression.

In *Epicene*, then, Jonson turned another corner in his career, leaving behind a world where majesty and law enforce the humane principles of comic theater. *Volpone* reassures us, though with less than half a heart, that comic justice is a function of a legal system that perceives and attempts to act upon moral values; *Epicene* pays no heed to such matters, appealing to us instead on the basis of the kind of gentlemanly fair play that licenses brutality put to the service of wit and style. In spite of the fact that the stakes have come down since *Volpone*, that is, no one is sexually assaulted, clapped in chains, or sent off to the galleys, and in spite of the fact that *Epicene* is a very funny play, it is in its own way as doggedly aggressive toward humanity in general as any of Jonson's previous plays. If this conclusion seems to contradict my earlier optimism about the play's spirit of resolution and accommodation, the discrepancy is an instructive one: it points toward the fact that for Jonson acceptance and rejection go hand in hand. Indeed, they pay each other's way. *Epicene* signals a new way of mediating the extremes. To put it in spatial terms, accommodation is a function of the play's surface, while just below the surface there is a great deal of hostility. Jonson has submerged his ambivalence toward his spectators, and this is a major development in his changing relationship to his audience. In the earlier plays, even *Volpone*, this ambivalence is expressed in conflicts that occur on the surface of the plays: moral and immoral, civil and uncivil move in a single plane. Asotus and his crew in *Cynthia's Revels* are set over against Crites and company, and the play's satire works to close the gap, to accommodate the outsiders to the utopian world. A spectator to this drama orients himself easily. If he is a fool he takes his medicine, and once he has faced his vices and assured himself that he is on the proper side of the line between the judging and the judged, he is beyond the satiric aggression of the author, free to vent his own aggressiveness on others.[8]

Jonson's move away from the world of clear morality did not exclude moral judgment—it only complicated it. One might say he buried the moral issues in his work, and the result is a break between the surface of his plays, that is, the dramatic action, and a new judgmental substrate. In effect, the plays delaminate; they acquire horizontal fissures to replace the vertical ones of the earlier plays. On the surface of *Epicene* everyone is permitted his pleasure because our pleasure is no longer tied to serious moral choices, but beneath the surface the battle continues over what values and responses are appropriate. Jonson accepts his audience with all its foibles and deficiencies in a superficial way, while he rejects them savagely behind his mask of geniality. Such is the Jonsonian pact, acceptance only at the cost of subtler and deeper rejection. The early plays are univocal, or relatively so; they say what they mean, are as they seem. But slowly we are made to deal with equivocal theater, with oblique, two-faced drama that enacts its meaning tendentiously. Satire is no longer a broadsword wielded in the name of social morality, but a rapier employed in personal combat—or just for the fun of it.

Nothing better exemplifies this process as it is worked out in *Epicene* than Jonson's depiction of women and the relations between the sexes. And the revelation of Epicene as a boy, the stratagem that concludes the play, serves as a splendid metaphor for the entire play. In the most obvious sense it is a comic stroke, the final "deflation" of Morose and a denial that there is real violence in the struggle between nephew and uncle. The joke is that "no woman" is involved in the plot, but beneath the surprise and laughter the revelation generates for an audience a good deal of relief, because, while the play acknowledges explicitly that control of a woman is part of oedipal conflict, it makes comedy of the issue of sexual aggression in a way that no previous Jonson play did. Instead of a son seeking access to the father's woman, here the "dauphin" offers the "patriarch" a non-woman. This is an ingenious way of dissipating the hostility that lies just beneath the comic surface of the play, but, from another perspective, it is an especially grim twist to the conventions of romance comedy, suggesting that whatever truth romance comedy represents about human society and individual maturation, in the end what really matters is man-to-man conflict, the business deal, necessary, unpleasant, but manageable without mortal combat. Furthermore, behind the epicene joke stands the conviction that women do not have to be taken seriously, or, to put it more precisely, the fear, based on what the play reveals about women, that maybe they *do* have to be taken seriously. Whereas most comedy lays the groundwork for satisfying relations between the sexes, this comedy sequesters male from female in all but the most debasing circumstances.

That the play treats women badly is undeniable.[9] Here there is no Celia, no pious natural beauty. Instead we have Mrs. Otter and her Collegiate friends, women "that live from their husbands; and give entertainment to all the Wits, and Braveries o' the time, as they call 'hem: crie downe, or up, what they like, or dislike in a braine, or a fashion, with most masculine, or rather hermaphroditicall authoritie" (I, i, 76-80). Otter is the epitome of the castrating female, a siren who "commands all at home," dominating the most minute aspects of her husband's existence, while enjoying Collegiate license for herself. The rest are loud, aggressive, adulterous, and, beneath their makeup, old and ugly. The president, Lady Haughty, owns an "autumnall face" and "peec'd beautie," and the disgust Clerimont registers in merely recounting her toilet is unmistakable: "There's no man can bee admitted till she be ready, now adaies, till she has painted, and perfum'd, and wash'd, and scour'd, but the boy here; and him shee wipes her oil'd lips upon, like a sponge" (I, i, 86-89). There are no ideals here, except those that people talk about. This is a world of Lady Wouldbes.

Nor is this treatment of women simply collateral to the main business of the play involving Dauphine and his uncle. The debate between Clerimont and Truewit in the opening scene of the play suggests that the issues of relations between the sexes and the nature of the female will be major concerns of the play. The terms of the debate seem to me less important than the context in which the debate takes place: both men start from the assumption that most women are inherently pretty awful, but the difference in their outlooks is that Truewit accepts this idea while Clerimont commits himself to the search for the exception to the rule. In the opening lines of the play, Clerimont mentions a song he has written for Lady Haughty, a song performed shortly thereafter by his boy:

> Still to be neat, still to be drest,
> As, you were going to a feast;
> Still to be pou'dred, still perfum'd:
> Lady, it is to be presum'd,
> Though arts hid causes are not found,
> All is not sweet, all is not sound.
>
> Give me a looke, give me a face,
> That makes simplicitie a grace;
> Robes loosely flowing, haire as free:
> Such sweet neglect more taketh me,
> Then all th'adulteries of art.
> They strike mine eyes, but not my heart.
> (I, i, 91-102)

This is some love song. In fact, it is a real act of aggression, and the message is one repeated throughout the play: males feel revulsion even imagining the hidden physical corruption of women. The debate is not whether women are corrupt, but to what extent men will accept it. Clerimont is won over

EPICENE

to Truewit's side as the play progresses and Dauphine is initiated into the herd of Collegiate studs, but a necessary corollary of the accommodation seems to be the venting of tremendous disgust, primarily through Truewit. Consider this exchange between Truewit and Clerimont:

> TRUEWIT. Women ought to repair the losses, time and yeeres have made i'their features, with dressings. And an intelligent woman, if shee know by her selfe the least defect, will bee most curious, to hide it: and it becomes her. If shee be short, let her sit much, lest when shee stands, shee be thought to sit. If shee have an ill foot, let her weare her gowne the longer, and her shoo the thinner. If a fat hand, and scald nailes, let her carve the lesse, and act in gloves. If a sowre breath, let her never discourse fasting: and alwaies talke at her distance. If shee have black and rugged teeth, let her offer the lesse at laughter, especially if she laugh wide, and open.
>
> CLERIMONT. O, you shall have some women, when they laugh, you would thinke they bray'd, it is so rude, and—
>
> TRUEWIT. I, and others, that will stalke i'their gait like an Estrich, and take huge strides. I cannot endure such a sight.
>
> (IV, i, 35-50)

The great worry expressed in this play is that men might glimpse the wreckage beneath the illusion of beauty; hence male-female relations might be described as imminent disasters. The fantasy that counters this fear throughout the play is that of creating attainable, sexually manipulable women, but this play makes it clear that women can be admitted as objects of desire only after being degraded[10] and exposed as degenerate, unfaithful, self-sufficent, and domineering. There are, however, momentary escapes from this reductive vision, as when Morose lovingly elaborates his feminine ideal for his bride-to-be:

> But heare me, faire lady, I doe also love to see her, whom I shall choose for my heicfar, to be the first and principall in all fashions; praecede all the dames at court, by a fortnight; have her counsell of taylors, linneners, lace-women, embroyderers, and sit with 'hem sometimes twise a day, upon French intelligences; and then come foorth, varied like nature, or oftner then she, and better, by the helpe of Art, her aemulous servant.
>
> (II, v, 68-75)

But, finally, this is just another futile expression of the impulse to control, and when his hopes are dashed by Epicene's roaring after the wedding ceremony, Morose retreats to his original belief that women are just intrusions on his precious peace. Truewit puts it nicely: "Nay, looke you, sir: you would be friends with your wife upon un-conscionable termes, her silence" (IV, iv, 45-46).

The catalogue of *Epicene*'s anti-feminism is impressive, but there is a logic to the hostility that goes beyond that of an anti-feminist tract. In part, this is a play about males managing the female rejection that seems to be an inescapable part of growing up. The essential male anxiety is that mother-wives are self-sufficient—they do not need men, or, to twist this proposition to reflect the fear implicit in the idea of female promiscuity, any man will do. The young men are caught in a psychological trap: growing up means establishing sexual relations with the opposite sex, but such relations are revealed to be regressive experiences. The women in the play want to make children, playthings, objects of their lovers, or, worse, to dismember them. In fact, Jonson offers us three stages of male development in *Epicene*. The first is prepubescent innocence; the second, single young adulthood punctuated by sexual episodes involving promiscuous women; the third, middle-aged celibacy either by choice, as with Morose, or by force of one's wife having abandoned marriage to "live apart" with the Collegiates. The first and third are, for all intents and purposes, equivalent. Tom Otter is just a child dominated by a termagant wife-mother. The young men occupy a precarious middle ground, and the ideal moment of development, as described in a conversation between Clerimont and his boy, seems to be the precise moment of puberty's onset, offering at once the widest sexual access and acceptance as a cuddly child:

> BOY. . . . I am the welcom'st thing under a man that comes there [the mansion of the Collegiate women].
> CLERIMONT. I thinke, and above a man too, if the truth were rack'd out of you.
> BOY. No faith, I'll confesse before, sir. The gentlewomen play with me, and throw me o' the bed; and carry me in to my lady; and shee kisses me with her oil'd face; and puts a perruke o' my head; and askes me an' I will weare her gowne; and I say, no; and then she hits me a blow o'the eare, and calls me innocent, and lets me goe.
> CLERIMONT. No marvell, if the dore bee kept shut against your master, when the entrance is so easie to you—well sir, you shall goe there no more, lest I bee faine to seeke your voyce in my ladies rushes, a fortnight hence.
>
> (I, i, 9-22)

Jonson's aggression toward women in this play serves two psychological ends: first, it is a confession, an acknowledgment of the fear suppressed in the earlier plays, that women are really nasty creatures; second, to portray them as nasty is revenge against them, not just for their malignancy but also for their rejection of males. And it is this bitter admission of his own hostility toward females that softens the male-to-male conflict and admits homosexuality as an acceptable activity. One might say there is a system of psychic compensation at work here—women being what they are, men must stick together.

Central to this psychology is the fact that more than any other Jonson play *Epicene* is about the successful negotiation of adolescence. The good-son satirists of the early plays are prepubescent; on the other hand, Ovid, Sejanus, and Volpone are exiled, torn limb from limb, or shackled for their oedipal aggressions. In *Epicene*, the world has passed to adolescents. There are no maternal or paternal forces either to order things or to muzzle youthful exuberance. The positive side to this is Truewit's wonderful theatricality, which can be indulged without reprisal; the negative side is the terrible sterility into which exuberance continually threatens to collapse. Clerimont asks Truewit in the opening scene, "Why, what should a man doe?" and the response, though offered flippantly, is finally hollow: "Why, nothing: or that, which when 'tis done, is as idle." Dauphine's quest for his knighthood, of which his uncle's fortune is an integral part, is by any conventional standard an empty one, a point which Morose makes with vicious precision:

> This night I wil get an heire, and thrust him out of my bloud like a stranger; he would be knighted, forsooth, and thought by that meanes to raigne over me, his title must doe it: no kinsman, I will now make you bring mee the tenth lords, and the sixteenth ladies letter, kinsman; and it shall doe you no good kinsman. Your knighthood it selfe shall come on it's knees, and it shall be rejected; it shall bee sued for it's fees to execution, and not bee redeem'd; it shall cheat at the twelvepeny ordinary, it knighthood, for it's diet all the termes time, and tell tales for it in the vacation, to the hostesse: or it knighthood shall doe worse; take sanctuary in Coleharbor, and fast. It shall fright all it friends, with borrowing letters; and when one of the foure-score hath brought it knighthood ten shillings, it knighthood shall go to the Cranes, or the Beare at the Bridge-foot, and be drunk in feare: it shal not have money to discharge one taverne reckoning, to invite the old creditors, to forbeare it knighthood; or the new, that should be, to trust it knighthood. It shall be the tenth name in the bond, to take up the commoditie of pipkins, and stone jugs; and the part thereof shall not

EPICENE

furnish it knighthood forth, for the attempting of a bakers widdow, a browne bakers widdow. It shall give it knighthoods name, for a stallion, to all gamesome citizens wives, and bee refus'd; when the master of a dancing schoole, or (How do you call him) the worst reveller in the towne is taken: it shall want clothes, and by reason of that, wit, to foole lawyers. It shall not have hope to repaire it selfe by Constantinople, Ireland, or Virginia; but the best, and last fortune to it knighthood shall be, to make Dol Teare-Sheet, or Kate Common, a lady: and so, it knighthood may eate.

(II, v, 100-131)

What Morose imagines is Dauphine as a knight without his inheritance to pay the bills, and the specter of knighthood reduced finally to a license to pander is a sobering one. What is intriguing about the speech, however, is that implicit in this vision is Morose's idea of the life of a knight *with* money, and it is scarcely better. Knights seem to spend their time and money in tavern crawling, chasing citizens' wives, and arranging commodity scams, and frankly we see nothing of Dauphine to suggest that his aspirations are much grander. The nephew does not want a princess or honor, nor does he seek to praise his king through valorous service; he wants none of these things, feels none of the responsibilities of the usual hero, and he is accorded none of the satisfactions. He wants his inheritance to make himself a fully enfranchised member of the foolish, sordid society he inhabits.

What is valued in this world is entertainment for its own sake, and, while this is a good deal in itself, it is Jonson's unwillingness to affirm anything beyond this that is telling, particularly in light of his earlier plays. *Epicene* is comedy that takes place only at the abdication of majestic authority, forcing us to suffer fools unless we wish to retreat to womblike seclusion. Ovid's festive spirit is brought to a strange rebirth: in Jonson's world, the son's gain is the father's loss, but the father always has a measure of revenge. Here Morose, on behalf of Ovid Senior, offers his heir a world of confused values and empty jests. For other writers this is well down the road to tragedy.

I have argued all along that it is a short step from the psychological drama of family politics to managing an audience in the theater, and one of the terms that bridges the distance for Jonson is "privilege." His commitment to entertaining the public meant the destruction of all privileged perspective (just as in the masque it meant extraordinary efforts to construct privileged perspective). His own account of this process is in terms of allowing all spectators a privileged perspective, but this situation conforms to the paradox of democracy: a privileged perspective for all is a privileged perspective for none. Gone from this play is the moral hierarchy headed by a Cynthia or Augustus, which confidently places its spectators through the sorting action of satire. Most critics have taken this release from moral seriousness at face value, chalking it up to Jonson's "mellowing," as if he were doing us a favor. But if one takes seriously the idea that he took with one hand what he gave with the other, one might expect that the change was not so simple or so cheerful as it seems. In fact, clear and simple moral hierarchy relieved Jonson of having to face the deep hostility he felt toward his audience. As the privilege went out of his theater, with it went the romance of the harmonious family, in terms of both oedipal psychology and social theory. Maternal and paternal pressures were no longer sufficient to suppress his anger, so the plays turned to examining the relationships upon which the early plays had unself-consciously relied. The result is the rejection of psychological privilege (after all, mothers and fathers are privileged family members) and the dissolution of certain social relations. Volpone and Sejanus attempt to usurp paternal privilege, but *Epicene* just dismisses both maternal and paternal privilege. The children rule this new world, but, instead of inheriting an adult world, they find their realm strangely diminished.

In other words, Jonson set about to deny his spectators

power over himself by using the *speculum consuetudinis* to show the audience to itself as it was, as a way of keeping them at a distance. Thus, his acceptance of his audience and his renewed commitment to entertaining them are inextricable from the grim assertion that those same spectators are essentially unregenerate souls. If we credit Truewit with any of Jonson's own sensibilities, we must admit that, for Jonson, the belief that noise, discord, extreme self-interestedness, foolishness, promiscuity, and blasphemy are all part of human recreation does not relieve them of their sordidness. Jonson was finally beginning to accept that the aggression of his audiences toward himself, and his toward them, was a natural and unresolvable consequence of the relationship, determined not only by their peculiar intractability but by his own as well. There is despair in such a commitment to playfulness.

FIVE

The Alchemist: "Yet I Put My Selfe on You"

WHEN LOVEWIT has finished justifying himself to the theater audience at the conclusion of *The Alchemist*, he instructs Face, "Speake for thy selfe, knave," and Face responds with what serves as the epilogue to the play:

> So I will, sir. Gentlemen,
> My part a little fell in this last Scene
> Yet 'twas decorum. And though I am cleane
> Got off, from Subtle, Surly, Mammon, Dol,
> Hot Ananias, Dapper, Drugger, all
> With whom I traded; yet I put my selfe
> On you, that are my countrey: and this pelfe,
> Which I have got, if you doe quit me, rests
> To feast you often, and invite new ghests.
> (V, v, 157-65)

Face begins, as Lovewit did, by evaluating his role and attempting to forestall what he thinks to be a likely criticism, the "fall" of his part. What he offers in his defense is decorum, an appeal not to our experience of *The Alchemist* but to a set of autonomous theoretical considerations. He suggests that his fate will be understood to be appropriate when considered in the context of classical comic conventions. Face's "fall" respects both the appropriate servant-master relationship and, at least from his own point of view, comic justice. It is not at all unusual to find Jonson buttressing his work with literary theory; in fact, it is the exception among his plays which is not so defended. But Face is no simple Jonsonian apologist. If we believe that Face ends decorously, if we allow him to slip " 'twas decorum" past us without question, we have ignored a great deal of indecorous behavior. Face has robbed all of those with whom he claims to have traded, yet his reward is the praise and protection of his master. The prologue to the play has promised us "wholsome remedies" and "faire correctives," yet Lovewit ends up straining his "candor," rejecting these comic conventions outright and reserving for himself the judgment of his behavior. Lovewit's answer to proper dramatic decorum is to assert the value of his own pleasure:

> Therefore, gentlemen,
> And kind Spectators, if I have out-stript
> An old mans gravitie, or strict canon, thinke
> What a yong wife, and a goode braine may doe:
> Stretch ages truth sometimes, and crack it too.
>   (V, v, 152-56)

Face and Lovewit have the capacity to regard their roles self-consciously within both the context of the play and the larger context of literary tradition. What is striking is that they use this capacity to define themselves as unique characters in a unique play, not as part of a comic tradition. Jonson insists repeatedly, as he does in the prologue to *The Alchemist*, that his work has moral significance for his audience, and he attempts to validate the claim by placing his work in the traditions of classical satire and comedy. We are asked to respond to his work with informed critical and moral judgment, and we are told again and again that the two go together, yet here are two of Jonson's creatures resisting us on both scores. If we judge Face and Lovewit as Jonson asks, we must reject their own standards of behavior.

Face is far more devious than his master. His glib use of the word "decorum" is just a single instance of the deception which defines his role. It is here in the epilogue, however, that Face attempts his most interesting imposture, toward his audience of theatergoers and readers. The conventional epilogue constitutes an actor's appeal for the praise of his audience. In this moment we are asked to recognize what we ordinarily are asked to ignore, the distinction between the actor and his role. Face satisfies the *pro forma* requirements of the epilogue by making his apologies and humbling himself to our judgment, flattering us as his jury and promising his ill-gotten goods as a kind of restitution against his acquittal. In one sense, this is a simple acknowledgment of the audience's power to determine the success of any play; our approval is literally the vital force of Face's role. But, whereas most epilogues attempt to simplify and minimize the judgmental problems involved in theater, Jonson's epilogues invariably do just the opposite. At the moment we regard the creature standing before us both as Face, a fictional character in a play called *The Alchemist*, and as the actor playing Face, we must consider two kinds of pelf as well. There is the strange pile of treasure toward which Face gestures, the orphans' goods and Mammon's brass and pewter, and there is somewhere in the theater the pelf from our own pockets. Face's promise to the audience, then, is a complex one. First, he suggests that his fictional pelf will remain for use in subsequent performances of *The Alchemist* and second, by pointing our thoughts toward the real pelf, he expands our sense of theater beyond this particular play to the financial reality of theater as a vital social organ. The price of our admission will sustain the theater, paying the actors, buying props, and renting the building. Face emphasizes the role of the theater as a fundamental enactment of human community by depicting it as a feast to which we come as guests. A good deal of Jonson's commentary on his work, including the epilogue to *Volpone* and the prologue to *Epicene*, is couched in the terms of feasting, and the feast is a prototype of one version of Jonson's ideal theater.[1] His poem "Inviting a Friend to Supper" defines the perfect entertainment as an action completed by the guest: "It is the faire acceptance, Sir, creates/The entertaynment perfect: not the cates."[2] In the same manner, though with considerably less sincerity, Face invites his audience to complete the

THE ALCHEMIST

theatrical event by playing the lead role in this self-renewing social experience.

Lest we exult in this privilege, however, we ought to remind ourselves that our ability to enact such an idealized role is always questionable for Jonson. He felt his audiences were inevitably subject to lapses in taste, if not to downright malice. Such spectators threatened Jonson's ideal theater, but there is another threat suggested in this epilogue, a threat from an unlikely quarter, the theater itself. The final twist in Face's role is his adumbration of the danger which the theater poses to itself through self-interestedness. Against the natural unmasking of the actor, which asserts the value of theater for its audiences, stands the characteristically Jonsonian threat that the actor will not rejoin the human community but will assert, instead, the independence that his fictional role allows him. Volpone resists us in this way in his epilogue, choosing finally to occupy his own private realm apart from both the play and its audience. In Face's speech, the problem is contained, *in potentia,* in the contrast between "feast" and "decorum," between justifying theater in terms of its audience and justifying it in terms essentially external to the experience of a play. Jonson frequently tries both, but, at moments like the conclusions to *Volpone* and *The Alchemist,* the latter becomes a defense against the former as Jonson attempts to avert the fear that the plays, once allowed to speak for themselves, may no longer say what he wishes. In other words, there are moments when Jonson uses the power of his fictions against his audience to protect his own interests in the theater. He will not allow us our communal moment without qualification.

The key to Face's final performance is the finely calculated ambiguity of his speech, specifically his use of the word "pelf." As we recall the money collected from all of us on admission to the theater, the clear inference is that we are in some way, like Mammon, Dapper, Surly, and the rest, Face's gulls. Such a suggestion was implicit in *Volpone,* and the induction to *Bartholomew Fair,* while addressing explicitly the question of the financial relationship between stage and audience, makes the suggestion again. There Jonson attempts to specify what it is we buy with our admission, offering us the right to judge in proportion to the percentage of the house we rent for that performance. Of course this is nonsense, but Jonson has us thinking about things that we normally take for granted. And, when he finally instructs us, "As you have preposterously put to your Seales already (which is your money) you will now adde the other part of suffrage, your hands" (*Bartholomew Fair*, Induction, 53-55), clearly he is twitting us about our gullibility: we have just given our money for something about which we are ignorant, and yes, we *will* now "adde the other part of suffrage" by applauding before the play begins.

Through the induction, Jonson makes us as conscious as he was himself about every facet of theatergoing, particularly the problem of valuing our experience. For Face, acting is gulling—he knows no other way of dealing with an audience. The question is what this means for us as his final, real audience. Initially, the epilogue flatters our privileged perspective as spectators. The reference to decorum is a joke between Face and us based on the perception that his fate is technically decorous while being in every other way indecorous. His characterization of the business with Subtle, Surly, and Mammon as "trade" requires the same kind of complex response. In the simplest sense, it is another private laugh. We know, as he knows, that it was not trade in any normal sense of the word, but there is a real, if oblique, sense in which "traded" is exactly correct. Face and Subtle have responded to the lunatic obsessions of their clients with the best approximation of magic we have, theater. There is no doubt that they have supplied those commodities which Jonson hoped his own theater would supply, wonder and delight. The clause which follows "traded" sustains the idea that Jonson is moving in oblique ways: "Yet I put my selfe/On you, that are my countrey." Face means ostensibly that, now that he has escaped the judgment of those in his private drama, he will try our judgment. But it seems to me impossible, in light of what has transpired on stage, to hear this character named Face speaking of putting himself on us without asking ourselves whether Face is not still Face, turning the basic premise of the theatrical medium, putting on faces, to gulling a new audience of readers and spectators. This Face seeks acquittal but knows that we will "quit" the theater with or without bestowing our favor, and leave him with our gold. Are we to congratulate ourselves as benefactors of the Jacobean theater or to consider ourselves cozened, like Mammon?

> MAMMON. And my goods,
> That lye i'the cellar: which I am glad they ha' left,
> I may have home yet. LOVEWIT. Thinke you so, sir?
> MAMMON. I
> LOVEWIT. By order of law, sir, but not otherwise.
> MAMMON. Not mine owne stuffe? LOVEWIT. Sir, I can take no knowledge.
> That they are yours, but by publique meanes.
> If you can bring certificate, that you were gull'd of 'hem,
> Or any formall writ, out of a court,
> That you did cosen your selfe: I will not hold them.
> MAMMON. I'll rather loose 'hem.
>
> (V, v, 62-71)

In this theater, the price of objecting to the play, of demanding one's wholesome remedies or one's money back, is a public admission of gullibility.

In the end, we must admit to our idea of theater as a social experience valued for its ability to affirm human community, the suggestion that theater might actually exclude its audiences from the communal experience it seems to promise. In this sense, the theater is apart from its audience, seeking its own ends and picking our pockets with ease. As he often does, Jonson cheerily sets out the ideal while leaving in the shadows, for anyone who will look to see it, the ugly side of things. Face is finally just a face inviting us to choose among his aspects. In speaking for himself he speaks for no one; his mask is a mirror in which we see of ourselves only what we wish to see. Far from urging a genial reconciliation between stage and audience, Jonson has actually escalated the risk attendant upon the judgment of his play. Approval and disapproval are not simply a matter of liking or disliking an entertainment: any response is perceived from the stage as a choice of a self-revealing social role. *The Alchemist* has not ended but, instead, begun a new act by calling on its audience to record publicly its judgment.

We are not dealing here with a Pirandello or a Camus; *The Alchemist* is not, in Robert Brustein's terms, the "theater of revolt." It is didactic drama which is uneasy about its work, theater which, because it will not offer theatrical solutions to the real problems it raises, willingly sows the seeds of its own destruction. The point is not that *The Alchemist* cheats us— the evidence is overwhelmingly to the contrary—but simply that, in light of Jonson's apparent eagerness to reach his audiences with morally significant drama, it is peculiar to find this play suggesting that the interests of stage and gallery might actually diverge. The entire weight of Jonson's critical commentary on his work rests on the side of poetry which seeks to improve its spectators, to educate them, to correct their foolish behavior and to expose their vices. Yet Lovewit and Face, who speak the final lines of the play with impunity, could never take such a task seriously.

In short, here as elsewhere in Jonson's work theory and practice do not conform. The portrait he offers of his play in the prologue scarcely resembles the play itself. Jonson is more insistent than ever on prescribing a standard of value which requires a judging response of the spectator:

> But, when the wholsome remedies are sweet,
>   And, in their working, gaine, and profit meet,
> He hopes to find no spirit so much diseas'd,
>   But will, with such faire correctives, be pleas'd.
> For here, he doth not feare, who can apply.
>   If there be any, that will sit so nigh

Unto the streame, to looke what it doth run,
  They shall find things, they'ld thinke, or wish, were done;
They are so naturall follies, but so showne,
  As even the doers may see, and yet not owne.
(Prologue, 15-24)

Not only does the prologue define appropriate and inappropriate responses to the play, it also rejects the notion that the significant activity in the playhouse takes place exclusively on the stage. *Poetaster*'s armed prologue defends the stage against the subversive portion of the audience bent on turning the stage action into an occasion for its own self-celebration. Here in *The Alchemist*, however, Jonson hopefully offers the stage to his entire audience, unthreatened by those who would "apply" and willing to please his audience as a means to improving it. All he asks is that we judge ourselves as we judge the play.

We might expect, then, on the basis of Jonson's own theorizing in the prologue, that our satisfaction with the play will be directly proportional to our willingness to play the role of judging spectators. But just the opposite is true. It is when we begin thinking about this play that it poses problems for us. This play makes it easy for us to enjoy ourselves in the theater. We do not worry in this play, as we do not worry for much of *Volpone*, about the questions of morality and dramatic form which might interfere with our immediate pleasure. *The Alchemist* has earned the reputation of a genial play, and so it is. What is the swindle played by Face, Subtle, and Dol compared to the vicious ambition of Sejanus, or even Volpone? Loss in this play seems carefully measured against the capacity to sustain it. There is never any suggestion that the victims suffer crippling setbacks; in fact, the cruelest theft of all involves neither cash nor goods, but expectation, Surly's loss of the widow he never really had. But as we bring to the play the critical perspective which Jonson began cultivating in his audiences in the comical satires, we qualify and in fact impair our ability to enjoy the play. In a theater which requires extreme self-consciousness, we find ourselves in the position of Narcissus: as long as we watch the reflections in the dramatic stream without recognizing their full implications for ourselves, the illusion is safe. With full self-consciousness, we find the stage turning on us, and the illusion is lost.

In the realm of the efficient morality, *The Alchemist* falters. When the time comes for him to do so, Jonson simply will not fully assert his moral authority. He will do so in his prologues and epistles, outside of his plays, but he is reluctant to do so *within* plays like *Volpone* and *The Alchemist*. John Enck's comment in *Jonson and the Comic Truth* is typical of critics who find the ending of the play faulty: "Lovewit's unexpected return to London creaks like a crane lowering a ponderous and desperate *deus ex machina*. He bears no warrant whatsoever except as owner of the house, and his judgments sound thoroughly whimsical."[3] Certainly this ending is an uneasy one in terms of the expectations set up in the play. It is a repetition of Jonson's refusal in *Volpone*, in the name of strict justice, to permit any of the characters any real satisfaction. In *The Alchemist*, we have the added twist that Lovewit, an interloper, gets everything. What Enck suggests is that the execution of the ending is a miscalculation on Jonson's part, when it is in fact the coldest calculation, the acknowledgment of comic convention through its conscious subversion. Do we want a wedding? We have one here that resolves none of the issues of the play, one that revels in its capriciousness. Marriage, which serves conventionally as one of the primary vehicles for comic justice, *guarantees* in this play that there will be no justice at all. Critics assert that, in overruling justice, Jonson rules in favor of wit; after all, it is a character named Lovewit who triumphs.[4] But this assumption strains the play considerably. Surly has as much wit as anyone in the play; he beats Face at his own game with a wonderful performance as Don John, and it is simply his misfortune to run out of time. It is Lovewit's good fortune to arrive just in time, while it is his authority and his willingness to strain his candor, not really his wit, that allow him his victory.

Jonson knew exactly what he was doing when he lowered his ponderous machine. How could it be otherwise? He knew the drama, classical and contemporary, inside out, and had he been desperate, as Enck suggests he was, he could have chosen any one of a number of more appropriate conventional endings. Indeed he remarks on the ease of just such a thing in Volpone's epistle:

> And though my catastrophe may, in the strict rigour of comick law, meet with censure, as turning back to my promise; I desire the learned, and charitable critick to have so much faith in me, to thinke it was done off industrie: For, with what ease I could have varied it, neerer his scale (but that I feare to boast my owne faculty) I could here insert.
>
> (Epistle, 109-14)

The point is that here, as in *Volpone*, it would have been easier for Jonson as a skilled dramatist to have conformed to convention and expectation. Instead, the entire force of Face's and Lovewit's concluding lines is toward the conscious manipulation of expectation. Jonson twists our expectations and tells us as he does it.

By far our most troubling discovery as judging spectators, however, is Jonson's impulse to reveal his theater as a mean and parodic version of Cicero's *speculum* and *imago*. The portrayal of self-interested activity is nothing new to Jonson's drama, but Face, Subtle, and Dol are more than just self-interested; they are professionally self-interested. Volpone is a magnificent amateur who assumes briefly, as Scoto of Mantua, the role of professional actor, whereas Face and his partners live by their acting, like Voltore who coins words into profit. No doubt Volpone would have scorned them as he scorns the lawyer. Volpone's amateur standing keeps him above the realities of professional theater, allowing him to despise, as Mosca despises, those who act to satisfy gut and groin. With Face and Subtle, we are confronted again and again with the seaminess of what they do, yet their venture is unquestionably theatrical in many of the ways any professional theater is theatrical. Playwrights create and actors enact roles in the hope of stimulating an audience to part with its cash.

Jonson seems fascinated by the fact that what distinguishes public theater from private, patronized theater is a special, unspoken contract among playwright, actor, and spectator. The nature of this contract troubled Jonson both because it kept poetry tied to commercialism and because it was inherently volatile. And, as Gerald Eades Bentley makes clear, the nature of this contract troubled all of English society in the late sixteenth and early seventeenth centuries.[5] From the beginning of his career Jonson sought to redeem theater from its commercial association by redefining profit and pleasure in ethical and moral terms. In 1610, we find him still tricking self-consciously with the words "gain" and "profit" in the prologue to *The Alchemist*. And yet his work actually moved closer and closer to examining fully the implications of theater-for-hire. It is as if the only way for Jonson to remove entirely the stains of lucre from his theater was to confess them from the stage. From *Sejanus* on, self-interestedness is defined more and more in terms of cash, and from *Volpone* Jonson took the mountebank as a tentative metaphor for professional theater and recast him fully formed in *The Alchemist*.

It is easy for us to watch Volpone perform as Scoto. While Jonson surely had a personal stake in Scoto's theatrical performance,[6] the multiplicity of theatrical perspectives keeps us from really feeling the force of the playwright's self-indictment. We know that Volpone is playing at Scoto of Mantua for reasons unrelated to self-conscious theater, and we have the action filtered through the eyes of Sir Pol and Peregrine. Consequently, we are relieved of the burden of dealing head-on with Scoto and what he represents. In *The Alchemist*, the mountebank has been transformed into the "venter tripartite," an alchemist and his two colleagues, and, because our

THE ALCHEMIST

theatrical perspective is largely their creation, we must deal with them fully. *Volpone* is fastidious about its existential dilemma: behind the illusion is a void. When the actor ceases to act he has no self left. But what threatens the illusion and the people who create it in *The Alchemist* is terrible squalor and degradation. Dol is a whore, Face a servant and pander, while Subtle clothes himself in rags "rak'd, and pick'd from dung-hills" and slowly starves. The threat is not extinction of the self but confinement to a subhuman world where one is reminded constantly of what he is not. This is a far different vision from *Volpone*'s. In that play, such confinement threatens the self-conscious participants only at the end, and by and large it is treated as a joke, as in Volpone's descriptions of his clients' infirmities or Sir Pol's reptilian rebirth.

Perhaps the combination of successes in the playhouse and preferment at court allowed Jonson in 1610 to confront openly what he had suppressed in the past, the fragile and ephemeral nature of success as a professional writer, or, more precisely, the consequences of failure as one. The threat of confinement, which had been reserved for the fools in the comical satires, has become in the mature comedies the worry of the creators of dramatic illusion. The fools in *The Alchemist* are insulated against real loss and real self-knowledge by their foolishness, and Jonson is content to leave them that way while he attends to other matters. Mammon's final speech is a perfect example: "I will goe mount a turnep-cart, and preach/ The end o'the world, within these two months" (V, v, 81-82). Not for a moment do we imagine Mammon mounting a turnip cart—this is simply his tireless imagination pumping out yet another peculiar fantasy. Surly tells us early in the play that his friend is not always a fool:

> Hart! can it be,
> That a grave sir, a rich, that has no need,
> A wise sir, too, at other times, should thus
> With his own oathes, and arguments, make hard means
> To gull himself?
>
> (II, iii, 278-82)

And we can imagine, as the play ends, that Mammon will go on, less rich than before, sometimes grave, sometimes wise, and sometimes a prey to confidence men. The fools in this play are left to themselves while Jonson examines the self-conscious participants, and the confidence man becomes the embodiment of Jonson's ambivalence about his own career, as he projects onto the stage the meanest version of professional theater.

Jonson chose for himself the task of reconciling the contradictory aspects of his professional role. On one hand, he saw himself as a philosopher and as the custodian of both the truths of the natural world and the treasures of classical culture. On the other hand, he found himself a member of a profession full of rakes, vagabonds, social climbers, and sundry self-seekers, individuals whose interests in the theater were undeniably self-gratifying. In addition, he was unhappy about the apparently irreconcilable requirements of pleasing an audience and remaining faithful to his muse. Alchemy offered Jonson a fascinating metaphor for theater. It was every bit as full of inconsistency and self-contradiction as Renaissance theater. Many of the professors of the art lived, like Subtle or the alchemists at court whom Jonson flayed in *Mercury Vindicated*, like the theatrical companies, always one step away from prosecution as vagabonds. Others like Roger Bacon were regarded as the great natural philosophers of their times, and tracts such as Bacon's *The Mirror of Alchimy* described the sanctity of their mission

> Know brother, that this our mastery and honourable office of the secret Stone, is a secret of the secrets of God, which he hath concealed from his people, neither would he reveal it to any, save to those, who like sonnes have faythfully deserved it, knowing bothe his goodnesse and greatnesse.[7]

The alchemists' professions of selflessness and their vows of poverty and chastity stood in stark contrast to the alchemical confidence game, just as Jonson's perception of poetry's place alongside philosophy conflicted with the actuality of the poet-

THE ALCHEMIST

aster's gimmickry. Both poetaster and alchemical impostor served up heaping portions of illusion concocted only to feed the public's appetite for the fantastic.

Moreover, alchemy dealt self-consciously in Art and Nature, the terms in which Jonson cast much of his thinking about poetry and theater. He accused the poetaster, as he accused the fake alchemist, of using art against nature, while he saw himself, on the other hand, using art judiciously to reveal the beauty of nature and to entice the spectator. This is precisely how the true alchemist understood himself as well. He projected his role in terms of his relationship to ancient Hermetic philosophy, and he considered at length the problems of textual exegesis which that relationship created. Out of the inscrutability of ancient and classical Hermetic texts the alchemists fashioned a serious theory of rhetoric: the use of words to safeguard art and nature by concealing them from "the multitude." In *The Alchemist*, Surly confronts Subtle with the familiar charge against alchemy:

> Rather, then I'll be brai'd, sir, I'll beleeve,
> That Alchemie is a pretty kind of game,
> Somewhat like tricks o' the cards, to cheat a man,
> With charming. . . . What else are all your termes,
> Whereon no one o' your writers grees with other?
> Of your elixir, your *lac virginis*,
> Your stone, your med'cine, and your chrysosperme.
> (II, iii, 179-85)

Subtle's response is by the book, and it establishes clear links between alchemy and poetry:

> And all these, nam'd
> Intending but one thing: which art our writers
> Us'd to obscure their art. . . .
> Was not all the knowledge
> Of the Egyptians writ in mystick symboles?
> Speake not the Scriptures, oft, in parables?
> Are not the choisest fables of the Poets,

That were the fountaines, and first springs of wisedom,
Wrapt in perplexed allegories?

(II, iii, 198-207)

Of course, Subtle is into his patter here, but from the pen of someone like Roger Bacon the argument is genuinely impressive:

My Sonne keep this most secret Booke, and commit it not into the handes of ignorant men, being a secret of the secretes of God: For by this meanes thou shalt attain thy desire. Amen.

I consider that the secrets of Nature contayned in the skins of Goates and sheep, are not spoken of, least every man should understand them. As Socrates and Aristotle willeth: for he affirmeth in his booke of Secrets, that he is a breaker of the celestiall seale that maketh the secrets of Art and Nature common: adding moreover that many evils betide him that revealeth secretes. And in the booke intituled *Noctes Attica*, in the comparing of wise men togither, it is reputed a great folly to give an Asse Lettice, when Thistles will serve his turne. . . . I speake of the Common sort, in that Sence, as it is heere distinguished agaynst the learned. For in the common conceytes of the minde, they agree with the learned, but in the proper principles and conclusions of Arts and Sciences they disagree, toyling themselves about meere appearances, and sophistications, and quirks, and quiddities, and such like trash, whereof wise men make no account. . . . Now the cause of this concealment among all wise men, is, the contempt and neglect of the secretes of wisedome by the vulgar sort, that knoweth not how to use those things which are most excellent. And if they doe conceive any worthy thing, it is altogither by chance and fortune, & they do exceedingly abuse that their knowledge, to the great damage and hurt of many men, yea, even of whole societies: so that he is worse then mad that publisheth any secret, unlesse he conceale

THE ALCHEMIST

it from the multitude, and in such wise deliver it, that even the studious and learned shall hardly understand it.[8]

It was in the humanist faith in the text, however, that alchemist and poet found their common denominator. Speaking of the magus, in his introduction to the Yale edition of *The Alchemist*, Alvin Kernan observes, "It is necessary to realize that at the time of the Renaissance a number of men of learning began to believe that the powers of the universe could be found and controlled by bringing together all knowledge from ancient books and manuscripts."[9] This was by no means a belief unique to the Hermetic philosopher—through Ramus it became the mainstream of Renaissance pedagogy:

> The humanist, like his medieval predecessor, was conditioned to learning by reading. The scholastic, scientific passion for fixity and exactitude, associated with dependence upon written documents, was extended by the humanists even to the matter of literary style. No longer left to the vagaries of the changing world of sound . . . style was to be controlled by modes of speech fixed in writing and thus freed of the transiency of present time.
>
> The humanists' apotheosis of the past enforced the assumption, if it did not articulate it, that the curriculum subjects had once been perfectly organized and that all that was needed was some sort of key to restore them to their normal simplicity and order.[10]

Jonson is clearly a major figure in this tradition, for his reverence of text, enacted in his extraordinary desire to publish his work and in the meticulous way he oversaw the process; for his reverence of classical literature and humanist education; and, as Jonas Barish has demonstrated, for his remarkable commitment to prose as a medium for fixing the eccentricities of human personality.

Finally, Jonson perceived his audiences in exactly the same way the alchemical writers perceived theirs, as split radically between fit and unfit members, the understanders and the "beast multitude." For the alchemist the split required a two-fold approach: the understanders were to be enlightened, the multitude confused. Jonson—to his everlasting frustration—felt more responsible than his alchemical counterparts for making nature available to the masses, but when it came down to practice, he was remarkably adept at limiting his audiences to the chosen few and protecting his work from the others with a formidable array of prologues, epilogues, inductions, and the kind of "perplexed allegories" found in *Cynthia's Revels* or *Sejanus*. There are Baconian echoes throughout Jonson's work, in his assessment of the multitude, in his defensiveness toward his audiences, in his idea of the "secret Cause":

> There is a more secret Cause: and the power of liberall studies lyes more hid, then that it can bee wrought out by profane wits. It is not every mans way to hit. They are men (I confesse) that set the Caract, and Value upon things, as they love them; but Science is not every mans Mistresse. It is as great a spite to be praised in the wrong place, and by a wrong person, as can be done to a noble nature.[11]

It is worth noting the ease with which Jonson revises our perspective in this passage to emphasize the conflict between author and audience. The passage initially appears to be concerned with abstract matters, "liberall studies" and "Science," and with the impossibility of "every mans" tapping their secrets. But the sense of Jonson's impersonal observation of the fruitlessness of prophane wits is shattered by the final sentence which brings us right back to the theater and to Jonson's own preoccupation with judgment. No longer is it a question of man and nature, but one of man versus man. Even in his prose, Jonson is constantly changing the scene.

In *Discoveries*, it is difficult to find a coherent expression of Jonson's philosophical views. The extoller of the "secret Cause" can be found, not one hundred lines later, claiming, "Truth and Goodnesse are plaine, and open."[12] Because Jon-

THE ALCHEMIST

son put theory to practice in the theater, however, a work like *Mercury Vindicated* is a more reliable record of what Jonson took to be the relationship between theater and alchemy. Those spectators of *Mercury Vindicated* who had been schooled in the masque at Jonson's earlier productions would have recognized in Mercury the figure of a poet-presenter. In a number of the early masques, Mercury essentially takes on the role of Jonson's spokesman, speaking for the truth of the masque and working the required theatrical tranformations. In the *Entertainment at Highgate*, it is Mercury who, "by the mightie power of Poetrie,"[13] creates the Arcadian landscape where the entertainment takes place. While the King and Queen look on, Mercury moves easily between the worlds of Highgate and Arcady, introducing the symbolic persons of the masque and explaining the action to the royal audience. In *An Entertainment at Theobalds*, the spectators were introduced to

> a gloomie obscure place, hung all with black silkes, and in it only one light, which the Genius of the house held, sadly attir'd; his Cornucopia readie to fall out of his hand, his gyrland drooping on his head, his eyes fixed on the ground.[14]

The Genius of Theobalds is distressed at the impending departure of its master, the Earl of Salisbury, but Mercury intervenes, and with a single line, "Despaire not, Genius, thou shalt know thy fate," dispels the gloom. He descends from the heavens, "in a flying posture," to conduct the masque and to instruct Genius that the loss of Salisbury will be more than recompensed by the arrival of James.

Mercury, then, was a familiar spirit to Jonson's masque audiences, and in *Mercury Vindicated* Jonson has given him his most ambitious role. Here Mercury plays not only in his usual role as herald of the gods but also as the physical element mercury. Vulcan and his alchemical colleagues open the masque in their workhouse, where they are seeking to liber-

142

ate Mercury from the grosser elements. The Cyclope's song makes clear the alchemist's relationship to art and nature:

> Soft, subtile fire, thou soule of art,
>   Now doe thy part
> On weaker Nature, that through age is lamed.
>   Take but thy time, now she is old,
>   And the Sunne her friend growne cold,
> She will no more, in strife with thee be named.[15]

The terms here are right out of the epistle and prologue to *The Alchemist*. The alchemists place art and nature in contention, the same charge which Jonson lays at the feet of the poetasters, and what permits this abuse is the willfulness of the age: "How e'er the age, he lives in, doth endure/The vices that shee breeds, above their cure."[16] Mercury bears the burden of the metaphorical progress of the masque by presenting the proper vision of things: he perceives his alchemical liberation from nature as no liberation at all but entrapment in Vulcan's self-serving art. Mercury will not submit; he breaks free and appeals directly to the audience for salvation. This is only appropriate. It is in Jonson's view the failure of judgment on the part of the general populace that has allowed the counterfeit artist to survive, and Mercury's appeal to the masque audience recognizes, hopefully, its special nature: "Now the place and goodnesse of it protect me."[17] Here is an audience that should know better than the public audience. In the antimasque, Mercury allows the "fire-worms" their moment on stage before he banishes them and commands the change of scene which transforms Vulcan's shop into Nature's bower. In this gesture, he affirms a great deal: he affirms the power of nature over alchemy, countering the dance of the imperfect and unnatural antimasquers with the perfection of the masque dances. He affirms James's majesty by casting him as the Sun, Nature's monarch. The dances affirm the nature of true procreation: the maids of the court are daughters of Nature and mothers-to-be, courted in the revels which Mercury empowers with his caduceus. Mercury

THE ALCHEMIST

has saved Nature from the rape threatened by Vulcan and his crew, and he alludes specifically to the phallic power of the caduceus: "You might wreste the Caducaeus out of my hand, to the adultery and spoile of Nature, and make your accesses by it, to her dishonour, more easie."[18]

With the appearance of Prometheus, the man-god who understood the value of fire for mankind, the masque opposes true heroism to the "smoaky familie" of alchemists and their vulgarized versions of Deucalion and Prometheus and to the list of social degenerates who have replaced mankind's real heroes:

> For, in yonder vessels, which you see in their laboratorie, they have inclos'd Materials, to produce men, beyond the deedes of Deucalion, or Prometheus (of which, one, they say, had the Philosophers stone, and threw it over his shoulder, the other the fire, and lost it.) And what men are they, they are so busie about, thinke you? not common or ordinary creatures, but of rarity and excellence, such as the times wanted, and the Age had a speciall deale of neede of: such, as there was a necessitie, they should be artificiall; for Nature could never have thought or dreamt o' their composition. I can remember some o' their titles to you, and the ingredients: doe not looke for Paracelsus man among 'hem, that he promised you out of white bread, and dele-wine, for he never came to light. But of these, let me see; the first that occurres; a master of the Duel, a carrier of the differencies. To him went spirit of ale, a good quantitie, with the amalgama of sugar and nutmegs, oyle of othes, sulphure of quarrell, strong waters, valour precipitate, vapor'd o're the helme with tobacco, and the rosin of Mars, with a dram o' the businesse, for that's the word of tincture, the businesse. Let me alone with the businesse, I will carrie the businesse. I doe understand the businesse. I doe find an affront i' the businesse. Then another is a fencer i' the Mathematiques, or the townes-cunning man,

a creature of arte too; a supposed secretary to the starres; but, indeed, a kind of lying Intelligencer from those parts. His materials, if I be not deceiv'd, where juyce of almanacks, extraction of Ephemerides, scales of the Globe, fylings of figures, dust o' the twelve houses, conserve of questions, salt of confederacy, a pound of adventure, a graine of skill, and a drop of trueth. I saw vegetals too, aswell as minerals, put into one glasse there, as adders tongue, title-bane, nitre of clyents, tartar of false conveyance, *Aurum palpabile*, with a huge deale of talke.[19]

I have quoted at length here because the passage is crucially important. What Mercury affirms, above all else, is true poetry and true theater. He wrests the Deucalion of Ovid from the alchemical writers, and he offers a masque instead of a theater which can only be the Jacobean playhouse—indeed the realm of the kind of drama which Jonson himself had created. We are offered a theater governed by James, as the Sun, and by Nature devoid of self-serving art. Here art is unnecessary; poetry is free of the artifice which conceals self-interest because it serves only to reveal Nature and true majesty. The alchemist deals in a version of theater which discounts heroes such as Deucalion and Prometheus—or James— for the man about town, the railer, the rhymer, the gamester. As Jonson reminds us repeatedly, the public playhouse was responsible, to a large extent, for creating and sustaining these monstrosities by giving them a place to be seen and to indulge their social quirks. And in this regard Jonson does not spare himself. For all his desire to use his art to free Nature in the playhouse, specifically to relieve his spectators of their noxious humors, he, more than any other playwright, had been responsible for shaping these new, grotesque heroes. He had put these roles before the public, and, as his rehabilitative plans failed, he was left with a parodic version of the theater he had intended. Through Mercury, Jonson accepts this responsibility, and this masque, entitled *Mercury Vindicated From the Alchemists at Court*, is in many ways

THE ALCHEMIST

Jonson's self-vindication from the aberrant and self-serving forms of art. Mercury describes the alchemists as playwrights: "They have inclos'd Materials, to produce men, beyond the deedes of Deucalion"; they are busy rewriting myths. The list of characters describes not only London society but also Jonson's stage, with a gloss on Dapper, Wasp, and, of course, Subtle, the "secretary to the starres." The antimasque, which features "imperfect creatures, with helmes of lymbecks on their heads," might be an embryonic Jonson comedy. Certainly it is Jonson, as well as Vulcan, who has offered "ridiculous monsters," though only with the hope of exposing them and restoring to them their manhood.

The crucial action of the masque is Mercury's banishment of the antimasquers when he vows to forsake them and pledges his loyalty to the Sun. With the pledge comes the tacit admission that he has been, in some way, the creature of the "philosophers." This is a remarkable moment in Jonson's dramatic career. It is an explicit affirmation from the stage of the masque form itself, and it offers a striking view of Jonson's changing commitment to the theater. The monarch offers the poet what the playhouse audience cannot, the authority which gives real meaning to mankind's myths as an articulation of Nature and defends that meaning against the multitude. In 1616, the year *Mercury Vindicated* had its performance, Jonson left the public playhouse for the theater at court, returning only when the death of King James, Mercury's "majesty of light," set him free in 1625.

The metaphorical relationship between theater and alchemy gave Jonson the chance to project onto the alchemists with vengence whatever sense of imposture and insubstantiality he felt about his own professional role. He was always clear in his critical writing about the distinction between poet and poetaster: it was not simply that the poetaster was unskilled or egocentric, but also that he cheated his audience. In *The Alchemist*, the epistle "To the Reader" warns about theater in the same terms Jonson might have warned about an alchemical confidence game: "If thou art one that tak'st up, and but a Pretender, beware at what hands thou receiv'st thy commoditie; for thou wert never more fair in the way to be cos'ned (then in the Age) in *Poetry*, especially in Playes" (Epistle, 2-5). But Jonson makes no such distinction among the alchemists. For him they are frauds, one and all, and his interest in Hermetic philosophy extends only to degrading it. Perhaps by willfully ignoring the ethical and intellectual complexities of alchemy, Jonson bought himself some relief from the complexities of his own profession and from the fear that the distinctions he sought to defend in the theater were fundamentally problematic. His reluctance to enact fully in his drama the principles he set out in the prologues, epilogues, inductions, and epistles suggests a flirtation with the parodic impulse to reveal from the stage the insubstantiality of moral drama. But Jonson does so only metaphorically, through characters like Volpone and Face who cheat their audiences in the name of "substance" while living free from the full force of justice.

The counterpart to Jonson's attempt to stress the significance of his work over our immediate experience of it is his campaign to define the proper mode of participation in this theater. He sought the understanders, the judicious among his audiences, in short the self-conscious spectators; yet in *The Alchemist*, as in *Volpone*, self-conscious response to the drama presents us with a set of special problems. For instance, as we enlarge the context of Face's closing remarks beyond the concerns of the immediate performance, we find that, even as this theater invites us to return, it threatens to exclude us with the suggestion that we have been gulled financially and intellectually. In other words, if we apply to this play the critical tools Jonson offers us, we may turn it into a pile of dramatic fragments. If we drag out our bag of terms, our "deus ex machina" and our "comic justice," for us the ending will suffer. It appears that Jonson is coming to terms in this play with something he has known all along: successful drama *requires* unself-conscious participation. It requires spectators willing to risk their money and willing to

THE ALCHEMIST

surrender temporarily the judgmental powers Jonson prized. This necessity contradicts his commentary on his drama, but I think Jonson found inescapable the conclusion that self-consciousness can be as great a threat as any to theater, while the spectator's search for self-knowledge can be the most pernicious kind of self-seeking.

This conclusion places Jonson's relationship with his audiences in an interesting light. We might consider his preoccupation with judging spectators a manifestation of his perception that they represented the greatest threat to his theater, not the least. There is a peculiar irony in the notion that judgment is antitheatrical, but in fact judgment attacks the mimetic heart of drama, processing experience as meaning. Something is lost along the way, just as something is lost from the communal aspect of theater as the individual resolves his experience into self-knowledge. And it is the critical and moral judgment of the truly judicious spectator which threatens to reject any given theatrical production as insubstantial, or worse, as the product of authorial self-interestedness.

Oddly enough, in light of Jonson's public campaign against the ignorant and self-serving spectator, the forces which really threaten his drama are internal, embodied in the self-conscious participants, not in their foolish audiences. The unselfconscious, those who have no fundamental understanding of theatricality, are never a problem. They are confined to everlasting gullhood and manipulated with ease. Jonson extols theater which educates, which literally leads its audiences out of their self-imposed bondage by allowing them to see themselves as others see them. Yet his work progressively suppresses this didactic potential of theater. The fools of the comical satires are shown their shortcomings, though we never feel that their fleeting insights are likely to admit them to the circle of the wise. But *Volpone* and *The Alchemist* deny their fools even minimal education. Sir Pol, Corvino, Voltore, Mammon, Dapper, and Drugger live out their lives in plays which do not care, one way or the other, about providing for their enlightenment, but instead exult in the ease with which such characters can be abused. The threat to these plays comes not from those who are victims but from those who understand and, in some cases, create them. Sejanus, Volpone, Mosca, Surly, Face, and Subtle are understanders who for various reasons jeopardize the plays in which they enact their roles.

The Alchemist opens exactly where *Volpone* leaves off, with the two major characters struggling to reach an agreement that would permit the drama to continue. It is the inability of Volpone and Mosca to reach "composition," as the latter terms it, that brings down the charade, and only when Face and Subtle set aside a portion of their self-substantiating zeal can this play get under way. It becomes, thereafter, a vehicle for their self-interests and a controlled medium for the release of their hostility toward one another. Such is the case when Face's affirmative response to Dapper's query about whether Subtle is a doctor recalls us, and no doubt Subtle as well, to Face's earlier deprecation, "Doctor dog." The aggression which always threatens to break into the open is the first major threat to the "venter tripartite"; Surly is the second. He is self-assertive, like the others, but he is also a model of the self-conscious, judging spectator, not one to be fooled by imposture. Thus, when he and Subtle take up the matter of alchemy in act 2, scene 5, the debate involves more than the philosopher's stone. Jonson debates with himself, in front of us, the issues of his own theatrical practice.

Subtle's defense of his art sounds a great deal like Ben Jonson in his epistles and prologues. When Mammom first appears, Subtle declares:

> I should be sorry
> To see my labours, now, e'ene at perfection,
> Got by long watching, and large patience,
> Not prosper, where my love, and zeale hath plac'd 'hem
> Which (heaven I call to witnesse, with your selfe,
> To whom, I have pour'd my thoughts) in all my ends,
> Have look'd no way, but unto publique good,

THE ALCHEMIST

    To pious uses, and deere charitie,
    Now growne a prodigie with men.

(II, iii, 10-18)

This could be Asper or "the Author" of *Poetaster* in the Apologetical Dialogue, or even the writer of *Discoveries*. Subtle speaks many of Jonson's own sentiments, the concern for "publique good" at the expense of "long watching" and "large patience," and the conviction that such things have "now growne a prodigie with men." When the alchemist finally claims, "All arts have still had, sir, their adversaries,/But ours the most ignorant" (III, ii, 217-18), surely Jonson is having a grim chuckle. In the art of verbal self-defense, he was Subtle's closest London rival. This scene, then, turns Jonson's own tricks against Surly, Subtle's judging spectator, and we take it, as it is meant, for a joke. But the implications of the scene are far more serious for the entire play, because *The Alchemist* provides much the same experience for its own surly spectators who wish to look behind the illusions.

    The theater which Face, Subtle, and Dol establish in Lovewit's house is characteristically Jonsonian. From *Sejanus* on, all activity that might be called "theatrical," in the sense of conscious role playing, is self-interested. Characters act, in other words, only to satisfy personal needs, and we no longer see the selfless action of Horace, Asper, Crites, and other figures in the comical satires whose sense of self is limited by their participation in a commonwealth. In fact, the selfless creatures of the mature comedies and *Sejanus*, Celia and Bonario and the Germanicans, are incapable of the kind of role playing which seems necessary to get on in the world, and they are left to look silly, even pitiful, for this lack. In the comical satires the satirist is a servant of the monarch, his actions the articulation of royal authority. *Volpone* and *The Alchemist* reveal the satirist in business for himself. He serves no higher authority; his art is his recreation or his means of subsistence. His business is still theater that causes its audiences, now clients, to reveal themselves as fools, but this aspect, once the end of satiric art, has become incidental to the flow of cash and goods and the sense of power. No longer content merely to provide spectators with self-revealing roles, the satirist now stimulates the client's sense of self to grotesque proportions by selling custom-made, inflatable fictions. Like any entrepreneur he is concerned to maximize the return on his investment, but he also has developed, like any playwright, a fascination for the performance as performance, for the perfection of his work for its own sake as the product of his imagination. Subtle's interest in Mammon, for instance, far exceeds the financial rewards:

> O, I did looke for him
> With the sunnes rising: 'Marvaile, he could sleepe!
> This is the day, I am to perfect for him
> The magisterium our greate work, the stone;
> And yeeld it, made, into his hands: of which,
> He has, this month, talk'd, as he were possess'd.
> And, now, hee's dealing peeces on't, away.
> Me thinkes, I see him, entring ordinaries,
> Dispensing for the poxe; and plaguy-houses,
> Reaching his dose; walking more-fields for lepers;
> And offring citizens-wives pomander bracelets,
> As his preservative, made of the elixir;
> Searching the spittle, to make old bawdes yong;
> And the high-waies, for beggars, to make rich:
> I see no end of his labours. He will make
> Nature asham'd, of her long sleepe: when art,
> Who's but a step-dame, shall doe more, then shee,
> In her best love to man-kind, ever could.
> If his dreame last, hee'll turne the age, to gold.
>   (I, iv, 11-29)

Subtle is running a con, but he lovingly imagines Mammon enacting this fantastic role simply because *he* has made it for Mammon. This is the Jonsonian "hero" in his great moment, relishing as a spectator the drama he has compelled another to enact. Satiric authority in Jonson's theater no longer substantiates the values of a monarch or even the consensus of a reasonable audience, but, rather, whatever can be made to work in the confrontation between self-interested parties.

In the course of his career, Jonson redefined the term "selfless." His early satirists are content to act on behalf of higher authority, for the sake of principle, and this sacrifice of self results in the clear and strong sense of self felt by Horace, Asper, and Crites. When principle and authority fail, however, when one is left to define himself by his own means, one finds himself in *Volpone* or *The Alchemist*, where selflessness is not a choice but a condition. Put another way, Horace is Horace, and nothing happens in the course of *Poetaster*, even his self-doubting talk with Trebatius, to call into question the essential integrity of his character. *The Alchemist*, by contrast, almost fails to get under way for the inability of the characters to define themselves. The constant but relatively contained anxiety generated in *Volpone*, as Volpone and Mosca deal with the problem of self-definition, runs out of control in the opening scene of *The Alchemist*. Face is not Face; he is a "wild sheep," while Subtle is a "mongrel," a "slave," or a "notorious whelp." And the name-calling expands into more coherent images hurled from one to the other:

> You were once (time's not long past) the good,
> Honest, plaine, livery-three-pound-thrum; that kept
> Your masters worships house, here, in the friers,
> For the vacations—
>
> (I, i, 15-18)

But I shall put you in mind, sir, at pie-corner,
Taking your meale of steeme in, from cookes stalls,
Where, like the father of hunger, you did walke
Piteously costive, with your pinch'd-horne-nose,
And your complexion, of the romane wash,
Stuck full of black, and melancholique wormes,
Like poulder-cornes, shot, at the 'artillerie-yard.

(I, i, 25-31)

Dol does not clarify matters any, labeling them an "abominable paire of stinkards (I, i, 117). Through it all, there is never any sense that these individuals are human beings. They are for each other only what they are for us, characters in a play. And each has his own version of what the play is.

These characters are defined by their roles: by their immediate behavior they are curs, by their past behavior they are butlers and vagabonds, by their current agreement they are a "suburb-Captayne" and a Doctor of Alchemy. They are, in short, not persons, not even characters in the usual sense, but a series of dramatic roles which have meaning only in relation to whatever drama is at hand and whatever other roles they encounter. What is significant, as Dol points out, is not the metaphysical consideration of Face's question "Who am I?" but the progress of the play. This is a disconcerting scene to confront as a spectator. It is a genuine problem to figure out who these people are and what they are doing. We have to deal with all of the conflict but without a context to give it significance. A "civil war" Dol calls it,[20] but we watch a long while before we know the nature of the republic. Nothing happens to change our relationship to the stage, either. There are none of Mosca's soliloquies to make us feel that we have gained a confidence, because, more than any other of Jonson's characters, these exist only to play their roles. If we think at Lovewit's return that Face, frightened and shaken from his role, takes us into his confidence with his asides, as Volpone does in act 5, our comfort is shortlived. Lovewit admits Face to a new play by offering him a new role, and we realize, if we take the epilogue seriously, that we are like "Subtle, Surly, Mammon, Dol, Hot Ananias, Dapper, Drugger, all," part of the multitude with whom Face has "traded." At the very most we are offered the role of patrons of a morally bankrupt and self-serving theater, and our consolation is Face's defiant suggestion that the show *will* go on.

The progress of Jonsonian theater roughly describes the progress of Renaissance English society away from adherence to accepted social authority toward increasingly self-reliant, self-substantiating commercial life. It describes as well the progress of Jonson's career as a professional satirist, from his initial commitment to classical satiric forms and his concern with the problem of satiric authority for himself and for his stage satirists, to the point at which surviving in the theater became a critical concern. He had created for himself the role of dramatic satirist, and all evidence suggests that it was never an easy role for him to sustain, in part because, like any satirist, along the way he only multiplied his contempt for his audience. As Jonson became increasingly self-conscious about the impact of his work, two things were likely to have occurred: first, he saw that the task of criticizing his spectators without alienating them was not simply the elected task of the compassionate satirist, as he suggests in the prologue to *The Alchemist*, but the condition of his success in the playhouse. The dramatic satirist seeking to make his living on the boards does not enjoy the freedom of the Stoic or the court poet. Second, he must have felt increasingly, as his work failed to produce an audience of judging spectators to insulate him from the volatility of the playhouse crowd, that the roles he had imagined for his spectators were becoming a parodic version of his intention.

Whatever the reason, Jonson's drama clearly becomes vindictive: Sejanus, Tiberius, Volpone, Mosca, Face, and Subtle push their victims as far as possible for the fun of it. Self-knowledge, that is, the fool's acceptance of his foolishness, is no longer the satirist's offer of freedom. In *Volpone*, it is the ultimate stroke in a game which confirms psychological determinism; in *The Alchemist*, it is the limit with which the con man flirts but dares not tamper. Both plays are about theater which enforces one's chosen sense of self. Face, Subtle, and Volpone sell self-substantiating drama, although Jonson makes it clear that the same self-gratifying impulse which is the source of this drama is essentially antitheatrical by virtue of its solipsism. Volpone and Mosca blow their scheme apart, and Face and Subtle nearly fail to get their play going because of the need of each to reduce the other to a minor role in his drama. Once they have accomplished the elusive "composition," however, they direct the bulk of their aggression outward at their clients.

Sir Epicure Mammon reveals as much of what is on Jonson's mind as Surly does. Taken together, the pair roughly describes the conflict between judgment and imagination experienced by any spectator. Imagination, as Mammon demonstrates, is entirely self-referential, whereas judgment deals with the relationship of self to others. In creating Mammon, Jonson chose to endow a gull with tremendous imaginative energy. Sir Epicure partakes of Volpone's spiritual vitality, and the implication is that theatrical energy is something to be shared by actor and spectator. In spite of Mammon's foolish, petty wants, we find attractive his capacity to create self-gratifying fantasy out of nothing. George Hibbard correctly argues that the play is about the nature of illusion, how far people can be pushed and how much they can be made to pay before they will part with their self-serving images.[21]

But Mammon resists the game through a peculiar, unconscious "heroism." Face and Subtle may be said to create Mammon by stimulating his imagination and offering him a role to play, but he transcends their little drama because he is genuinely impervious to loss. Both the stone and the widow are in his head, safe from the "venter tripartite." Surly and Mammon show us something important: to judge fiction is to reduce illusion to intention and motivation and, by discounting the immediacy of experience, to risk certain kinds of re-creation. Imagination completes the fictional action but threatens it from another direction. To the extent that it excludes judgment, it divorces the spectator from reality, jeopardizing his self-respect, not to mention his cash.

In Jonson's creation of Mammon there is disturbing self-implication. Sir Epicure's poetry is real poetry, some of Jonson's best, yet, for all its power, it reprocesses all of Jonson's revered classical learning as foolish and empty. Again Volpone comes to mind. When the Venetian magnifico reveals his mountain of gold, our sense of heroic possibility is strong,

THE ALCHEMIST

and even when Volpone loses it all he can, by virtue of the theatrical authority he has established, stand apart from the world that seeks to value his action by putting him in chains. But Mammon is from the outset one who is taken, not one who takes, and, while we feel the force of his imagination, he spends it turning the Golden Age to lead while he seeks the philosophers' stone in order to do just the opposite. Mammon nearly completes for Jonson the process, begun in *Sejanus* and continued in *Volpone*, of turning the classical world inside out. Whatever there is for us in *Sejanus* in terms of ethical lessons, there is a tremendous sense of the failure of classical ideals. The entire Germanican line is blasted and withered, Tiberius is vicious, and the opposition impotent. Even the treatment of classical religion is equivocal. Volpone, too, reduces and inverts in his poetry. His gold displaces the sun as the center of the universe, and Ovid becomes a lovers' handbook. The pairing of Surly and Mammon adds a new dimension, however, because Surly debunks Mammon's poetry on the spot. In other words, while Mammon speaks Volpone's poetry, Surly reveals him to be another Sir Politic Wouldbe.

Finally, *The Alchemist* offers us a clear glimpse of the contradictions inherent in fictional experience. In the extreme, both judgment and imagination threaten theater. To the myth of poetry as the Word made flesh, Jonson adds one of his own, the flesh made word, poetry as the scarcely mediated confrontation between parties bent on self-gratification. Out of the cautious prosecution of self-interest, on all sides, come the fictions we value. For Jonson they never came easily, only in the company of terrible self-scrutiny.

SIX

Bartholomew Fair: Jonson's Masque for the Multitude

> Is there a bridle for this Proteus
> That turns and changes like his draughty seas?
> Or is there none, most popular of men,
> But when they mock us, that we mock again?
> (William Butler Yeats, "At the Abbey Theater")

ADAM OVERDO'S offer to have everyone home to supper at the conclusion of *Bartholomew Fair* marks a point of rest in Jonson's struggle to establish satisfactory relations with his playhouse audience. Moreover, the fact that this offer represents for Jonson a rare gesture of accommodation, coupled with the fact that *Bartholomew Fair* is the last of his great plays, suggests that he rested after some significant accomplishment. What Jonson had accomplished was a play that brought him as close as he ever came to freedom from his anxieties about the nature of commercial theater. *Volpone* and *The Alchemist* suggest to us the possibility that professional theater is a confidence game, in which the parties of the stage and the parties of the gallery meet to indulge selfish and aggressive impulses and in which recreation is like gold or silver, just another currency in the transaction. As an examination of theater, *Bartholomew Fair* follows directly from these two plays. The fair, like Volpone's chamber, Scoto's bank, and Subtle's laboratory, is a theater born of self-interest and sustained by self-gratification. But *Bartholomew Fair*'s depiction of self-interestedness is not something its audiences have found threatening; this play has earned a reputation for geniality and conciliation, and nothing has appeared in the last fifty years to render Herford and Simpson's comment obsolete:

> Whatever, in any case, the assuaging influences may have been, in *Bartholomew Fair* the most masterful of playwrights appears once more disposed to meet his unruly audience more than half-way; to give them as much as he in conscience could of what they wanted, instead of as much as they could stomach of what they ought to want; and above all, to resent no man's disapproval. The impersonal severity, the censorious sternness, which makes comedies like *Volpone* and even *The Alchemist* but equivocal examples of the comic spirit, have as far as the playgoing public are concerned wholly vanished from *Bartholomew Fair*. The preacher has descended from his pulpit, the censor has stripped off the robes of his authority and of his chartered scorn; he mingles with the people, with the mob of "ordinary readers" and the vaster mob of the unreading and the cannot-read, takes part in their least refined exhibitions and amusements and, as the chief exhibition of all, pillories for their ridicule the embodiments of the censorious spirit itself.[1]

Implicit in this vision of Jonson pressing the flesh is the assumption that giving an audience what it wants is essentially an act of generosity and accommodation. This seems a romantic notion, however, particularly when there is so much else in Jonson's work to suggest that appealing to an audience at its own level is at least in part an act of contempt. There is, for instance, the repeated criticism of playwrights who write plays "wherein, now, the Concupiscence of Daunces, and Antickes so raigneth, as to runne away from Nature, and be afraid of her, is the onely point of art that tickles the *Spectators*."[2] As late as *Catiline* Jonson subtly disparages his reading audience in the epistle prefacing the 1611 Quarto, "To the Reader in Ordinary." And nothing has really changed in *Bartholomew Fair*: if in the induction it appears that Jonson is turning the theater over to the multitude by writing to "the Scale of the grounded judgements here," he makes it clear that he is turning it over to boobs.

In a peculiar way, *Bartholomew Fair* is both genial and hostile toward its spectators, which is to say that Jonson is at once accepting and contemptuous.[3] This is no paradox: one of the lessons to be taken from the prologues, epilogues, and inductions to Jonson's plays is that the author's expression of his contempt for certain portions of his audience is a condition of his willingness to allow them in his theater. *Bartholomew Fair*'s particular triumph is in permitting Jonson's impulse to reject his audience to exist side by side, in a delicate suspension, with his desire to accept them.

Thus, Jonson used the theater to enact his personal conflicts by projecting his anxieties about authority onto his audience. As judges of his work, and, therefore, of his self in an intimate and immediate way, his spectators embodied the terrible threat of powerful, arbitrary, and vindictive authority, and in his quest to govern that authority, to make it his own, Jonson faced an intriguing crux. He saw two ways to dominate an audience, to teach them or to entertain them. Though he pledged himself to the Horatian ideal, *utile, dulci*, experience taught him that this was easier said than done. Stage satirists like Asper engage in glib theorizing that never quite deals with the reality of the playhouse:

> Good men, and vertuous spirits, that lothe their vices,
> Will cherish my free labours, love my lines,
> And with the fervour of their shining grace,
> Make my braine fruitfull to bring forth more objects,
> Worthy their serious, and intentive eyes.
> (*Every Man Out*, Induction, 134-38)

The attempts to teach, Jonson concluded on the basis of his reception in the theater, were not having their intended effect, and he felt the responsibility for entertaining as a demand from the vile, ignorant, and self-gratifying portion of his audience. After his rejection of comical satire, Jonson associated recreation more openly with aggression and with the control and exploitation of an audience. In other words, he acknowledged the parasitic side of satire and his own interests in self-indulgent theater which affirms moral values only incidentally. Finally, in *Bartholomew Fair*, the most purely recreative of his plays, Jonson struck a rough and precarious balance between entertainment and aggression.

The relationship between the structure of *Bartholomew Fair* and Jonson's personal interests in the theater at this point in his career is nowhere more apparent than in the play's handling of the marriage theme. Northrop Frye's essay "The Argument of Comedy" explains that marriage is a convention of New Comedy:

> In all good New Comedy there is a social as well as an individual theme which must be sought in the general atmosphere of reconciliation that makes the final marriage possible. As the hero gets closer to the heroine and opposition is overcome, all the right-thinking people come over to his side. Thus a new social unit is formed on the stage, and the moment that this social unit crystallizes is the moment of the comic resolution. In the last scene, when the dramatist usually tries to get all his characters on the stage at once, the audience witnesses the birth of a renewed sense of social integration. In comedy as in life the regular expression of this is a festival, whether a marriage, a dance or a feast.[4]

Frye assigns Jonson to this tradition—too easily I think, because what is most interesting about Jonson's use of the conventions of New Comedy is his refusal to use them conventionally. The conclusion of *Epicene* is based on the revelation that there is no heroine for anyone to wed, while the marriage that concludes *The Alchemist* is entirely whimsical, resolving none of the social or moral issues alive in the play.

Bartholomew Fair is no different. In fact, here Jonson has perfected the technique of unconventional conventionality. On one hand the play is one of Jonson's most schematic. A character named Winwife acquires a wife named Grace Wellborn, and the arrangement of their betrothal is one of the main concerns of the plot. The other suitors, Quarlous and Cokes, who has already taken out a license to wed Grace when the play begins, must be disqualified. In addition, Adam Overdo's authority must be subverted, since he is a double authority as both Grace's guardian and a justice of the peace. Of course, all of the necessary shuffling is accomplished at the fair.

On the other hand, this play which is bursting with people looking to marry or, like the Littlewits, enjoying the fruits of marriage, does a great deal to stand the institution of marriage on its ear. Much energy is spent within the play reducing marriage and all other forms of human companionship to their basest levels. This is comedy which shares Thersites' reductive vision, "All the argument is a whore and a cuckold."[5] The fair levels all male-female relationships to whoring and epitomizes male-male relationships in the game of vapors. When we get to Winwife's winning of Grace, there is not much left in the way of triumph. They stand together in the swirl of sexual energy which is the vitality of *Bartholomew Fair*, but they are aliens. Their union marks no affirmation, no renewed sense of social integration, no reconciliation, just a chance pairing that saves Grace from the immediate predicament of her betrothal to Cokes. If her romantic hopes ring hollow in this play, "I must have a husband I must love, or I cannot live with him" (IV, iii, 15-17), in other ways she is a realistic woman, able to face squarely the impossibility of her position, as her response, when faced with the choice between Quarlous and Winwife, indicates: "How can I judge of you so farre as to a choyse without knowing you more? You are both equall, and alike to mee, yet: and so indifferently affected by mee, as each of you might be the man, if the other were away" (IV, iii, 29-32). And she explicitly rejects the two conventional paths open to her, the politic wife and the romance heroine:

Gentlemen, this is no way that you take: you do but breed one another trouble, and offence, and give me no contentment at all. I am no she, that affects to be quarell'd for, or have my name or fortune made the question of mens swords. . . . I have profest it to you ingenuously, that rather then to be yoak'd with this Bridegroome is appointed me, I would take up any husband, almost upon any trust. Though Subtilty would say to me, (I know) hee is a foole, and has an estate, and I might governe him, and enjoy a friend, beside.
(IV, iii, 1-15)

Winwife's and Quarlous' choices of names from the mainstream of romance convention, Palamon and Argalus, only points out how far we are from romance in every other respect. The working of chance in conventional romance confirms preordained, "correct" choices of partners, whereas Grace's device is an expression of despair.

Bartholomew Fair, then, is a farrago of attitudes toward marriage and sexuality—exactly those likely to have been embraced by Jonson's audience—set off against romance convention. The play begins with the Littlewits' exhibition of what Jonas Barish calls a "gluey fondness," anchored in the proposition that "man and wife make one fool," and characterized by John Littlewit's sense of Win as a sartorial articulation of his wit and advancing social status:

This Cap do's convince! you'ld not ha' worne it, Win, nor ha' had it velvet, but a rough countrey Beaver, with a copperband, like the Conney-skinne woman of Budgerow? Sweete Win, let me kisse it! And, her fine high shooes, like the Spanish Lady. . . . Is there the Proctor, or Doctor indeed, i' the Diocesse, that ever had the fortune to win him such a Win. . . . 'Slid, other men have wives as fine as the Players, and as well drest.
(I, i, 19-42)

When Winwife parodies the proctor's linguistic voracity, Littlewit misses the point:

LITTLEWIT. I envy no man, my delicates, Sir!

WINWIFE. Alas, you ha' the garden where they grow still! A wife heere with a Strawbery-breath, Chery-lips, Apricot-cheekes, and a soft velvet head, like a Melicotton.

LITTLEWIT. Good y'faith! now dulnesse upon mee, that I had not that before him, that I should not light on't, as well as he! Velvet head!

(I, ii, 13-19)

After the Littlewits, we meet Winwife, the widow hunter, and hear of the bizarre quest of Dame Purecraft:

WINWIFE. Sir, my mother has had her nativity-water cast lately by the Cunning men in Cow-lane, and they ha' told her her fortune, and doe ensure her, shee shall never have happy houre; unlesse shee marry within this sen'night, and when it is, it must be a Madde-man, they say.

(I, ii, 45-50)

We learn of Zeal-of-the-Land Busy, whose idea of courtship is a more-than-square meal, and then Quarlous arrives to deliver his astounding diatribe against widow hunting. Finally, Wasp and Cokes round out the group as a trenchant comment on the practice of arranged marriage.

Once assembled, this bizarre romance moves to the fair, a world which embodies Quarlous' sexually reductive imagination and regards social convention as deceit and as the unnatural restriction of basic human needs like "pig and punk." Satisfying sexual appetite is as easy here as dining on pig and ale, a simple transaction. Here human community is affirmed not by marriage but by unabashed feasting and copulation. The center of this vital but crude society is Ursula, the Body o' the Fair, on one hand "punk pinnace and bawd," on the other the "mother o' the pigs," alive with her "litter of pigs, to grunt out another Bartholomew Fair."

One point about which Frye can be taken to task is his

contrasting of New Comedy, with Jonson as one of its main practitioners, with Shakespearean Comedy:

> It is only in Jonson and the Restoration writers that English comedy can be called a form of New Comedy. The earlier tradition established by Peele and developed by Lyly, Greene and the masque writers, which uses themes from romance and folklore and avoids the comedy of manners, is the one followed by Shakespeare. . . . We may call this the drama of the green world, and its theme is once again the triumph of life over the waste land, the death and revival of the year impersonated by figures still human, and once divine as well.[6]

Frye goes on to explain that Shakespeare's conception of a second, "green" world places him outside the tradition of Menandrine Comedy because the opposition of the green world to the normal world generates a new kind of comic resolution, "a detachment born of this reciprocal reflection of two illusory realities."[7] The fact is that *Bartholomew Fair* is very Shakespearean in Frye's terms, almost to the point of parodying a play like *A Midsummer Night's Dream*. Instead of the world of the fairies we have the fair, but the energies swirling around in both are remarkably similar. Oberon and Titania live in the same pansexual world that Ursula does, and Puck tends to Nature's needs as Ursula to her pigs and punk. In addition, many of the basic contrasts between Athens and the forest in *A Midsummer Night's Dream* hold up in *Bartholomew Fair*. Both plays pit morality and social convention against license, warrant against whim, legal discourse against poetry. The green worlds of both plays accommodate chance, error, whim, foolishness, and victimization in ways which mitigate their grim personal and social repercussions. They are, in short, holiday worlds which suggest that human relationships and the human community in general must accept even the most subversive influences if they are to be true and vital. In *A Midsummer Night's Dream*, the lovers must come to terms with the repressed material of nightmares and with the possibility that they are not, in fact, meant for each other as the conventions of heroic romance suggest. Hermia and Lysander trade Cupid, Venus, Dido, and Aeneas for Jack and Jill: human choice is reduced to animal instinct, and epic poetry to doggerel:

> When thou wak'st,
> Thou tak'st
> True delight
> In the sight
> Of thy former lady's eye:
> And the country proverb known,
> That every man should take his own,
> In your waking shall be shown.
>   Jack shall have Jill
>   Nought shall go ill;
> The man shall have his mare again, and all shall be well.
>   (III, ii, 453-63)

The structural resemblance between *Bartholomew Fair* and *A Midsummer Night's Dream* is almost uncanny when one considers that each concludes with a play within the main play that raises questions about the relationship between theater and its audience. *A Midsummer Night's Dream* ends with Nick Bottom's production of "A Tedious Brief Scene of Young Pyramus and his Love Thisby," and *Bartholomew Fair* with John Littlewit's puppet motion, "The Ancient Modern History of Hero and Leander; or The Touchstone of True Love." Bottom's play sets up a very sophisticated framework of dramatic perspective based on the fact that *A Midsummer Night's Dream* itself was performed as a dramatic epithalamion to celebrate an aristocratic marriage. Thus, the theater audience stands in the same relation to the play as Theseus, Hippolyta, and the rest stand to Bottom's interlude. This is precisely the point of Puck's epilogue:

> If we shadows have offended,
> Think but this, and all is mended:

> That you have but slumb'red here,
> While these visions did appear.
> And this weak and idle theme,
> No more yielding but a dream,
> Gentles, do not reprehend:
> If you pardon, we will mend.
> And, as I am an honest Puck,
> If we have some unearned luck
> Now to scape the serpent's tongue,
> We will make amends ere long;
> Else the Puck a liar call:
> So, good night unto you all.
> Give me your hands, if we be friends,
> And Robin shall restore amends.
>
> (V, i, 423-38)

Puck collapses the perspective framework by explicitly putting to us the same problems of response and judgment that all of the characters of the play confront. We are asked to consider our roles as spectators, to evaluate what we have seen and choose either to reject or accept it.

One of our options is to mend the vision by confining it to the world of dreams, thereby pardoning the players through an act of good will. Puck encourages us in this choice, which, we should recall, is the choice of majesty, made by Oberon and by Theseus. When Oberon instructs Puck to reconcile the Athenian lovers, he resolves that, "When they next wake, all this derision/Shall seem a dream and fruitless vision" (II, ii, 370-71); and when he addresses the problem of bringing Titania back, he declares, "I will undo/This hateful imperfection of her eyes" (IV, i, 65-66). Theseus assumes essentially the same role, that of mender of vision, when he views the rustics' nonsensical play. Philostrate counsels him against permitting the performance.

> It is not for you. I have heard it over,
> And it is nothing, nothing in the world;
> Unless you can find sport in their intents,

Extremely stretched and conned with cruel pain,
To do you service.
                                    (V, i, 77-81)

Hippolyta presses the point, but Theseus has an entire dramatic theory ready for her:

HIPPOLYTA. I love not to see wretchedness
    o'ercharged,
  And duty in his service perishing.
THESEUS. Why, gentle sweet, you shall see no such
    thing.
HIPPOLYTA. He says they can do nothing in this kind.
THESEUS. The kinder we, to give them thanks for
    nothing.
  Our sport shall be to take what they mistake:
  And what poor duty cannot do, noble respect
  Takes it in might, not merit.
  Where I have come, great clerks have purposed
  To greet me with premeditated welcomes;
  Where I have seen them shiver and look pale,
  Make periods in the midst of sentences,
  Throttle their practiced accent in their fears,
  And, in conclusion, dumbly have broke off,
  Not paying me a welcome. Trust me, sweet,
  Out of this silence yet I picked a welcome;
  And in the modesty of fearful duty
  I read as much as from the rattling tongue
  Of saucy and audacious eloquence.
  Love, therefore, and tongue-tied simplicity
  In least speak most, to my capacity.
                                    (V, i, 85-105)

The point of Theseus' remarks is that the monarch is the ultimate spectator, charged with interpreting and responding to the actions of his subjects.

The rustic players enact an episode from Ovid's *Metamorphoses*, and quite by accident they manage a metamorphosis of their own, transforming tragedy to farce. In a sense, this has been the progress of the main action. Oberon takes the potentially tragic drama of the lovers as nothing but foolishness, and the play itself resolves this tragic potential into comedy. Theseus and Puck make it clear that the question of response to experience is at least partially in our own hands, and several other kinds of vision compete in the play with this essentially comic vision. Egeus embodies totally reductive, self-reflexive response; he sees his daughter as a possession and Lysander's suit as a potential violation of his property rights. Oberon extends this vision into the forest, demonstrating what happens when this kind of destructive vision rules the natural world. Oberon's temper tantrum over Titania's boy has disrupted all of the normal processes of nature and eventually victimizes even Titania when he casts her in love with Bottom. However, Oberon reasserts his majesty and resumes his custodianship of the natural world, in part because Titania gives him what he wants and in part because he finds what he has done hateful. He feels pity for Titania, but it is clear that she does not share the response: she is having a wonderful time. The hateful imperfection of her eyes is hateful only to Oberon. In short, the restoration of harmony in the natural world is a function of Oberon's choice, and his choice is a function of his response to a drama he has invented for himself. His decision is both personally and socially responsible: majesty, in its dual role as chief actor and chief spectator in the social drama, chooses to act benevolently toward its subjects because the rewards are reciprocal.

This is the lesson Theseus "learns" between act 1 in which he substantiates Egeus' legal claim, and act 4, in which he rejects that claim in favor of the lovers. Oberon makes it easy for him by reshuffling Hermia, Helena, Demetrius, and Lysander into a proper comic arrangement, but Theseus makes the proper choice. As a counterpoint to the theme of social renewal through benevolent majestic response we have Bottom, whose totally unself-conscious response to the world admits him to the richest experience of any mortal in the play.

Bottom's "dream" is the measure of Shakespeare's unwillingness to fake his comic resolution. To Bottom he has given the charge of nurturing that irreducible portion of life that resists articulation, that we can accommodate only as "experience." The weaver speaks the real truth of the play: "I have had a most rare vision. I have had a dream, past the wit of man to say what dream it was. Man is but an ass, if he go about to expound this dream" (IV, i, 204-7), and his topsy-turvy syntax in the description that follows captures perfectly the confusion of his experience. This is the opposite of self-conscious response, and Shakespeare makes it clear that it has its own rewards. We must sacrifice to sustain a social community; we must abandon Egeus and Oberon's entirely self-referential mode, and we must abandon Nick Bottom's uncritical mode, but only after we have enjoyed him. In a sense, *A Midsummer Night's Dream* is a play about the possibilities and responsibilities of the spectator in the *theatrum mundi*.

In *Bartholomew Fair*, the significance of Littlewit's motion in relation to the rest of the play and its audience is much the same, but, as we might expect, when there is a different audience involved, there is a different set of conclusions. Like Bottom, Littlewit unwittingly debases Ovid; "The Touchstone of True Love," like "Pyramus and Thisbe," is a simpleton's attempt to be a poet, but far more important than what the motion reveals about its author is what it reveals about Jonson's perception of its audience. Leatherhead complains about authors who "put too much learning i'their things nowadays" (V, i, 15-16), and worries that Littlewit's motion will suffer from such an attempt. Littlewit himself assures Cokes that learning and poetry will not spoil his work:

> I have onely made it a little easie, and moderne for the times, Sir, that's all; As, for the Hellespont I imagine our Thames here; and then Leander, I make A Diers sonne, about Puddle-wharfe: and Hero a wench o' the Banke-side, who going over one morning, to old fish-street; Leander spies her land at Trigsstayers, and falls

in love with her: Now do I introduce Cupid, having Metamorphos'd himselfe into a Drawer, and hee strikes Hero in love with a pint of Sherry, and other pretty passages there are, o' the friendship, that will delight you, Sir, and please you of judgement.

(V, iii, 120-30)

One cannot imagine a worse wrenching of Ovid and Marlowe, but it is hard to deny that it is beautifully matched to its audience: Cokes, the most avid of playgoers, pretending to judgment and making a general nuisance of himself; the gallants there to watch and partake of the social intrigue of the playhouse; the drunk citizens' wives on the verge of prostitution; the pimps; Wasp, whose idea of good acting is good vapors; and the Puritans and the Magistrates who, along with serious playwrights, were foolish enough to take all of this to heart. And this audience must have been very close to Jonson's own, or at least to his perception of his audience, particularly in light of *Catiline*'s recent failure.

The fairgoers assemble for the puppet show just as Jonson's audience had assembled for *Bartholomew Fair*. Filcher and Sharkwell, by their very names, recall the seaminess of the commercial side of theater. Cokes arrives to assert his gentlemanly status by paying twelvepence instead of the required twopence, and once inside he enters immediately into a discussion of "the matter" with Littlewit and Leatherhead. Clearly Jonson mocks, through Cokes' behavior, the kind of self-centered, disruptive spectator encountered in Jacobean social climbers, like the grocer couple, George and Nell, in *The Knight of the Burning Pestle*. Attending the theater because it is their idea of what they ought to do but understanding nothing about the theater and the conventions by which it works, they violate every notion of decorum. Like the grocers, Cokes feels no inhibition about interrupting a play to ask questions or make suggestions, because he has no sense of what is going on. The epitome of Cokes's foolishness is his confusion of the puppets with real actors, capped by his defense of himself against what he takes to be Leatherhead's imputation of improper sexual interest in the females: "I warrant thee, 1 will not hurt her, fellow; what dost think me uncivill? I pray thee be not jealous: I am toward a wife" (V, iv, 6-8). The other members of the audience are easily recognizable members of Jonson's own audience, gathered on stage to watch a play.

Furthermore, the action which immediately precedes the motion itself serves the important function of allowing Jonson to expand the context of the interlude beyond that of a fictional puppet show in a fictional fair. At the opening of act 5, when Leatherhead instructs Filcher and Sharkwell in their duties, his chatter about his puppet experience makes the motion we are about to see a part of the real tradition of English puppetry:

> O the Motions, that I Lanthorne Leatherhead have given light to, i' my time, since my Master Pod dyed! Jerusalem was a stately thing; and so was Ninive, and the citty of Norwich, and Sodom and Gomorrah; with the rising o' the prentises; and pulling downe the bawdy houses there, upon Shrove-Tuesday; but the Gunpowder-plot, there was a get-penny! I have presented that to an eighteene, or twenty pence audience, nine times in an afternoone.
>
> (V, i, 6-14)

Leatherhead and his puppets transcend the bounds of the purely fictional to claim a place in the realm of the actual. In this same way, Cokes, for all his idiocy, translates the world of the puppet show into real theater. We get the physical sense of the playhouse when he asks for the tiring house so that he, like all gallants, might drink with "the young company," This mention of the young company, together with Leatherhead's comment, "we are but beginners," and Littlewit's description of the company as "Pretty youthes, Sir, all children both old and yong," reminds us that *Bartholomew Fair* itself was being played by a new company that was, in

R. B. Parker's words, "an eccentric and, as it proved, unstable amalgam of the adult Lady Elizabeth's Men and the Children of the Queen's Revels."[8]

The high point of this increasing self-consciousness about the play-within-a-play is Cokes's allusion to Taylor, Burbage, and Field, three living actors, two of whom, Taylor and Field, may well have been on stage at that very moment. Thus, the prelude to the puppet show emphasizes, like the induction, that we are at a play about to watch a group of actors watch what is very nearly another play. The suggestion is that we, as an audience in the playhouse, are about to watch *ourselves* watch a play, only what we see of ourselves is an assembly of dull-witted, cantankerous, thieving, promiscuous, and conniving playgoers. The analogy between stage audience and playhouse audience is even clearer if one considers that the same process by which *Hero and Leander* becomes "The Touchstone of True Love" has been at work since the beginning of *Bartholomew Fair*. This is not to say that Ben Jonson had come to see himself as another John Littlewit or that he meant his play to be another "Touchstone," but rather that he was greatly concerned about what happens when a self-conscious playwright bows to the tastes of his audience, when he writes to the level of the grounded judgments. The debate is as much between Jonson and us as between Littlewit and Cokes or Busy. In his induction, Jonson promises us exactly what Littlewit promises his spectators, and the rest of the play works out the implications of that promise. Littlewit's motion impoverishes heroic romance, but so does Jonson's. For all the power of the play to entertain, it offers none of the comic resolution of *A Midsummer Night's Dream*. What is lacking in Jonson's theater is the impulse to mend this degraded comic vision; it is lacking in the world of the fair, by implication in Jonson's playhouse audience, and, finally, in Jonson himself. There is no majesty left.

Jonson's drama, the fair, and the puppet motion are perpetually defending themselves against the overly enthusiastic Cokes, who fondles the players and chatters during the play;

against the killjoys; against apathy and ignorance. And there is no energy left to reconstitute social order, except in the most minimal, *pro forma* way. This is theater devoid of majesty, until *real* majesty in the person of King James views the play—and then Jonson offers his play in the same manner Puck offers *A Midsummer Night's Dream*:

> Your Majesty hath seene the Play, and you
>   can best allow it from your eare, and view.
> You know the scope of Writers, and what store
>   of leave is given them, if they take not more,
> And turne it into licence: you can tell
>   if we have us'd that leave you gave us, well:
> Or whether wee to rage, or licence breake,
>   or be prophane, or make prophane men speake?
> This is your power to judge (great Sir) and not
>   the envy of a few. Which if wee have got,
> Wee value lesse what their dislike can bring,
>   if it so happy be, t'have pleas'd the King.
>   (Epilogue, 1-12)

Otherwise, the play undermines authority, revealing it as false and stupid, but from this reductive process comes our entertainment. Unlike Jonson's early satiric comedy, however, there is no authority to reconcile our pleasures with the social renewal which is supposed to complete the meaning of the word "recreation."

Tom Quarlous comes closer than anyone to supplying this majestic vision, and close enough to have caused some critics to consider him our means to evaluating the play.[9] No one will dispute Jonas Barish's observation that "it is chiefly by his agency and that of his companion Winwife that the procession of fools who visit the Fair is effectively ridiculed,"[10] but it does not follow, as Richard Levin has argued, that "these men can be said to function as our representatives at the fair, guiding our response, in the manner of chorus.[11] In the first place, Quarlous and Winwife, unlike the proper chorus, are not on stage throughout the play; second, and even more significant, there are severe limits to Quarlous' vision of the fair. He generates satire primarily at the level of his own interests; his is a performance devoid of higher vision, or, for that matter, lower. At several points he rejects the fair as below his dignity. Though he is not precisely an enemy of the fair, he is a parasite, there to entertain himself at the expense of others, watching and helping them make fools of themselves. Without the unself-conscious spectator like Cokes, willing to pay his money and accept the risk of bad drama or "stale bread, rotten egges, musty ginger, and dead honey," no fair to theater will survive for long. In the end, Quarlous offers what nearly everyone else in the fair offers, a partial version full of its own peculiar energy, but denying a great deal to the fair.

In an extremely interesting essay entitled "Infantile Sexuality, Adult Critics, and *Bartholomew Fair*," Judith Gardiner examines the psychological themes of the play. Her line of reasoning parallels Levin's: where Levin talks of "symmetrical relationships developed between comparable characters and groups,"[12] Gardiner talks in terms of shifting oedipal triangles, and she reaches essentially the same conclusion, that Quarlous is the hero of the play:

> Quarlous' role in the play is drawn so that through him the audience can enjoy Oedipal fantasies of rebelling against the "stepfathers" and of gaining sexual access to the "mother." . . . Even Overdo, who should feel most threatened by Quarlous, accepts him at the end of the play like a lost son. If these comic distortions show us that Quarlous is not so very bad, Jonson's irony also protects us from the other direction by persuading us that we have not identified with Quarlous at all and are more like good Ned Winwife.[13]

I think the play is far less certain of itself than Gardiner would have us think, but her perception of Quarlous and Winwife as matched pieces of a single psychological dynamic points toward one of the cruxes of the play. In his treatment of

Quarlous and Winwife, Jonson registers his inability to affirm fully the romance conventions which provide the characteristic satisfactions of comedy. Instead of one full-fledged hero, Jonson offers us two semi-heroes who divide the compensation in the play. Quarlous is by far the more vivid and attractive of the two, yet Winwife is "good Ned Winwife." Each winds up in an extremely ambiguous position: Quarlous gets the widow Purecraft and her six thousand per year, but as he reconciles himself to his decision to accept her we feel all of the comic energy of his diatribe against widows in act 1 going sour on him. Winwife gets Grace, but, instead of presiding over the ending of the play, he and his betrothed retire to the sidelines while Quarlous takes on this part of the hero's role. This schizoid approach to comic resolution is the measure of Jonson's unwillingness to accept what the fair and the romance world represent to him.

Again, Gardiner points us in the right direction:

> Most references to sexuality in *Bartholomew Fair* are infantile and immature. Naughty talk in the play centers about masturbation, castration, exhibitionism, and urination and defecation, especially in public. The frequent association between urination and female sexuality in the play relates to the child's confusion about adult genital functioning, and Quarlous' tirades against female sexuality reflect the fears and disgust of the son who will not believe that his own mother is sexual. In Quarlous' speeches, the male is small as a child; the woman is perceived as monstrous and engulfing.[14]

Jonson's fair, like Shakespeare's forest, is clearly a world of infantile sexuality, and conventional comic resolution requires acceptance of this world as a condition of the hero's reaching adulthood and the society's reaching harmony.

In *Bartholomew Fair*, Quarlous' inability to accept the fair disqualifies him as heroic material, and no one else can mend the comic vision by reconciling social authority with infantile sexuality and license. The sides are clearly drawn between the denizens of the fair and the outsiders, and no one crosses the line. Quarlous comes closest, but he is finally ambivalent: he uses Edgeworth but feels sullied, and he harshly rejects the fair at other points as well. His final choice is a limited one; he must be content with his financial reward and with the fact that his failure has made his friend's triumph possible.

In a sense, Quarlous is Winwife's scapegoat: onto him are dumped all the unconscious adolescent fears about marriage, the fear of falling in and never getting out, of literally losing oneself, and of growing old, which Quarlous expresses so beautifully: "We shall ha' thee, after thou hast beene but a moneth marryed to one of 'hem, looke like the quartane ague, and the black Jaundise met in a face, and walke as if thou had'st borrow'd legges of a Spinner, and voyce of a Cricket" (I, iii, 79-83). Quarlous makes the point with striking clarity as he concludes his execration upon widows; rather than marry a widow, he boasts, "I would een desire of Fate, I might dwell in a drumme, and take in my sustenance, with an old broken Tobacco-pipe and a Straw." (I, i, 85-87). We might recall here the sexual punning on "drum" in *The Alchemist* and the image of the infant of Saguntum, whom Jonson addresses in his ode "To the immortall memorie, and friendship of that noble pair, Sir Lucius Cary, and Sir H. Morison":

> Brave Infant of Saguntum, cleare
> Thy comming forth in that great yeare,
> When the Prodigious Hannibal did crowne
> His rage, with razing your immortal Towne.
> Thou, looking then about,
> E're thou wert halfe got out,
> Wise child, did'st hastily returne,
> And mad'st thy Mothers wombe thine urne.
> How summ'd a circle didst thou leave man-kind
> Of deepest lore, could we the Center find!
> . . . .
> As, could they but lifes miseries fore-see,
> No doubt all Infants would returne like thee.[15]

The psychological issues involved in Quarlous' choice are clear: marriage represents the willingness to accept the realities of adulthood and, in terms of oedipal conflict, to deal with the infantile fears associated with women who have belonged to other men; the other option is perpetual fetal existence. Quarlous chooses the widow, but it is not an entirely happy choice, and he makes it only by dehumanizing it, by marrying Purecraft's fortune: "It is money that I want, why should I not marry the money, when 'tis offer'd mee?" (V, ii, 80-82).

The inability of this play to affirm romance convention has important implications for Jonson's theater. Denying his audiences the conventional satisfactions of comedy was for Jonson a means of maintaining control in the theater, and this control was necessary because of his uneasiness about the relationship between recreation and license. To entertain his audiences freely, Jonson had to put some distance between himself and his theater; he had to insist, as Quarlous does, that he stands apart from it, even as he creates and enjoys it. *Bartholomew Fair*, then, is another attempt to come to terms with a public audience. From *Epicene* onward, Jonson wrote for himself a new role as the genial poet looking to satisfy, within reasonable limits, the wishes of his spectators, but this reconciliation is contingent upon qualified rejection; geniality goes hand in hand with contempt. Behind the mask, Jonson was writing himself out of a theater which he had come to regard as the realm of fools. He found it increasingly difficult to see the playhouse as a place of enlightenment; instead, he saw it as a marketplace for self-interest. Whereas he had used his authority to argue for reform in his early work, he seemed content later to depict his audiences as he saw them, to leave them to deal with the portrait—or not—and to suggest that theater might exist just for the pleasure of taking fools' money. The plays entertain, but they offer recreation with an edge to it. The author promises recreation while his plays deal equivocally with the audience, frequently by juxtaposing the concern for theater that addresses moral questions and reasserts the values of human community with theater's self-interestedness, its need to keep its hand in its spectators' pockets. The prefaces and the prologues become more and more elusive as we approach *Bartholomew Fair*, and Jonson's aggression is buried in difficult syntax or recondite allusion. In other words, Jonson's work records the fact that his commitment to recreative theater was made at the considerable cost of facing up to a great deal of contempt for both himself and his audience, contempt generated by his abandonment of morality drama and projected onto his dealings with paying customers. His coming to terms with this contempt is signified in *Bartholomew Fair* by his portrayal of theater as a socially acceptable, self-gratifying ritual, as a fair.

The induction to the play begins Jonson's meticulous depiction of theater as ritual by particularizing the activity of playgoing. Not since *Every Man Out of His Humor* had Jonson gone to such length to preface a play, and this induction, like its predecessor of fifteen years, examines minutely the assumptions underlying the theatrical event to follow. It stresses the fact that the opening performance of the play is an event unique in the history of theater, and it isolates the individual spectator, defining him progressively by his presence in a particular theater on a particular day in a particular seat with a particular set of expectations shaped by unique prior experience in the theater. The most significant aspect of this examination of theater, however, is Jonson's attempt to cast the play as a fair. We are instructed to regard *Bartholomew Fair* as a fair in itself, not as a play *like* a fair. Jonson asks that his fair be judged against other fairs, like Smithfield; he counters imagined objections to the absence of little Davy and Kindheart not by claiming that the play is a fiction, his to do with as he pleases, but by asserting that he has merely updated Smithfield, substituting "a strutting Horse-courser" and "a fine oyly Pig-woman" for the others. In addition, as Eugene Waith argues in the introduction to his Yale edition of the play, there is good reason to believe that Jonson meant the staging of the play to keep before his audience the atmosphere of the fair.[16] Just before the play begins, Jonson depicts himself as a chapman about to offer this play as his ware:

> Howsoever, hee prayes you to beleeve, his Ware is still the same, else you will make him justly suspect that hee that is so loth to looke on a Baby, or an Hobby-horse, heere, would be glad to take up a Commodity of them, at any laughter, or losse, in another place.
> (Induction, 161-65)

Here Jonson makes it clear that the analogy between fair and theater goes to the heart of the author-spectator relationship. He who will not laugh at Jonson's play, he who rejects this ware, is a fool, a potential mark for real swindlers and for theater which is ultimately interested only in victimizing its spectators.

Jonson's self-consciousness about fairing in the induction prepares us for the proposition which *Bartholomew Fair* itself considers, that the fair represents the truest expression of commercial theater. This is to say nothing of Jonson's concept of ideal theater, only that, given the two aspects of commercial theater which distinguish it from its privately financed relatives, its need to be financially self-sufficient and its need to grapple with the self-gratifying urges of a diverse audience, the fair is Ben Jonson's vision of truly democratic theater, a masque for the multitude. A fair is theater reduced to its component parts, a series of contractual agreements between the individual fairgoers and the entrepreneur, just as theater might be thought of as the sum of the relationships between a playwright and his individual spectators or, from an even wider view, as the sum of all the choices made by spectators from the beginning of commercial theater, to see this play, to disregard that play, choices which determined the nature of the theater in 1614 as much as did the personalities of the actors and playwrights. The entire force of the induction is to isolate the components of this theater, on one hand the role of the paying customer on October 31, 1614, on the other hand, the entire panorama of playhouse history from "Jeronimo" to Caliban, from Adams and Tarleton to Brome. The bookholder reminds us of the financial arrangement by which we participate in the theater, even if his version is only Jonson's wishful thinking. In short, we are asked to examine all of the facets of our relationship to the stage and consider the basis of our role in the theater a contract between us and the playwright. The point of this contract is not simply that it allows Jonson to meet his audiences halfway, but that it allows him to meet them only halfway. It protects him, allowing him a basis on which to reject portions of his audience and permitting him that essential distance.

Like the most sophisticated of Jonson's antimasques, then, the induction sets for the play a problem, in this case the creation of a theater which can accommodate, even satisfy, the myriad expectations of a public audience, while permitting its author some protection from the extremes of the self-gratifying urges of his spectators. The solution offered by the fair is two-fold: first, it offers its spectators an individualized experience. The profusion of experience presented by a fair recognizes, above all, the fact that different fairgoers enjoy different pleasures. If one likes pig, he may eat until his stomach or his purse gives out, while another may avoid such things altogether. A fair allows each to please himself according to his desire and his capacity. Second, a fair is by nature a commercial enterprise, one which largely removes self-gratification from its aggressive associations. Volpone's ruse works only on the denial of its commercial aspect, whether in his chamber or in the street before Celia's house. In *The Alchemist*, money changes hands only with apologies. But a fair is fundamentally commercial, a celebration of individual purchasing power. The essence of fairing is the transaction which satisfies both buyer and monger. In the comedies previous to *Bartholomew Fair*, the exchange of money, that is "purchase," is little but an occasion for one party to victimize another. Money is pelf, to be kept in a trunk, in a cellar, or behind a curtain, and Sir Epicure Mammon's dreams are the closest we come to seeing that money can be *used* deliberately to acquire something of value. Most often, the exchange of money simply binds and deludes. Because the fair, however, is explicitly commercial yet removed from the risks of the real world, its patrons, like the patrons of the theater, are assured of some insulation from real loss. They bring to the fair only what they are willing to lose, even if losing it makes them unhappy. And in *Bartholomew Fair*, coin jingles unabashedly from start to finish, small coin not massy plate. There is Littlewit's "six-shilling beare" and Ursula's business: "Then 6. and 20. shillings a barrell I will advance o' my Beere; and fifty shillings a hundred o' my bottle-ale. . . . five shillings a Pigge is my price, at least; if it be a sow-pig, six pence more: if she be a great-bellied wife, and long for't, six pence more for that" (II, ii, 94-122). There is Cokes's "Little scurvy white money" and his forty-shilling masque. Purecraft's six thousand pound and her Volponesque sport are of another world: "These seven yeeres, I have beene a willful holy widdow, onely to draw feasts, and gifts from my intangled suitors" (V, ii, 53-55). What we sacrifice to *Bartholomew Fair* from *The Alchemist* and *Volpone* is all sense of the grandeur of Mammon's fantasies and Volpone's vision:

> Good morning to the day; and, next, my gold:
> Open the shrine, that I may see my saint.
> Haile the worlds soule, and mine.
> *(Volpone*, I, i, 1-3)

In return we get a world of copious and varied delight. Here the commercial aspect of recreation is something to be celebrated.

Perspective is one of the means by which a playwright determines the nature of his spectator's experience. In Jonson's early work, such as *Every Man Out* or *Cynthia's Revels*, he is relatively clear about perspective. We are meant to respond to the action of *Cynthia's Revels* exactly as Crites does, and the elaborate induction to *Every Man Out* leaves us no doubts about the issues in that play and our relation to them. From *Poetaster* on, however, the perspective is blurred. The characters through whose eyes we watch, by whose actions and opinions our understanding is shaped, are no longer transparent personifications of simple authorial judgments. But even with the judgmental complexities in plays like *Volpone* and *The Alchemist*, dramatic perspective is not so difficult as it might be: we see the action from the vantage of the gullers, not the gulls. By contrast, the experience of *Bartholomew Fair* is kaleidoscopic; we perceive the action through many eyes, and the problem of resolving those perceptions into a coherent understanding of the play is largely our own. This is the closest Jonson came to James Joyce's invisible and indifferent creator.

As spectators in such a theater, we have a good deal of choice about what we value in our theatrical experience. Like fairgoers, we are bombarded with versions of the fair offered by the various parties to the event. What we purchase in this theater is the right to exercise our own judgment, a point which Jonson makes explicitly in his induction:

> It shall bee lawfull for any man, to judge his six pen'orth, his twelve pen'orth, so to his eighteen pence, 2. shillings, halfe a crowne, to the value of his place: Provided alwaies his place get not above his wit. And if he pay for halfe a dozen, hee may censure for all them too, so that he will undertake that they shall bee silent. Hee shall put in for Censures here, as they doe for lots at the lottery: mary, if he drop but six pence at the doore, and will censure a crownes worth, it is thought there is no conscience, or justice in that.
> (Induction, 87-96)

Judgment is a form of authority, here to be purchased like a place on a bench. The contract fixes a theme which runs throughout Jonson's drama, the relationship between coin and language.[17] Both are forms of authority, and Jonson is clear about how the absence of one can be compensated by the masterful use of the other. Figures like Crites and Macilente are comforted in their poverty by the fact that verbal virtuosity admits them to social privilege. Others like Volpone, Face, and Subtle use theatrical discourse to acquire cash. Mosca strokes the lawyer Voltore with a piece of flattery far more applicable to himself or his master: "Every word/Your worship but lets fall, is a cecchine!" *Bartholomew Fair* is extremely self-conscious about the relationship between money and language and about the use of language to value one's experience. The interaction between the inhabitants of the fair and the visitors is as much a matter of language as of money.

Quarlous, for example, brings no money to the fair, at least no substantial amount, for Edgeworth passes over Quarlous and Winwife as marks with the observation, "These fellows were too fine to carry money." Later Winwife does manage to come up with twel'pence for Whit, but he uses it to get rid of the pander, not to buy his product. Quarlous is an outsider, and his use of language confirms this; he uses language to fix people, to keep them at a distance, and to manipulate them for his purposes without compensating them. He rewards Edgeworth for his services in procuring the license from Wasp by responding to the pickpocket's offer of some free punk with, "Keep it for your companions in beastliness; I am none of 'em, sir. . . . The hangman is only fit to discourse with you" (IV, vi, 20-25). In short, he refuses to enter into mutually beneficial transactions. He responds to the hawking of Leatherhead and Trash by fixing them as mythological characters, Orpheus and Ceres. Knockem becomes Neptune, Ursula the "Body o' the Fair." This extreme self-consciousness allows him to control others, but it also allows him to stand outside the fair, to consider it a play to be observed and not enacted. He has inherited this role directly from Volpone, Truewit, and Face, although, as Barish points out, Quarlous is unable to keep himself entirely out of the swirl of the fair.[18] Quarlous' denial of the fair and his hostility toward its inhabitants are the measure of Jonson's own rejection of what he has made of the theater in writing to the level of the grounded judgments. Although it is a partial vision, and although it does not deny a fascination with the fair, Quarlous' vision does carry a great deal of weight in the play. The unrelenting impulse to reduce the world and to use its other inhabitants as objects upon which to drain one's anger is very similar to the refusal to spend one's cash to express value and judgment.

The opposite of this tendency is Cokes, willing to spend on everything; the clear implication of his behavior is that to value everything equally is to value nothing at all. Where Quarlous uses words to distance, Cokes renames things to give them entirely personal significance. And the complete lack of reference in the naming process makes the objects all the more precious. Why should Hero be Cokes's "fairing" or Leander a "fiddle," except that the terms are Cokes's alone? The relation of money and language to authority is underscored by Cokes's financial and physical stripping. His litany of loss is astonishing; with Trouble-all at his side, in a bizarre recollection of Lear on the heath, he describes his predicament:

> Friend, doe you know who I am? or where I lye? I doe not my selfe, I'll be sworne, doe but carry me home, and I'll please thee, I ha' money enough there. I ha' lost my selfe, and my cloak and my hat; and my fine sword and my sister, and Numps, and Mistris Grace (a Gentlewoman that I should ha' marryed) and a cut-worke handkercher, shee ga' mee, and two purses to day. And my bargaine o' Hobby-horses and Ginger-bread, which grieves me worst of all.
> (IV, ii, 78-86)

Not only is he unable to use language to control his experience, he is terribly susceptible to the language of others. The scene in which Edgeworth and Nightingale pluck Cokes's second purse is *Volpone* or *The Alchemist* in miniature, the use of poetry simultaneously to enthrall, stimulate, and rob its audience while explaining the con to increase all the more the pleasure of the game.

Overdo's foolish attempts to use language self-consciously parallel his mistaken faith in rhetoric and theatricality as means to truth. His encounter with Lantern Leatherhead and Joan Trash is exactly to the point. Leatherhead threatens to ruin Trash's business if she hinders his "prospect." The threat leads to a quarrel over the quality of the gingerbread woman's wares:

> LEATHERHEAD. Hinder not the prospect of my shop, or I'll ha' it proclaim'd i'the Fayre, what stuffe they are made on.
> TRASH. Why, what stuffe are they made on, Brother Leatherhead? nothing but what's wholesome, I assure you.
> LEATHERHEAD. Yes, stale bread, rotten egges, musty ginger, and dead honey, you know.
> (II, ii, 4-10)

Overdo, disguised as mad Arthur and overhearing their spat, assumes without question the truth of Leatherhead's allegation, and Trash, after her first denial, resorts to impugning her attacker:

> Marre my market, thou too-proud Pedler? do thy worst; I defie thee, I, and thy stable of hobby-horses. I pay for my ground, as well as thou dost, and thou wrong'st mee, for all thou art parcell-poet, and an Inginer. I'll finde a friend shall right me, and make a ballad of thee, and thy cattell all over. Are you puft up with the pride of your wares? your Arsedine?
> (II, ii, 13-19)

They go on to imagine a session in the court of Pie-Powders with Overdo presiding, and Trash concludes, "I'll be found as upright in my dealing, as any woman in Smithfield, I, charme me?" (II, ii, 25-26). If Ursula is any measure, this would be no vindication, but the point is that this squabble offers neither Overdo nor us any means of judgment. We have in fact witnessed a court session with Overdo in attendance, but all we have in evidence is a stream of self-assertive language. In this round, perhaps the Justice is correct, but he loses one in his assessment of Edgeworth, and he draws with Knockem when Overdo takes the horse-courser for a cutpurse on the strength of Ursula's roaring. What is wonderful about this encounter is Overdo's attempt to test his judgment with Mooncalf:

> JUSTICE. Is this goodly person before us here, this vapours, a knight of the knife?
> MOONCALF. What meane you by that, Master Arthur?
> JUSTICE. I meane a child of the horne-thumb, a babe of booty, boy; a cutpurse.
> MOONCALF. O Lord, Sir! far from it. This is Master Dan. Knockhum: Jordane, the Ranger of Turnebulle. He is a horse-courser, Sir.
> JUSTICE. Thy dainty dame, though, call'd him cutpurse.
> MOONCALF. Like enough, Sir, she'll doe forty such things in an houre (an you listen to her) for her recreation, if the toy take her i' the greasie kerchiefe: it makes her fat, you see. Shee battens with it.
> (II, iii, 27-39)

Amid much self-congratulation, Overdo changes his mind: "Here might I ha' beene deceiv'd, now: and ha' put a fooles blot upon my selfe, if I had not play'd an after game o' discretion (II, iii, 40-42). But who knows for sure? In large measure, Overdo's task of sorting out the evidence is our task. It is a frustrating one, complicated by the clear and frequent reminders that those who attempt to judge in this play make fools of themselves more often than not.

If the others represent a spectrum of various relationships among language, money, and authority, Trouble-all stands at both extremes. For him all language, all authority, all value center in Adam Overdo's warrant, but, even if the Justice's signature is for Trouble-all the essence of meaning, it has, by virtue of his insanity, no actual significance. It is all-powerful, but Trouble-all has no use for it. When Knockem offers him a drink and Trouble-all refuses for lack of warrant, Knockem simply forges the signature, and everyone is happy. The relationship between control of language and self-definition is underscored in act 5 when Quarlous, having deprived Trouble-all of his gown and cap, impersonates him and finally makes some use of the character. Like Bottom, Trouble-all has no capacity for controlling himself, and yet he is in touch with the fundamental realities of his world. It is his act of interpretation—which is no interpretation at all—that resolves the romance plot and allows Winwife to wed Grace. And his response to the world of warrant has its own peculiar logic: one solution to the problem of dealing with questions of value and authority is to give oneself over entirely to the authority of others, to refuse even to "stale" without someone else's permission.[19]

Bartholomew Fair manages to accommodate all varieties of verbal self-definition, accepting freely that language is not only self-expressive but self-gratifying in its capacity to fool, entrap, anger, and expose its audiences and even simply to expend itself with no thought to the consequences. The fair handles linguistic aggression as it handles everything else, as recreation and as transaction, and in this way self-interested language is liberated from much of the hostility it expresses in plays like *Sejanus* or *Volpone*. Ursula's roaring is all part of her business, and the game of vapors turns out to be the perfect forum from someone whose use of words never seems to get beyond belligerence. One of the consequences of the ultimately self-referential use of language, however, is that the function of language as communication is diminished. As language is atomized, exploded into a myriad of individual jargons, it ceases to express community or to define principles by which a society might order itself. In short, it is devoid of authority beyond individual authority. Vapors and roaring and poetry that picks pockets are the result.

It is at this point that *A Midsummer Night's Dream* and *Bartholomew Fair*, plays equally concerned about the verbal universe (to use Frye's term), diverge. When language becomes the articulation of majesty, when it is used to constitute human community, as it is in Shakespeare's play, full comic resolution is possible. Jonson's fair is communal, but it is an odd community, one which is never comfortable with itself. It threatens continually to fall apart, to scatter its members like marbles. The only majesty, in fact the only real authority, in this theater is the majesty of King James, and the epilogue stresses his special nature as a spectator, the power which is his alone, not the power of a public audience: "This is your power to judge (great Sir) and not/The envy of a few" (Epilogue, 9-10). We can repeat this judgment, mending the comic vision, but Jonson is not optimistic about our willingness to do so or the significance of it if we did. Instead of Theseus' masque dances, *Bartholomew Fair* offers us the mixed blessings of supper with idiots and the cheerful oblivion of drowning the memory of all enormity in drink.

The condition of our full enjoyment at the fair is our acceptance of its chaos, its hostility, its degeneracy, its unstinting self-gratifying energy, its threat to social convention, and, finally, our acceptance of the fact that our own responses are our own responsibility. Jonson refuses to save us from our judgment; indeed, he makes it very difficult for us to exercise it in any comprehensive way. We must settle for small, qualified resolutions. In this sense, Jonson may be said to have written himself out of the theater as an authority. It is no secret that as successive human generations progress toward adulthood, they repeat, even as they modify, the authority relationships of their own childhoods. Gardiner and Parfitt both suggest that Jonson, deprived of a gentleman father before he ever knew him, invested a great deal of energy in a psychological quest for an "absent and ideal father." This quest figures importantly in his work, and *Bartholomew Fair* represents a tentative resolution: Jonson most freely accepts the recreative aspect of theater and admits his audience to it only as he disqualifies himself as a didactic playwright. One might say that he becomes to his audience the absent father he sought for himself, and, as he stands away from his work, this time he permits his spectators real, self-indulgent entertainment, instead of rejecting them as he had done in *Sejanus*. Acceptance is qualified, however, by the concern which runs from induction to epilogue, that what is made for and taken up by fools may not be more than foolish.

SEVEN

Beyond *Bartholomew Fair*

I

IN THE fourteen years between *Poetaster* and *Bartholomew Fair*, Ben Jonson gradually surrendered his work to his playhouse audience. The idea that he could be satisfied to "prove the pleasure but of one,/So he judicious be" was unworkable for both financial and artistic reasons, so Jonson turned his energy to proving the pleasure of all, judicious or not. It was a struggle. Certainly the sense of confrontation between stage and gallery was intense in the early years of the seventeenth century, but Jonson magnified it, identified the threats to his theater, and attempted to fashion his work to deal with them. His concern was not simply getting his spectators to be silent and remain in their seats; he wished above all to remain faithful to his belief that theater ought to reflect its audience, and he meant his own theater to comprehend the foolishness, hostility, and ignorance of individual spectators without impairing his commitment to recreation. The satire of his early work had offended too many too often; the new theater required the inclusion of the fools and troublemakers instead of their satiric exclusion. Therefore, Jonson grew less and less eager to discriminate morally among various kinds of self-seeking, and conceded, as the condition of including the previously subversive members of his theater audience, that self-seeking is an expression of fundamental human energy. If it is sometimes aggressive, foolish, and unpleasant, it can be nonetheless grand and invigorating. The comic worlds of *Volpone, Epicene, The Alchemist*, and *Bartholomew Fair* are fragile: they show clear signs of Jonson struggling to keep his moral judgments of his audience at bay, but they entertain us wonderfully.

The terms of the settlement Jonson reached with his spectators in the period of his great comedies are complex and provisional, and *Bartholomew Fair* by no means settled the conflict. After 1614, however, Jonson never again fully embodied in his drama the most difficult problems of theatrical authority. In 1615, after *The Devil Is an Ass*, he left the public theater for a decade, and in that time he wrote his finest court masques. For whatever reason—exhaustion, indifference, absorption in the masques—Jonson stayed clear of the playhouse, and when he returned with *The Staple of News* in 1625 he bullied his audience as he had in the comical satires: "If that not like you, that he sends to night,/'Tis you have left to judge, not hee to write" (Prologue for the Stage, 29-30).

The Staple of News shows Jonson seriously at odds with his audiences and with himself. The induction and the intermeanes which follow each act, featuring the gossips Mirth, Tattle, Expectation, and Censure, take us back to Mitis and Cordatus in *Every Man Out of His Humor*, but whereas the early play might be said to be optimistic by virtue of encouraging its spectators to respond judiciously, the later play is clearly dour, confronting its audience with a satiric version of itself and actively seeking to thwart certain kinds of response. The distance between stage and gallery has widened again, and Jonson is back dealing with the multitude as beast, not as humankind. Most telling, however, is Jonson's difficulty with the tone of the play itself. The morality aspect of the play, the allegory, as Jonson calls it in the address to the readers after act 2, creates real problems for him. He wishes Pecunia, for instance, to represent money, which takes its character from the person who uses it; yet she is also a character in a play which is not rigorously symbolic or allegorical. The result is a strange mixture of passivity and aggression. She chides Peniboy Senior for his miserliness, as if she has a clear, satiric sense of things but lacks the ability to control her fate:

> Cannot my Grace be gotten, and held too,
> Without your selfe-tormentings, and your watches,
> Your macerating of your body thus
> With cares, and scanting of your dyet, and rest?
> (II, i, 22-25)

In the same act, however, she throws herself at Peniboy Junior with abandon, as if Jonson meant to underscore the natural affinity between prodigals and money:

> And I have my desire, Sir, to behold
> That youth, and shape, which in my dreames and wakes,
> I have so oft contemplated, and felt
> Warme in my veynes, and native as my blood.
> When I was told of your arrivall here,
> I felt my heart beat, as it would leape out,
> In speach; and all my face it was a flame,
> But how it came to passe I doe not know.
> (II, v, 50-57)

These two aspects of character are not consistent, and the problem is reflected most clearly in the epilogue spoken by Pecunia:

> And so Pecunia her selfe doth wish,
> That shee may still be ayde unto their uses,
> Not slave unto their pleasures, or a Tyrant
> Over their faire desires; but teach them all
> The golden meane: the Prodigal how to live,
> The sordid, and the covetous, how to dye:
> That with sound mind; this, safe frugality.
> (V, vi, 60-66)

Again one is struck by the inconsistency, this time between her sense of herself as forced to be a slave or a tyrant and her wish to teach the prodigal, sordid, and covetous how to manage money. In the first case, her role is determined by the behavior of the master; in the second, she actively controls him, and Jonson, though in his best work extremely careful about such matters of perspective and authority, here lets the incongruity pass.

The Peniboys, most notably the nephew and uncle, suffer from the same confusion. The former resembles Jonsonian fools like Asotus, Kastril, and Cokes, but in rare moments he contributes the kind of worldly wisdom that makes Truewit an attractive character. He poses a question about the Staple of News which, ten years earlier, might have interested Jonson enough to have become a significant issue of the play:

> Why, me thinkes Sir, if the honest common people
> Will be abus'd, why should not they ha' their pleasure,
> In the believing Lyes, are made for them;
> As you i'th' Office, making them your selves?
> (I, v, 42-45)

But in this play Jonson heavily dismisses such intriguing matters:

> Hee prayes you . . . to consider the Newes here vented, to be none of his Newes, or any reasonable mans; but Newes made like the times Newes, (a weekly cheat to draw mony) and could not be fitter reprehended, then in raising this ridiculous Office of the Staple, wherein the age may see her owne folly, or hunger and thirst after publish'd pamphlets of Newes, set out every Saturday, but made all at home, & no syllable of truth in them: then which there cannot be a greater disease in nature, or a fouler scorne put upon the times.
> (To the Readers, 7-16)

The father's perception that "all the whole world are Canters" and the son's resolve to build a canters' college have remarkable potential, metaphorically and dramatically, but Jonson never develops it.

It is finally the uncle, however, who is most problematic. In act 3, feigning infirmity like Volpone, he traps the greedy Cymbal, who has come to woo Pecunia, and delivers a splendid diatribe, Juvenal and Seneca perfectly melded, before throwing the man out of his house. A comparison of the conclusion of Peniboy's speech with the Senecan original, translated by Jonson in *Discoveries*, reveals the care with which Jonson is working at this point in the play. The original maintains throughout the perspective of Seneca as the spectator:

> Have not I seen the pompe of a whole Kingdome, and what a forraigne King could bring hither also to make himselfe gaz'd, and wonder'd at, laid forth as it were to the shew, and vanish all away in a day? And shall that which could not fill the expectation of a few hours, entertaine, and take up our whole lives? when even it appear'd as superfluous to the Possessors, as to me that was a Spectator. The bravery was shewne, it was not possess'd; while it boasted it selfe, it perish'd.[1]

Seneca is not concerned in a particular way with theater: he uses the terms of shows and entertainment to lend point to his comments. Through some careful rearrangement, Jonson brings the problem of theater and the relationship between actors and audiences to the fore:

> Say, that you were the Emperour of pleasures,
> The great Dictator of fashions, for all Europe,
> And had the pompe of all the Courts, and Kingdomes.
> Laid forth unto the shew? to make your selfe
> Gaz'd and admir'd at? You must goe to bed,
> And take your naturall rest: then, all this vanisheth.
> Your bravery was but showen; 'twas not possest:
> While it did boast it selfe, it was then perishing.
>   . . . All that excesse
> Appear'd as little yours, as the Spectators.
> It scarce fills up the expectation
> Of a few houres, that entertaines mens lives.
>   (III, iv, 57-67)

Here Jonson makes the most of his material; he is keenly aware of the dramatic potential of the Senecan original. In fact, Jonson takes the example as an opportunity to create a miniature theater for Cymbal, putting the Master of the Staple on stage with the leading role. Finally, the point becomes a double-edged one, remarking not simply on the ephemeral nature of pomp and bravery but on the insubstantiality of shows as well. We have before us again, momentarily, the question of the value of theater, excess, and bravery that "scarce [fill] up the expectation of a few houres" to entertain men's lives. Jonson's doubts about the stage rise powerfully to the surface. In many ways, Peniboy is another Morose, but he makes far more compelling demands on our sympathies.[2] This justification of extreme frugality and isolation is squandered, however, when Peniboy goes mad at the loss of Pecunia and falls victim to the jeerers in a way that renders him pathetic. Cymbal the fool has his revenge on Peniboy, who turns out to be an even bigger fool, not a vital personification of the Juvenalian spirit.

In *The Staple of News*, then, Jonson offers an unsettling mix of satire, farce, morality, allegory, and romance. There is no consistent, coherent perspective to order things in any powerful way. The intense commitment to theatrical problems, to public theater as a celebration of its audience and as a profoundly inclusive act of human community, is gone, partially, I suspect, because the court masque had become the forum for Jonson's best thinking about theater. There, even if people did not always understand or appreciate him, he felt he could express himself without fear of the rejection threatened by the playhouse audience. Confirmation of this idea comes, I think, in the relationship between *The Staple of News* and Jonson's Christmas masques for 1624 and 1625, *Neptune's Triumph for the Return of Albion* and *The Fortunate Isles and Their Union*. The first thing one notices upon examining all three is Jonson's easy manner of borrowing. The master cook and several of his speeches appear in both the play and the antimasque to *Neptune's Triumph*, and various other terms and phrases indicate the free exchange from one to the other. What is important, however, is that Lickfinger and his poetic musings seem out of place in *The Staple of News.* The play is not concerned seriously with abstract and theoretical questions of poetry and audience, though it might have been, just as it might have followed through on the implications of "all the whole world are Canters." The cook has a real home in *Neptune's Triumph*, in which Jonson considers earnestly the problems of theater. Moreover, when Jonson remade this masque for the following Christmas, he recorded with striking clarity the nature of the revision that his sense of theater had undergone between *Every Man Out* and *Bartholomew Fair*. For this reason the masques deserve a closer look.

II

When Ben Jonson recast *Neptune's Triumph for the Return of Albion* as *The Fortunate Isles and Their Union* for Twelfth Night 1625, he made several changes. It was necessary to alter the political basis of the 1624 masque because the matter of Prince Charles's return from Spain, which had been scarcely current in 1624, was not at all so one year later. Far more interesting in terms of the artistic design of the masque, however, is the complete revision of the antimasque. *Neptune's Triumph* offers in its antimasque a discussion between fictional versions of the court poet and the master cook about the nature of poetry. The cook is an exuberant sort, oblivious to the strains in the analogy he constructs between his own role and the poet's and eager to accept the capriciousness of his audience as a challenge to his art. The poet is a bit of a grump, complaining of his treatment at court and expressing reservation about the idea of pleasing "the palates of the ghests." His skepticism about this peculiar "brother poet" is clear, but it does not prevent his joining a discussion about one of Jonson's favorite topics, the anxieties of the professional poet. The heart of the problem is how to deal with the wishes of an audience, wishes which here, as elsewhere in Jonson's work, acquire a kind of independent life as "Expectation." Poet and cook take the two sides of an argument which had been in Jonson's blood since the comical satires. On his generous days, he saw himself as a cook determined to satisfy Expectation; on his less generous days, as a poet, he defended himself against those same expectations, now a "pressing enemie."

The antimasque to *The Fortunate Isles* is very different. The cook is nowhere to be found, and the role of the court poet is filled by "Jophiel, an aery spirit, and (according to the Magi) the Intelligence of Jupiter's sphere" (*Fortunate Isles*, 1-2). Jophiel introduces the masque to the King and in the main masque takes the lines the poet had spoken (or not spoken) in *Neptune's Triumph*, but first he encounters Mere-Foole, the "Melancholique Student" who wanders on stage just after Jophiel himself appears. Mere-Foole is an overweight, budding Rosicrucian seeking a sign from the Brotherhood, and the "sport" which Jophiel makes at his expense proceeds along lines familiar to any Jonsonian audience: the quick-witted satirist Jophiel exploits the foolishness of the gull Mere-Foole. He convinces Mere-Foole that Father Outis (nobody), the head of the Rhodostaurotick Brethren, has died in order to confer on him the leadership of the Order, and as a sign of Mere-Foole's new powers Jophiel offers his services, in the manner of Satan to Faustus, for calling forth a vision or two. Mere-Foole makes a number of choices culled primarily from the ranks of the Hermetic philosophers, while Jophiel puts him off with a series of tall tales about why such figures as Zoroastres, Hermes Trismegistus, Ulen-Spiegle, and Pythagoras are momentarily unavailable. The game concludes when Jophiel brings out the poet-jesters Skelton and Scogan, and Mere-Foole, after witnessing an antimasque performed by characters assembled from an assortment of English poems and plays, professes gratitude for "the first grace/The company of the *Rosie Crosse* hath done me." Thereupon Jophiel explodes with indignation at Mere-Foole's misapprehension, and dismisses him:

> The company o' the Rosie-crosse! you wigion,
> The company of Players. Go, you are,
> And wilbe stil your selfe, a Mere-foole; In,
> And take your pot of honey here, and hogs greace,
> See, who has guld you, and make one.
>
> (*Fortunate Isles*, 431-35)

This antimasque is one of Jonson's longest and most recondite, but reference to the earlier version in *Neptune's Triumph* offers a useful perspective. One might say that in the 1624 antimasque Jonson considers the role of poet specifically in terms of dealing with audience expectation. In theatrical terms, the question is: on whose authority, the poet's or the spectators', is the nature and value of theatrical experience determined? If the poet writes to satisfy the tastes of his audience, then expectation is the real source of theatrical authority, and what a poet accomplishes can be judged rightly on the basis of audience response. However, if the poet creates according to his own impulse, *he* commands the stage, and the judgment of his audience becomes only part of the complex problem of valuation. This is the issue the poet and cook debate. The poet will not ignore the defects in the cook's vision of a happy union between Poetry and Expectation, but, as far as the antimasque is concerned, the cook holds sway. He employs a particularly Jonsonian trick to deal with disruptive spectators: they wind up in the pot as seasoning. In other words, the cook puts them on stage to expose them for what they are, just as Jonson has done throughout his career to his own potentially subversive spectators.

Except for a small contribution from the cook at the conclusion, the main masque is entirely the poet's. What we see, then, is Jonson's side-by-side consideration of two roles which fascinated him, the poet as custodian of audience taste and the poet as representative of the learned community. *Neptune's Triumph* allows Jonson to depict an uneasy union of the two, something far more elusive in real life. And what makes the union possible, appropriately, is King James, whose royal authority settles all questions of value and response. While the masque celebrates James as "The mightie Neptune, mightie in his styles,/And large command of waters, and of Isles (*Neptune's Triumph*, 130-31), the unity of masque and antimasque celebrates him as the ideal spectator and, therefore, as the co-creator of the theater.

In *The Fortunate Isles*, Jonson's examination of theatrical authority begins at the point where the cook and poet leave off. Instead of having his creatures merely debate the problem of expectation, Jonson gives us Mere-Foole, his incarnation of the self-seeking spectator. Jonson's argument turns on a peculiar irony: Mere-Foole is finally condemned for his misapprehension, for mistaking players for spectres, and yet the entire demonstration is conducted by an aery spirit whom we are clearly meant to perceive as such, though he is himself a player. The point is that Mere-Foole cannot discriminate the proper relationship between theater and reality. In his self-seeking zeal he confuses all of the Rosicrucian nonsense with reality, and in his ignorance he cannot distinguish real theater from his delusions. He cannot, in other words, discern imposture, and he makes the crucial overreach characteristic of all Jonsonian villains of the theater, real and fictional: he asks for what he has no right to expect. In this theater he is therefore a fool; in another he might have been a hero.

While Mere-Foole is abused for his desire to see spirits, we can watch Jophiel at no risk of Jonson's scorn because we understand the nature of his existence. He is a creature of the theater, Ben Jonson's creation, on one hand less "real" than any of the figures Mere-Foole asks to meet, on the other hand part of a world which, by virtue of its metaphorical expression of King James's actual authority, is very real. Herford and Simpson offer this comment on *The Fortunate Isles* and the problem of spectator perception:

> Satire and Lucianic fancy appear to contend in Jonson's mind, leaving it uncertain whether we are meant to conceive the show of ancient worthies and modern vaga-

bonds whom Merefool does not wish to see but puts up with, as a mocking vision conjured up by the airy spirit, or as merely (what they of course actually were) the company of players in disguise. The realist in Jonson was always liable to encroach upon the fancy of which the Masque was the proper sphere.[3]

Herford and Simpson characteristically oversimplify the masques, and what they fail to understand here is that Jonson means us to conceive both the mocking vision and the company of players, for it is our ability to accomplish this complex conception of theater that distinguishes us from Mere-Foole and from the mere fools of the audience. The masque form in Jonson's hands defines itself by its movement from the world of the antimasque, where complex distinctions are required of the spectator, to the world of the masque, where all such distinctions are finally resolved. This particular antimasque serves to distinguish proper from improper modes of response in the theater. Jonson has created Mere-Foole just to cast him out, and the same process which reveals Mere-Foole's ignorance confirms the ideal spectator in his perceptions.

What Jophiel offers Mere-Foole is the opportunity to become the omnipresent spectator, to "see and commaund," to make the world his gallery, but, because he does not understand the proper exercise of his power, Mere-Foole becomes only the ultimate gull, an unwitting actor in Jophiel's little drama. Each of Mere-Foole's requests is countered with a witty refusal derived from a zany but equally erudite perception of the historical figure in question, Archimedes "inventing a rare Mouse-trap" or Pythagoras "keeping Asses from a feild of beanes." Mere-Foole responds neither to Jophiel's wit nor to the fact that he is being ridiculed, but when he gets to Aesop in his list, Jophiel stops him with a mild rebuke:

Things askt out of season
A man denies himselfe. At such a time
As Christmas, when disguising is a foote,

> To aske of the inventions, and the men,
> The witts, and the ingine[r]s that move those Orbes!
> Me thinkes, you should enquire now, after Skelton,
> Or Mr. Scogan.
>
> *(Fortunate Isles, 274-80)*

Mere-Foole has no perception of any context beyond his own petty wishes, and Jophiel makes this clear in the remaining portion of the antimasque. He offers Skelton and Scogan in place of Hermes and Howle-glas because this is a Christmas masque at the English court and the former are court poets and masque makers, Scogan "that made disguises/For the Kings sonnes" and Skelton "the worshipfull Poet Laureat to K. Harry." They recommend to Mere-Foole, in place of his conjurers' hall of fame, a list of figures from English poetry and the English stage, though a decidedly inauspicious and unheroic group. Elinor Rumming, Doctor Ratt, and the rest counterpoint both the philosophers of Mere-Foole's world and the heroic world of the main masque, and they are fit company for the new head of the Rosicrucian order, the stage's latest nonhero.

However, Jonson had far more in mind than counterpoint: in the space of just one hundred lines, from the entrance of Skelton and Scogan, he manages to develop a rich, if quirky, sense of the history of English literary life. This seemingly random assortment of characters is held together most surely by its lack of social distinction (a comment on Mere-Foole for both his own commonness and his ignorance of literature), but, in addition, its members or the works from which they have come nearly all have had some association with court entertainment. Skelton and Scogan present a parade of the oddities of English letters, but they are essential to Jonson's claims for his masque in spite of their oddity. They are all specks in the background against which *The Fortunate Isles* makes sense, pieces in the tradition of which Jonson has chosen to make himself and his masque a part. With remarkable economy Jonson has made himself a place beside Skelton and

Scogan in the line of court poets and his masque a place in the history of English letters, and if the company includes Elinor, Meg, and Mary, so what? Jonson himself has contributed Mere-Foole, transformed from would-be spectator to another oddity of the English stage. Moreover, Jonson has affirmed the tradition of court entertainment and offered his spectators a place in this tradition according to their capacities to understand and appreciate the antimasque. He has taken a far more tortuous route in *The Fortunate Isles* to the same destination he reached in the antimasque to *Neptune's Triumph*, but the result is a far better view of the literary landscape. The antimasque stands opposed to the main masque in its obvious features, the world of the English commons against the world of classical heroism, but this opposition should not obscure the fact that in its subtler aspects the antimasque educates its spectators by providing a context for what follows in the main masque. The antimasque, in short, creates the audience for the masque.

If we consider the antimasques to *Neptune's Triumph* and *The Fortunate Isles* as two approaches to the same problem, there are some conclusions to be drawn. In *Neptune's Triumph*, the problem of spectator expectation is precedent to what transpires in the theater: both cook and poet seem to agree that the problem of how to deal with the audience is something best resolved by the artist before he ever brings his work to the guest. The "poet" of *The Fortunate Isles*, who is Jonson and yet not all of Jonson, has rejected this idea and addresses the problem of dealing with those who "expect more than they understand," not as something anterior to the performance but as a legitimate function of the theater itself. He chooses, in other words, to make the preparation of his audience and the elimination of disruptive or unqualified members a part of the performance. The poet of *The Fortunate Isles* remains behind the curtain, but his spokesman Jophiel is witty and confident—neither oppressively enthusiastic like the cook nor weary and defensive like the poet of *Neptune's Triumph*. And this poet, like Jonson himself, has embraced the antimasque as an integral part of the form. There is a new sense of control in the 1625 antimasque, stemming from a radical reinterpretation of theatrical space. The characters in the antimasque to *Neptune's Triumph* maintain the boundaries between stage and gallery except for the brief moment when the cook's antimasque is performed and we encounter a potful of the kinds of people we might expect to be unsuitable spectators at a court masque. Stephen Orgel's comment on this strange dance of meat and vegetables is just to the point:

> In this masque, the antimasquers are those who "know all things the wrong way," and the deformity of their minds is embodied in the person of the real court figure who is identified as their leader. He has already been allegorized by the poet in his summary of his masque as "The Sea-Monster Archy" (line 172), the circulator of "tales and stories" that formed part of "th'abortive, and extemporall dinne" at Albion's return three months earlier. Archy is Archibald Armstrong, the court dwarf, who had accompanied the prince to Spain; he leads the antimasquers as the chief promulgator of false tales, and his dancers embody whatever in the court world threatened the truths of the poet's allegory.[4]

Except for this moment in which the potentially subversive members of the audience find themselves represented on stage, the distinction between stage and audience is clear, to be resolved only in the action of the main masque. In *The Fortunate Isles*, Jonson returns to develop the cook's idea and suggests, through Jophiel's ruse with Mere-Foole, a defense of the stage by discarding theatrical boundaries instead of enforcing them. Jophiel nullifies the threat posed by the self-seeking spectator by fictionalizing him, committing him to the gallery of fools. The unwitting Mere-Foole becomes a part of the drama for which Jophiel provides the script, and therefore he surrenders any power to define what transpires on stage.

The reemergence of *Neptune's Triumph* as *The Fortunate Isles* suggests that more than a decade after *Bartholomew Fair* Jonson was still intensely concerned about the relationship between stage and gallery, but at this point in his career real solutions to the conflict were possible only in the court theater. The royal presence imparted the order and meaning that the playhouse could never offer, and, able to assume this kind of authority, in the sense both of relying on it and taking it on himself, Jonson easily dramatized the problems of response and judgment which were the crux of his misgivings about his spectators. The great masques enact such problems in their antimasques, then resolve or banish them in the display of majesty. While Jonson never quite became a Crites to King James, he was afforded for ten years the luxury of dealing with the concerns of his playhouse spectators only in the rarefied atmosphere of the banqueting house.

Neptune's Triumph and *The Fortunate Isles* seem to have absorbed some of the energy from the renewal of hostilities in the playhouse, and the antimasques, taken together, represent for Jonson an act of self-justification, an expression of his commitment to theater. Like Jophiel, Jonson has turned the conflict between stage and spectator into part of a larger drama through which he defines himself as a playwright. As if, in a single motion, to answer for both the immediate problems of *The Staple of News* and those which extended all the way back to *Every Man Out* and *Cynthia's Revels*, Jonson declares that it is the presence of majesty in the theater, the power of royal authority, that completes his sense of himself as a poet and gives full meaning to the theater.

The two masques, then, portray in miniature the revision that Jonson's idea of theater underwent in the period of his most important drama. Stephen Orgel, speaking of *Comus*, makes this remark about Jonson's perception of the masque form. "To Milton, as to Jonson, the function of the court masque is the making of viable myths."[5] This statement embraces much more than the masque, however. It describes Jonson's entire sense of poetry, including all kinds of theater.

For Jonson "viable" meant not simply "true" or "workable" but also appropriate to a specific audience in terms of what they might understand, appreciate, and learn. The greatest impediment to the creation of viable myths for the playhouse was inherent in Jonson's perception of his public audience. He saw his spectators as molecules energized by self-interest, which, assembled, threatened the stage as the monolithic Expectation. By the time he finished *The Alchemist*, this conviction went far beyond the overtly disruptive behavior of a portion of his audience to include, as a potential challenge to the poet's mythmaking, all self-seeking, even the Socratic ideal of seeking to know oneself. After *Poetaster* Jonson outgrew the idea that the fine print in the "contract" between stage and gallery guaranteed a beneficent monarch to supply whatever authority the poet lacked to enforce his judgments. With this realization came another, that theater without such authority verged on a free-for-all, a competition between spectator and poet for the right to determine the meaning and value of drama. In place of the royal protector, Jonson found the harsh reality of an arrangement which was, at base, financial. What he faced, in other words, was the commercialization of his ideal theater.

After *Poetaster* Jonson's interests become far less identified with social authority, whether legal, royal, moral, or ethical, and he seems much more interested in the struggle for various kinds of authority than in the outcome. The progression from *Sejanus* through *The Alchemist* registers a decrease in the stakes for which characters compete, and the threat to both sides eases. Finally, *Bartholomew Fair* depicts a workable relationship between the parties to the theatrical contract. The level of hostility recedes within the plays and within the critical addenda, but there remains enough in places like the induction to *Bartholomew Fair* and the epistles to the readers of *The Alchemist* and *Catiline* to suggest that the overt conciliatory gestures elsewhere must be taken as provisional. In fact, Jonson becomes increasingly subtle and self-conscious about his power to deal with audiences. Instead of open conflict, he chooses passive modes of aggression, acceding superficially to what he took to be the demands of his audiences while reminding them of the conditions under which they participate in the theater. He stresses both the limitations imposed by convention, primarily the financial arrangement, and the limitations inherent in the individual spectator such as ignorance, belligerence, and sundry kinds of self-seeking. What was initially the greatest threat to his theater Jonson makes his strongest line of defense. The aggression in the mature plays is far more subtle because the plays themselves, in becoming vehicles for Jonson's consideration of theatrical problems, absorb the energy which was directly vented on the audience in a play like *Every Man Out*. Early in his career Jonson felt, like the poet of *Neptune's Triumph*, that the audience threatened his attainment of his artistic goals. However, as the topic of theatrical authority became the explicit concern of his work, the threat became less of a destructive conflict and more the energy which informed his drama.

This is not to say simply that Ben Jonson labored to settle a vendetta. His commitment to viable myths did not abate, but his belief that in the playhouse he was dealing with "the beast multitude" conflicted with his growing sense of the need to entertain. What did not change was his self-imposed task of presenting to the spectator, whether monarch or grocer, a comprehensive image of himself. By confronting in the theater problems like the nature of theatricality and the relationships it implies, Jonson was not just working out his idiosyncrasies; he also was asking his spectators to consider their roles as players in life's comedy.

CONCLUSION

The Theater of Self-Interest

The Concupiscence of Daunces, and Antickes so Raigneth, as to runne away from Nature, and be afraid of her.

I shall raise the despis'd head of poetrie againe, and stripping her out of those rotten and base rags, wherwith the times have adulterated her form, restore her to her primitive habit, feature and majesty, and render her worthy to be imbraced, and kist, of all the great and master-spirits of our world.

I

THE IDEA that meaning, like value, is something negotiated between the parties of the stage and gallery lies at the heart of Jonson's sense of theater, though this point is easily obscured if we accept uncritically his portrait of himself as a poet. He presents himself as a playwright whose work has clear personal meaning for its audiences, if only they have the good sense to pay attention. In the prologues and inductions to his plays, he is unabashedly moralistic, preaching the power of his work to reform its spectators, and by and large we have taken him at his word. Even recent studies that show considerable sophistication about Jonson's use of rhetorical tactics like irony and personae generally assume that meaning precedes drama, that his dramatic genius spent itself to make a point about this or that.[1]

The problem with this line of argument is that it inevitably bestows on Jonson more conscious control of his material and his relationship to his audience than his plays suggest he had. It devalues the bitter, aggressive energy of his plays, be-

CONCLUSION

cause, to the extent that Jonson's hostility is taken as the expression of a consciously executed role, one does not have to deal with it as a real part of his work and his feelings toward his spectators. Perhaps worst of all, once such feelings have been attributed to a role, the knowing reader can place himself beyond the reach of Jonson's intense aggression. Even when there is no overt intent on the part of a critic to save Jonson from his nasty self, this kind of argument leads to attempts to polish him up: we are urged to imagine behind the proliferation of masks and roles the "real" Jonson, controlled, angry only with fools, but never so angry as to forswear another essentially goodhearted attempt at educating his spectators.

But the impulse to write plays went deeper in Jonson than his pursuit of the Horatian ideal of profit and pleasure comingled. He wrote to find an audience, and the commitment to meaning, matter, and sense is one side of his extremely ambivalent feelings about this activity. The practice of stressing instruction and discursive meaning can become, finally, a way to qualify and delimit the recreative aspect of theatricality, a way to avoid coming to terms with what it means to please an audience. There is no denying the moral force of Jonson's satire, but one can suggest that it is part of a larger context complicated by difficult artistic and psychological issues. After all, meaning is always a function of interpersonal drama, and, beyond the simplest level, communication between human beings is an intricate pattern of motive, disguise, caution, compromise, and self-revelation. In Jonson's case, the pattern is particularly rich and the drama particularly available to public view.

The change in Jonson's relationship to his audience can be summarized in terms of his response to a fundamental dilemma: that, given the diversity of his playhouse audience, pleasing all the people all the time was a remote possibility. As he saw things, the playhouse forced a choice between the approval of a select audience of judicious spectators and the approval of the "beast multitude." For other playwrights who lived more easily on the middle ground, the choice was not so radical, but Jonson was disposed toward extreme positions, radical choices, and the mutually exclusive in general. What is important is his investment in the dichotomy, his *choosing* to develop a polarity that was immanent in his audience. Something in Jonson could not tolerate the idea of a homogeneous, undifferentiated audience, and he did his best to stress conflict where he found it and fuel animosity when he could. In short, his sense of a divided audience was a reasonable but not a necessary response to the playhouse—an idiosyncratic condition of his working for a public audience.

In the comical satires, Jonson continually badgered his spectators, forcing them to choose sides on a host of issues, and when he had raised a real tumult in the theatergoing community, when one might have expected him to seek the widest possible audience, he wrote *Sejanus*, a play that offered most of his audience almost nothing. This was no simple miscalculation. Jonson was as ambivalent about success as he was fearful of failure, because unmitigated success was, in its own way, a trap. What it meant to be validated by fools was for him one problematic issue, but an even subtler one was the price an artist pays to be kept by the moral, intelligent, grave—and dull. At the level of conscious choice, Jonson stuck with the judicious, but his plays reveal the strain in that commitment.

Roughly speaking, Jonson's dichotomy pits the judicious spectators against the dullards and the foolish cranks. The induction to *Every Man Out of His Humor* distinguishes between "attentive auditors" who "come to feed their understanding parts" and "monstrous fellows" who have "neither arte, nor braine"; the prologue to *Cynthia's Revels* rejects "ev'rie vulgar, and adult'rate braine" in favor of "gracious silence, sweet attention,/Quicke sight and quicker apprehension"; and the prologue to *Poetaster* arrives dressed in armor as "proofe against the conjuring meanes/Of base detractors, and illiterate apes." But even as these examples establish the dichotomy, they complicate it: judgments apparently made

CONCLUSION

on the basis of intelligence or social class frequently merge with or conceal questions of behavior in the theater or response to Jonson's work. Thus, a spectator's dislike for a play is prima facie evidence of stupidity, and, while there is plenty of room in this theater for commoners to reveal themselves sages by approving, there is no room at all for a person of intellect and manners to disapprove. Invariably the lines of distinction are blurred in this way, and at times the structure collapses on itself, as it does in the Apologetical Dialogue appended to the Quarto text of *Poetaster*. Stung by the play's rejection in the playhouse, Jonson was moved to his most extensive and vitriolic attack on his audience. Here there is no counterweight to the massive, brutal stupidity of the multitude. The "Author" of the Dialogue is beset by:

> These vile Ibides, these uncleane birds,
> That make their mouthes their clysters, and still purge
> From their hot entrailles.
> (Apologetical Dialogue, 219-21)

He finally rejects both comedy and his public audience:

> And, since the Comick Muse
> Hath prov'd so ominous to me, I will trie
> If Tragoedie have a more kind aspect.
> Her favours in my next I will pursue,
> Where, if I prove the pleasure but of one,
> So he judicious be; He shall b'alone
> A theatre unto me.
> (Apologetical Dialogue, 222-28)

Anger overwhelms the usual discrimination, although the historical evidence suggests that *Poetaster* was not, as the Dialogue implies, the nadir in a steady fall from favor with the public but, rather, another step toward respectability. W. David Kay has made a strong case for the argument that at this time Jonson was making considerable headway with his career, building a reputation as a first-rate playwright, particularly with his preferred audience among the elite, educated portion of London society.[2] The fact that *Sejanus* was acted by the King's men at the Globe and that, following its stage failure, Jonson was able to persuade figures like Marston and Chapman to write commendatory poems for the Quarto weighs heavily against his notion that he was headed for an audience of one.

The disparity here is both real and significant, and Jonson's attempts at self-allegorization in the prologues and inductions are evidence of anxiety about questions of authority and judgment that go deeper than his quarrels with boorish spectators. This is not to say the quarrels are beside the point, only that they are one aspect of a fundamental conflict. One of the recurrent themes of Jonas Barish's work on Jonson, stated most cogently in his essay "Jonson and the Loathed Stage," is that an "anti-theatricalism," a "deep suspicion toward theatricality as a form in the world," coexisted with Jonson's great theatrical gifts.[3] Surely one concomitant of such suspicion is contempt for the part of oneself given to theatrically—contempt easily projected onto the audience that comes to the theater to share in this suspect behavior. The act of splitting an audience along the lines of its intelligence and ability to judge is one defense against self-contempt: it removes the select portion of the audience to a realm where theater serves morality and learning, and makes it possible to unload onto the multitude one's disgust with theatricality as mere "self-tickling." One's better half, identified with the better audience, can be redeemed or exempted altogether from criticism by making scapegoats of the others.

Thus, the bipolar distinction that Jonson insisted upon can be seen as a psychological strategy allowing him to provisionally separate impulses that ran strongly together for him, contempt and praise, exuberance and decorum, rejection and acceptance. The strategy was simple in conception, but Jonson found it extraordinarily complicated at both extremes. At one extreme, his identification with his judicious spectators was threatened from two directions. First, experience repeatedly confronted him with the fact that the judicious spectator was finally a figment of his imagination, and under his withering scrutiny very few of his real spectators escaped his contempt. His fondness for throwing verbal rocks at his betters and benefactors is well documented. As he makes it clear in *Discoveries*, the chosen company is indeed a small one: "To judge of Poets is only the facultie of Poets; and not of all Poets, but the best" (*Discoveries*, 2578-79). Beneath the serious pedagogical point here is the reflection of the fact that in times of stress Jonson's ideal audience melted quickly away toward solipsism and self-congratulation. The second threat to Jonson's identification with his judicious spectators was his fear that acceptance is a kind of death, even when it is acceptance by one's chosen audience: one is defined, stifled, limited, engulfed by an audience, and spurred, like Volpone, into an exhausting repetition of his role in an attempt to escape the bondage. And as Volpone learns, the attempts succeed only in further enthralling the victim. In short, Jonson found success with the judicious a clog to the substantial portion of himself that loved license and unbridled exuberance.

Oddly enough, at the other extreme, where contempt lies thickest, there is a strange hopefulness as well. Certainly Jonson's dislike for his playhouse audience was mitigated by the need to instruct them and save them from themselves, but, more important, he was driven by a deeply held desire to entertain them and by the corresponding suspicion that, until he had reconciled himself to this task, he could not be a complete poet. Shakespeare's popular success must have pushed him in this regard, but at heart Jonson was an entertainer who wished to reach even the dullest and most disruptive members of his audience. History has emphasized, because Jonson himself emphasized, his impulse to reform and educate his spectators, to offer them entertainment only on his terms. But the course of his career suggests just the opposite: while he talked morality most of the time, he was learning to entertain. In a general way, this observation is corroborated by the critical consensus on Jonson's "mellowing." As they move toward *Bartholomew Fair*, the plays are less hectoring toward their audiences; the didactic pressure subsides and the governing mood swings from exclusion and rejection to accommodation.

It was onto the playhouse audience that Jonson projected his ambivalence about license and exuberance. This is the realm of emotion, not intellect. All of his sneering at "affection" notwithstanding, he understood that if theater could do no better than scourge vice in the wicked and permit the virtuous to enjoy the spectacle, it was a cripple.

The realm of license and exuberance is also the realm of genuine theatricality, acting as free, playful human activity—fun—as opposed to the rarefied regions of the learned and circumspect, where acting must be justified in terms of meaning. But to open the theater to these elements was to humanize it in a frightening way as well. With exuberance goes a Pandora's box of things that Jonson was much less certain about: chaos, anger, sexuality, aggression, noise, disrespect, competition, dirt, disease, and ignorance. In this realm, language is no longer the servant of majesty, learning, and morality; one must now deal with its capacity to tease, seduce, entrap, and destroy. This is a joyous but also a terrifying world. The reverse of a world where roles become stifling is one which there are no roles at all, where individual intent and action dissolve in the caldron of human activity, or, to use another metaphor, where the artist faces the fate of Orpheus torn to pieces by his audience. One must pay for license as for nobility. Jonson was keenly aware that play is a regressive activity which cannot ever be fully reconciled to the adult world of decorum and responsibility. In playfulness there is always the threat of destruction and limits breached, yet the human community might as well be dead without it. This paradox haunted Jonson, and the sequence of plays ending in *Bartholomew Fair* shows him exploring the nether end of the audience spectrum, learning to make a place for playfulness in his theater and defining the conditions under which it was possible. For whatever reason, Jonson could not maintain within himself the extreme polarity he initially imposed on

CONCLUSION

his audience. He had to find a middle ground, but what makes his case interesting is that, unlike those writers for whom such issues never pose a serious problem, Jonson had to proceed by unpacking an astonishing amount of psychological baggage. He had to work at it; consequently, we have a fascinating record of an artist's struggle to define himself through, and against, his audience.

Finally, it is this psychological baggage that provides the essential link between what takes place on Jonson's stage in the plays themselves and the drama he enacted between himself and his spectators. The plays are at once metaphors, that is, representations, of the conflict between artist and audience and rhetorical instruments that shape the conflict; and one critical language particularly suited to discussion of this simultaneity is psychoanalysis. Psychoanalytic theory insists on the relatively simple principle that every human utterance and gesture is significant both for its metaphorical relation to psychological issues crucial to the subject and for its part in transference, the immediate, temporal relation of subject to analyst. Applied in simple terms to the theater, it suggests that a playwright reenacts private conflicts as public art for, but also with, an audience.

There are several psychological themes that Jonson played on with varied intensity throughout his career, perhaps the most basic of which was his conviction that love and hate, acceptance and rejection—though they seem by definition polar opposites of human experience—are inextricably bound together. Moreover, he felt keenly the irony that accompanied this conviction, that both poles of the untenable dichotomy are painfully ambiguous: acceptance is fulfilling and stifling; rejection is both loss and the means by which human beings establish their independent selves. From these paradoxes follows a series of terms, antonyms that in Jonson's world continually threaten to collapse into synonyms: victory and defeat, beauty and deformity, virtue and depravity, disgust and desire. In the terms of Freudian psychology, the achievement of adult male potency is both a triumph, a tribute to one's own father, and a state of terrifying vulnerability because of the fear that adulthood can be purchased only at the expense of a vengeful father. Women are loving mothers, queens, the source of all nourishment and support; they are also treacherous wives, incestuous seductresses, and whores; they are beautiful, wise, simple, ignorant, chaste, false, loyal, painted, and ugly, and one suspects repeatedly that Jonson sensed with fascination and horror that the extremes lay closer together than most of us like to think. At some point he could not distinguish fatherhood from vengefulness, filial gratitude from patricidal aggression, or seduction from betrayal. What characterizes Jonson's response to the world in general is his difficulty in maintaining as emotionally valid the distinctions to which he was intellectually and morally committed. Profusion, in other words, inevitably meant confusion.

But Jonson's work does not simply repeat these conflicts. The plays from *Every Man Out* through *Bartholomew Fair* develop the conflicts in a way that uncannily recapitulates the historical development of the individual human personality. Pre-oedipal psychology describes the emergence of the human infant into an environment that is both satisfying and frustrating, nurturing and hostile, or at least imagined as hostile.[4] Later, as a child resolves that environment into personal relationships, gender begins to matter, and the initial ambivalence is projected into a sexual world. Jonson, too, moves out of the chaste and maternal world he creates at the end of *Every Man Out* and sustains through *Cynthia's Revels* into a world where gender relationships are extremely problematic. Cynthia's realm, where the poet-satirist serves as a good son to the motherly queen and where there are no kingly fathers, gives way in *Poetaster* and the plays that follow to a progressively bleaker drama of oedipal conflict. In these plays, males dominate the authority structure, and women are relegated, for the most part, to the role of pawns in the struggles between men. The Emperor Augustus, presented in *Poetaster* as the epitome of all things to be respected and admired in a ruler, continues to value the satirist as a good son, but Au-

CONCLUSION

gustus cannot accommodate another poet, Ovid, whose lifestyle and poetry embrace the libertinism that the satirist and the circumspect emperor eschew. In subtle ways, Jonson takes the emperor to task for this limitation, so that finally the play questions the nature of paternal authority. *Sejanus*, immediately following *Poetaster*, is a play of brutal oedipal defeat in which a would-be usurper is crushed at the threshold of his victory. This play represents an extreme version of Jonson's oedipal drama: Rome is specifically identified as ambiguously sexual and maternal femininity; thus, Sejanus' aggression toward the emperor Tiberius and his wish to rule Rome are implicitly oedipal. The instrument of his destruction is a letter from Tiberius, who is absent from Rome debauching himself at his island resort of Capraea. The message is clear: even absent fathers can assert their interests with astonishing severity.

Thereafter, in *Volpone, Epicene,* and *The Alchemist,* oedipal aggression assumes a more private cast. Empires are no longer at stake, and the would-be usurpers go underground, in *Volpone* and *The Alchemist* to an outlaw world, in *Epicene* to an elaborate drawing-room entertainment. The reassuring maternal background of Cynthia's world is gone, and, perhaps as a consequence, conflict is deflected from confrontation and mortal combat into gulling and satiric exposure. In an oblique way, *Volpone* also is about fathers and sons. Volpone himself kicks free of all natural family ties to establish his own procreative system based on theatricality instead of socially sanctioned sexuality: "Whom I make,/Must be my heire: and this makes men observe me." He spends his time enacting a ruse which appears to generate heirs but in fact only adds to his own substance. In a sense, this is the ultimate mediation of oedipal conflict: a man who is a father and no father, a son and no son, all at the same time. What is more important, however, is that *Volpone* initiates a new relationship between Jonson and his audience. With *Sejanus* he killed off his wholehearted commitment to the values of an idealized Imperial Rome or Cynthian England, as well as his commitment to satiric theater as a tool of social engineering. In *Volpone*, he begins to deal obliquely, equivocally with his audience: Volpone is punished for his crimes, but we have shared the power of his fantasy life, and when he walks out of the play at the end to deliver his epilogue—itself a cryptic piece of work—he clearly stands beyond the reach of Venetian law.

Epicene teases its audience, after providing another drama of filial succession, with the revelation that its heroine is not even a woman. More significantly, however, it takes on an issue that has lurked in the background since the appearance of "the Queen" at the conclusion of *Every Man Out*: female sexuality. Here the failure of strong paternal authority leaves Jonson's satirist-hero, multiplied in the threesome of Clerimont, Dauphine, and Truewit, a wider field in which to define his values, and a part of this process is negotiating the terms of relations with the opposite sex. Truewit does succeed in launching Dauphine into the company of the Collegiate women, but the play disparages this accomplishment by painting the Collegiates as a group of thoroughly unattractive women. They are shown to be nasty, promiscuous, and self-seeking in the extreme, embracing a lifestyle that excludes two essential social values, marriage and motherhood. In this context, the stratagem by which Epicene is revealed to be a boy is as much a relief as it is a surprise. The play seems to argue that for the moment in Jonson's world men and women are not required to have any serious relations, and it is this almost forcible exclusion of certain social values, accompanied by the renewed interest in the nature of women, that underlies the basic change in Jonson's relationship to his audience.

Lovewit's appearance at the end of *The Alchemist* to claim a silly wife and a fortune he does not need vitiates any appeal to traditional comic justice. Jonson seems finally to have come out in favor of whim; he has traded the role of stern, righteous satirist, tied to the structure of social authority, for the role of immanent authority, there but not there, teasing and manipulating always, but permitting us a great deal of not-

CONCLUSION

necessarily-clean fun in the bargain. The "venter tripartite" suggests yet another peculiar family configuration—the by now familiar woman who is both whore and queen, who cements the relationships but also serves as a pawn in the struggle between the two males to assert primacy.

Oddly, *Catiline* repeats the psychological conflicts of *Sejanus*, but here the usurper begins as an exile attempting to reenter the society from which he has been excluded. *Catiline* is the last spasm of bleak oedipal drama before *Bartholomew Fair* in which, for a number of reasons, the kind of accommodation that allows for real satisfaction is possible. *Bartholomew Fair* does what it can to discredit marriage as the basis of social values, but this is a play that is as genuinely comfortable with male aggression and female sexuality as the previous plays were not. And this fact bears a very close relationship to Jonson's new commitment to theater based on the "contract" he negotiates with his audience in the induction to the play. In return for our assurances that we will judge only in accordance with the amount we pay to enter the theater, Jonson formally relinquishes certain proprietary interests in the play, giving over self-consciously the whole concept of hierarchical theater based on majesty and morality. Although this induction is meant in part as a joke, and though one might argue that it should be taken as a cynical reaffirmation of the power of the poet and the degeneracy of the audience, when considered in terms of the experience the play offers us it heralds a major concession for Jonson. The play itself is more nearly a romance comedy than anything Jonson had written in fifteen years. Boys meet girls, boys get girls, but not before complications are worked out in Jonson's version of Oberon's fairy world—Overdo's fair. There romance and sexuality are completely demystified as they are dragged through the dirt, noise, depravity, and exuberance of Smithfield.

Thus, in the course of his career from *Every Man Out* to *Bartholomew Fair*, Jonson radically altered his sense of the theater and his relationship to his audience. Quite apart from the question of whether the change was for the better, it is clear that it was necessary, or at least that Jonson felt it was necessary. It is equally clear that the change had to be bought and paid for in the currency of emotion and imagination: the geniality of *Bartholomew Fair*, highly qualified though it may be, was accomplished at the expense of some painful examinations of issues which early in his career Jonson had been unwilling to address. This self-directed disillusionment, which made new illusions possible, can be described as a function of family psychology: Jonson staged various versions of family relations—maternal hegemony, paternal hegemony, filial hegemony, and a number of hybrid versions—only to discover that none offered the complete satisfaction he was looking for. By staging and thereby confronting the disquieting sides of these relations, he was able to strike a precarious balance between naive faith and horrified despair. And this balance in turn permitted him to put aside his stern satiric autocracy and expand his sense of theatrical entertainment. In this sense, one might say that Jonson's coming to terms with oedipal conflict and female sexuality is a significant factor in the development of his work and his relationship to his audience. It is one condition of his progress as an artist.

Inevitably there is the question of the relationship between psychology and biography. Ideally one would like to be able to judge with some confidence how this event or that person in Jonson's life influenced his artistic development, but, because we have little reliable information about his personal life, relationships between life and literature are unusually difficult to establish. There are, however, a number of intriguing circumstances. Jonson's natural father died one month before Ben was born, leaving his son with little besides some interesting family mythology. If we credit Jonson's report to Drummond, there was a title and a fortune on the father's side which was lost in the religious persecution of Queen Mary's reign.[5] This is a noteworthy detail in the life of a writer whose sense of his social position was very important to him. Jonson was a proud man forced, as he saw it, to live below his station

CONCLUSION

for most of his life. In the worst of times, he had to beg favors and money of men questionably his "betters." His mother eventually supplied a bricklayer for a stepfather, and while there is no record of the tenor of the relationship between father and son, it is reported in *Conversations* that young Ben, when put to his stepfather's trade, could not endure it. We know the mother only by way of one of Jonson's own anecdotes, recorded by Drummond:

> He was delated by Sir James Murray to the King for writting something against the Scots in a play Eastward hoe & voluntarily Imprissonned himself with Chapman and Marston, who had written it amongst them. The report was that they should then had their ears cutt & noses. After their delivery he banqueted all his friends, there was Camden Selden and others. At the midst of the Feast his old Mother Dranke to him and shew him a paper which she had (if the Sentence had taken execution) to have mixed in the Prison among his drinke, which was full of Lustie strong poison & that she was no churle she told she minded first to have Drunk of it herself.[6]

One can reasonably infer at least two things from this report. First, Jonson's mother was no shrinking violet; she seems to have shared with her son a certain aggressive theatricality. Second, she must have played a substantial part in his adult life—this brush with the law occurred when Jonson was in his mid-thirties, over a decade after his marriage and during or shortly after a five-year estrangement from his wife. His mother was there when he needed her, and not just as a comfort but as a co-conspirator.

Causation in the matter of the psychological development of the human identity is an intellectual quagmire if there ever was one, but one can make the case and hope the evidence of biographical fact and literary inference will support it. Certainly ambivalence toward authority and fascination with betrayal are preoccupations Jonson shared with nearly every other playwright of his generation, but his own coming to terms with these issues, at least as reflected in his plays, seems substantially colored by his particular family situation. Jonson had to deal with three parents. In his third year, he was forced to accommodate his mother's choice of a stepfather to head the family, indeed a man who dramatically lowered the social standing of the family. This was a double betrayal, a betrayal of the son's interests in the mother and a betrayal of the dead father-husband. We know nothing of either father, but, given what we do know of Jonson's sensitivity as an adult to matters of social position and authority, one can guess that the disparity between the two registered early and heavily on the boy, the more so since his notion of the natural father, unqualified by real experience, must have been easily shaped to set him against the stepfather as a foil. There are two major reflections of these circumstances in the plays: first, an unwillingness or inability to distinguish wives from mothers from lovers, and, in response to this confusion, a fear of betrayal by women in general, a fear defended against by alternately sanctifying and degrading them; second, an intense struggle with the problem of identification with authority. We all must decide in the process of claiming our adulthood how to present ourselves in relation to various kinds of authority, how to manage an acceptable balance, but in the world of Jonson's middle plays vertigo is the rule, stability the exception. Questions of paternal authority always seem to present themselves to him as extreme choices (serve the king as pageant poet or insult him and wind up in jail), and this makes perfect sense, I think, in light of his having had two fathers.

Yet it is not enough to say simply that Jonson is ambivalent about authority, or even that he is extremely ambivalent, for that is scarcely unique among artists. The distinctive and most interesting aspect of the interplay between Jonson's work and his family history is his effort, represented in the plays from *Every Man Out* through *Bartholomew Fair*, to recover his natural father by progressively identifying himself as a playwright with absent authority, immanent eminence, eminent immanence, as you wish. In other words, Jonson asserts his authority in *Bartholomew Fair* by abdicating the didactic power

CONCLUSION

he claimed in the early plays, by removing himself from his theatrical world and leaving it to his spectator-progeny. Here abdication is not a defeat but a triumph. In psychoanalytic terms, the role of absent authority is a remarkably efficient compromise formation: it allows him to enact at the same time the conflicting roles of strict authoritarian and generous benefactor. We have our freedom, but Jonson reminds us in subtle ways that he gave it to us and that it is conditional on our appropriate behavior. This is a tenuous and meticulously wrought balance, but then Jonson took fifteen years to work it out.

The intricacies of this arrangement help to explain why acceptance never comes without rejection in Jonson's world, and why, as the plays grow more accommodating toward their audiences, Jonson grows more elusive as an author, more and more subtly complicating our attempts to exercise judgment and derive the simple, conventional pleasures of theater. The peculiarities of his work, the marred endings, the defeated expectations, the inconsistent moral vision, while they may be flaws in the strictest aesthetic sense, can also be understood as strategic moves in a recondite game based on Jonson's idiosyncratic perception of his audience. *Bartholomew Fair*, at once the jolliest and most elusive of his plays, is the culmination of this maneuver. The fair itself is the soul of commercial theater, offered to us as a metaphor with the astonishing mixture of wonder and cynicism that Jonson brought to the Jacobean playhouse. He abandons us to make of it what we will, to spend our wit and judgment as fairgoers spend coins to define the nature of their experience. But even as he takes leave, setting aside his vindictive scrutiny, he suggests that more likely than not we will treat his play badly, behaving as fools and self-seeking monsters. In short, he leaves us to our pleasures, but as always he exacts his price.

II

There is one more link—and in Jonson's case a particularly useful link—between the psychology of the artist and the relationship between artist and audience established by a text or performance: the link is genre. We do not usually point to a writer's choice to write poems or novels instead of short stories, or even to write tragedy instead of comedy, as a clear indication of one or another set of psychological preoccupations, but Jonson's two major theoretical commitments to the theater, satire and the masque, are just that. They are typically treated as the two opposing poles of Jonson's artistic character, the impulse to flatter versus the impulse to castigate, but what is important in the context of this study is their common origin. They are children of a single conception of theater as a place of confrontation between stage and gallery. And drama, therefore, is an approach to an audience, quite apart from considerations of poetic form or artistic tradition. What distinguished satire and masque for Jonson was the nature of their respective audiences; the distinction, in turn, involved Jonson's belief in theater as a political force. The masque represented a theatrical ideal to which the plays aspired but never arrived because the masque audience was a social ideal against which Jonson found his playhouse audience wanting.[7] And while the masques celebrate this ideal audience, the plays examine the shortcomings of their spectators, using satire as an instrument of demographic investigation.

Although in the portrayal of Horace in *Poetaster* we sense that the satiric cast of mind is as much a trap as a gift, no mode of expression could have been better suited to Jonson than satire, for satire exists in the moment of confrontation between author and audience. Satire insists not just on representing experience or making argument but on imposing the satirist's vision of things on his audience through ridicule and abuse. The satirist confronts at least a portion of his audience with its existential deficiencies, relying on the complicity of the rest to establish his authority and increase the force of the indictment. Moreover, he mobilizes hostility against the object of his satire by using the sympathetic audience as both a vehicle and a source of power. Because it depends on the participation of its audience to make good its intentions,

CONCLUSION

in a way that comedy and tragedy, for instance, do not, satire is a specific kind of dramatic form that incorporates as part of its meaning "action" which extends beyond the stage. Like the masque, satire takes its form from the nature of its audience, then spends itself defining and refining the image of that audience. In this particular way, both forms are "occasional," and what Stephen Orgel observes about the Jonsonian masque can be applied with only minor adjustments to Jonsonian dramatic satire:

> It attempted from the beginning to breach the barrier between spectators and actors, so that in effect the viewer became part of the spectacle. The end toward which the masque moved was to destroy any sense of theater and to include the whole court in the mimesis—in a sense, what the spectator watched he ultimately became.[8]

Satire, which also attempts to "breach the barrier between spectators and actors" by inviting real and specific identifications between stage and spectator, moves "to destroy any sense of theater" because its meaning finally must exist in the real world as moral and social lessons or it has failed.

In the notion of the spectator becoming what he watches lies the crux of satiric impact. The satirist's fondest hope has been the reformation of the audience through its recognition of its fictionally portrayed faults. More often than not, recognition has occurred but reformation has not. The spectator becomes what he watches, but only in the most limited sense, by confirming his degeneracy. It is difficult to think of a genre that keeps the issue of artistic self-interest before its audience more intensely than satire. Certainly this is due, in part, to the taste for aggression and obscenity which the satirist traditionally has exhibited, but it must also have to do with the fact that satire's success at social and moral reclamation has always been ephemeral. Satire succeeds most obviously in enraging its audiences and calling forth their abuse; it seems appropriate, therefore, to question the personal motives of anyone who, like the satirist, time and again proclaims the loftiest intentions while exciting the lowliest passions. Human behavior that repeatedly generates the risk of extreme personal rejection is a curious phenomenon.

Considered yet another way, satire might be said to emphasize the relationship between judgment and authority. It is conceived in the act of the satirist judging his world, and effective satire requires of its spectators judgment of themselves and their culture. The satirist initiates a process which is completed by the response of an audience, but that response allows the satirist another chance to judge, that is, to accept or reject his audience on the basis of what it has revealed about itself through its own judgment. Thus, satire resembles a judicial proceeding in which response determines the guilt or innocence of the spectator. What Jonson understood, though perhaps only intuitively, is that this judicial aspect, taken a step further, can be used to maintain a margin of control in a theater full of self-seeking spectators. Making immediate demands on one's audiences is one way to prevent their making immediate demands on oneself. Such an insight, however, could not be reconciled easily to his belief in the moral and public nature of poetry and the socially affirming power of satire; finally, he was insufficiently cynical to discuss openly, or perhaps even to face privately, the self-serving implications of much of his drama. Perhaps it requires an entirely modern consciousness to explore fully the self-gratifying side of satiric theater, to demonstrate how judgment can be used to manipulate audiences and how, in turn, this manipulation becomes the vital energy of the poet.

In a sense, then, satire and the masque are, in Jonson's hands, closely related sets of rules for negotiations between author and audience that work to define, and hence to celebrate, authority. In the banqueting hall, the king is the primary actor and the primary spectator, and the masque acknowledges this by expanding the stage to embrace the monarch. In the playhouse, the satirist articulates authority he has amassed through a combination of artistic skill, personal integrity, common sense criticism, and reference to historical or contemporary models of moral and ethical virtue. His articulation of this authority is also an attempt to share and thereby multiply it by soliciting the judgment of others. In the theater, perspective *is* authority, and Jonson was more self-consciously aware of this fact than any other playwright of his generation. Indeed it is his fascination with this idea, his hypersensitivity to his spectators, that encourages one to speak of psychology and theater craft in the same breath. The masque offered Jonson a chance to celebrate something he lacked in his own experience, invulnerable paternal power. Satire offered him the best chance to create for himself, but also out of himself, that same power in the playhouse. In the public theater, the process was far more complex and troublesome, and more explicitly linked to the peculiar circumstance of his family history. The task of making a place in society for Poesy, selecting from the multitude an audience fit to share the poet's responsibility to defend her against her ignorant and spiteful enemies, was for Jonson synonymous with the psychic reconstitution of the family, that is, the recovery of a majestic father to protect and cherish a pure and nurturing mother. But there is an inherent conflict in all such oedipal drama: confusion between the safety of chaste filial service and the desire to accede to the role of father-husband-lover. For a while, in *Every Man Out, Cynthia's Revels*, and *Poetaster*, Jonson's satirist was content with filial submissiveness in return for the position of favored child-subject to the monarch, but Jonson could not sustain the commitment. Since psychological development and family experience are, like theater, matters of perspective and the privilege it confers, one might describe the relationship between dramatic form and oedipal psychology, as it evolved through the comical satires, in terms of Jonson's attempting to create for himself and his audience a privileged perspective based on shared social vision (whereas the masque takes this idea as its point of departure). But because he could not produce in the playhouse an authority structure sufficient to anchor his theatrical ideal, Jonson turned against privilege. He found it impossible to remake his audience into a group of kingly spectators, just as it was impossible in a more private realm to remake a bricklayer into a gentleman. The alternative was to level all distinction, to scrub one's theater clean of the traces of autocratic authority, to democratize it, and although this was ultimately impossible, since no artist can entirely escape responsibility for influencing his audience, Jonson made an interesting attempt at it.

By frustrating his spectator's attempts to infer the kind of authority that gives stable meaning to drama, Jonson acquired in his later masterpieces the somewhat perverse authority to refuse to be any authority at all. He also found the satisfaction he had mistakenly sought in Crites, Asper, Horace, Sejanus, Tiberius, Volpone, Face, Lovewit, and others: finally, he enacted the role of absent father, successfully identifying himself as an artist with his own father. What began as a clumsy program of including good fathers, bad fathers, good mothers, bad mothers, good sons, and bad sons acquired considerable sophistication as the boundaries between good and bad, strong and weak were blurred. This blurring permitted Jonson's theater to grow increasingly exuberant and forgiving, but it also permitted Jonson himself to be much more subtly oppressive. He finally gave himself the unique perspective and authority he accorded the monarch in the masque, taking his place above and beyond the others as both primary actor and primary audience in this remarkable theater.

Proclaiming Jonson a maker of masques for both private and public theater will never entirely resolve the complexities of his drama, but it can correct our perspective enough to make possible certain observations about his career. Perhaps the most important is that the sequence of plays from *Every Man Out* through *Bartholomew Fair* can be seen as a series of attempts to find a masque form, based on dramatic satire, appropriate to the playhouse. *Cynthia's Revels* is an early prototype, abandoned for forms more clever about their involvement with the audience. The process culminates in *Bartholomew Fair*, the closest Jonson ever came to his masque for the multitude.

NOTES

INTRODUCTION

1. Stephen Orgel, *The Illusion of Power* (Berkeley: University of California Press, 1975), 2.
2. This is a difficult assertion to substantiate, first, because the term "theatrical production" is itself hard to define and, second, because such cultural phenomena are not easily quantified. Certainly much of what passes for human entertainment does not fit the description of "theater" as we generally understand the term; in fact, much of what is theatrical is not theater. Perhaps I can best describe the difficulty by noting that much medieval drama was acted without a "theater," while activities such as bearbaiting, which we never consider "theater," took place in theaters. On the other hand, I do not wish to confine my use of the word "theater" to drama, because this excludes too many other kinds of performances: masques, tournaments, and festival entertainments, for instance. The point I wish to make is that Renaissance culture made room for an increasingly secular and commercial theater, with the term referring to public gatherings that involved actors, scripts, props, in short, *theater capital*. This change tended to homogenize the theatrical perspective of the audience, even where social stratification according to seating and admission rates was still apparent. I believe the work of people like Glynne Wickham and Robert Weimann supports this contention.
3. The term is one of Jonson's favorite epithets, but it should not be taken to mean that his spectators in the public playhouse were necessarily the rabble of London. To the contrary, as Ann Jennalie Cook has shown in her recent book, *The Privileged Playgoers of Shakespeare's London, 1576-1642* (Princeton: Princeton University Press, 1981), the audience was largely a group privileged in terms of wealth, education, and general socioeconomic background. Jonson's perception of his audience as "the masses" is not a socioeconomic judgment but a value judg-

ment based on a comparison with court audiences. He wanted educated spectators who believed in humane values and had the authority and the inclination to defend them; the playhouse supplied him, however, with spectators who appeared to reflect the values of an increasingly commercial and materialistic culture. In short, the playhouse audience, regardless of its social status, was clearly lacking when compared to an audience of philosopher kings. It is in this sense that Jonson used such disparaging terms as "the masses" and "the beast multitude."

4. Citations from Jonson throughout are to the Oxford edition, *Ben Jonson*, ed. C. H. Herford and Percy and Evelyn Simpson, 11 vols. (Oxford: The Clarendon Press, 1925-52), hereafter referred to as H&S. Where I have cited material from plays and other longer works, generally I have given act, scene, and line references within the text. Otherwise, I have used endnotes with references to volume and page in H&S. This particular citation is to *Cynthia's Revels*, Prologue, 20.

5. William Wycherley, *The Country Wife*, ed. Thomas H. Fujimura (Lincoln: University of Nebraska Press, 1965), 56.

6. Judgment and judging are crucial to Jonson, and these issues are discussed in relation to his audience and his sense of himself as an artist in an essay by Peter Carlson, "Judging Spectators," *ELH* 44 (1977), 443-57.

7.   To the Reader in Ordinarie

The Muses forbid, that I should restrayne your medling, whom I see alreadie busie with the Title, and tricking over the leaves: It is your owne. I departed with my right, when I let it first abroad. And, now, so secure an Interpreter I am of my chance, that neither praise, nor dispraise from you can affect mee. Though you commend the two first Actes, with the people, because they are the worst; and dislike the Oration of Cicero, in regard you read some pieces of it, at Schoole, and understand them not yet; I shall finde the way to forgive you. Be anything you will be, at your owne charge. Would I had deserv'd but halfe so well of it in translation, as that ought to deserve of you in judgment, if you have any. I know you will pretend (whosoever you are) to have that, and more. But all pretences are not just claymes. The commendation of good things may fall within a many, their approbation but in a few; for the most commend out of affection, selfe tickling, an easinesse, or imitation: but men judge only out of knowledge. That is the trying faculty. And, to those works that will beare a Judge, nothing is more dangerous than a foolish prayse. You will say I shall not have yours, therfore; but rather the contrary, all vexation of Censure. If I were not above such molestations now, I had great cause to think unworthily of my studies, or they had so of mee. But I leave you to your exercise. Beginne.

To the Reader Extraordinary

You I would understand to be the better Man, though Places in Court go otherwise: to you I submit my selfe, and worke. Farewell.

Ben: Jonson

8. H&S, vol. 8, 64.
9. H&S, vol. 5, 163.
10. See Jonson's report to Drummond about the royal "membrana," H&S, vol. 1, 142.
11. H&S, vol. 1, 41.
12. The question of Jonson's ambivalence to authority, though often noted by scholars in passing, is treated at length in an important essay by E. Pearlman, "Ben Jonson: An Anatomy," *English Literary Renaissance* 9 (1979), 364-93.

Chapter One

1. Oscar James Campbell, *Comicall Satyre and Shakespeare's Troilus and Cressida* (San Marino, Calif.: Huntington Library, 1959), 8.
2. This line of argument assumes that Asper represents Jonson, if not as a carefully drawn self-portrait at least as the embodiment of important authorial conflicts. Yet this assumption has been seriously questioned, most cogently in Alvin Kernan's study, *The Cankered Muse: Satire of the English Renaissance* (New Haven: Yale University Press, 1959). Kernan wants to put some distance between the actual author and what he calls "the more unsalutary aspects of the character of the satirist," that is, the satirist whom the author creates as a fictional character. He argues that biographical and historical investigation distorts our perception of satire:

   These methods have been applied with varying degrees of sophistication, but even at their best they inevitably lead us to such unanswerable questions as, "Was first-century

Rome as completely debased as Juvenal painted it?" or "Did Swift hate mankind as extravagantly as Gulliver hated the Yahoos?" Our attention is thus directed away from the satiric work itself and toward some secondary object, the personality of the author or the contemporary social scene. In this way satire is denied the independence of artistic status and made a biographical and historical document, while the criticism of satire degenerates into discussion of an author's moral character and the economic and social conditions of his time (Kernan, *Cankered Muse*, 2).

I have found Kernan's work very helpful as a corrective against the kind of methodological errors he describes, but my own response to satire has been that, one way or another, satiric personae represent their authors. The relationship may be oblique or difficult to explain, and an extremely skilled satirist may give a character a great deal of independence or even use him as a satiric object. Nevertheless, satire has value, I think, only when we intuit that it bespeaks the deeply held personal beliefs of a human being more or less like ourselves. Again, it is a matter of authority. Any work that attempts to deal seriously with morality is ultimately a sham unless it moves beyond the purely fictional to tap some source of real social authority, whether kingly majesty or the personal virtue of the satirist.

3. H&S, vol. 3, 599.
4. Edmund Wilson, "Morose Ben Jonson," in *The Triple Thinkers*, rev. ed. (New York: Charles Scribner's Sons, 1948). Reprinted in Jonas A. Barish, ed., *Ben Jonson: A Collection of Critical Essays* (Englewood Cliffs, N.J.: Prentice-Hall, 1963), 60-74.
5. Jonas A. Barish, *Ben Jonson and the Language of Prose Comedy* (Cambridge: Harvard University Press, 1960), 121.
6. George Parfitt, *Ben Jonson: Public Poet and Private Man* (London: J. M. Dent and Sons, 1976), 49.
7. Parfitt, *Public Poet and Private Man*, 61.
8. The words are Parfitt's.
9. Ernest W. Talbert, "The Purpose and Technique of Jonson's *Poetaster*," *Studies in Philology* 42 (1945), 225-52. Talbert's is clearly the minority position. Eugene Waith's essay, "The Poet's Morals in Jonson's *Poetaster*," *Modern Language Quarterly* 12 (1951), 13-19, best summarizes the majority position with which Campbell, Herford and Simpson, and Parfitt essentially concur.

NOTES TO PAGES 37-76

10. Robert C. Jones, "The Satirist's Retirement in Jonson's 'Apologetical Dialogue,' " *ELH* 34 (1967), 448.
11. Horace, *Satire, Epistles and Ars Poetica*, ed. H. R. Fairclough (Cambridge: Harvard University Press, 1966), 126.
12. H&S, vol. 8, 93.
13. Horace, *Satire*, 126.
14. The term is Parfitt's.

Chapter Two

1. Ben Jonson, *Sejanus*, ed. Jonas A. Barish (New Haven: Yale University Press, 1965), 24.
2. Jonson, *Sejanus*, 23.
3. Arthur Marotti, "The Self-Reflexive Art of Ben Jonson's *Sejanus*," *Texas Studies in Literature and Language* 12 (1970), 197.
4. Jonson, *Sejanus*, 22.
5. Marotti, "Self-Reflexive Art," 214-15.
6. As Barish's notes to the Yale edition point out, Jonson elected to develop the incident with Apicata well beyond the material offered by his sources: "The description of Apicata's despair far outdoes in turbulence and grandeur the brief mention of it in Dio (History 58.11), where she is said simply to have gone away, after viewing her children's bodies, in order to compose her statement concerning Drusus' death. Jonson makes the scene a final off-stage climax to the terrible events of the day, conferring on the bereaved Apicata some of the towering passion of a Hecuba or a Medea" (Jonson, *Sejanus*, 203). Apicata does speak for the interests of mothers in the play, and I think it is interesting that motherhood is allowed to speak for itself only after it has been dispossessed of its children.

Chapter Three

1. David McPherson, "Rough Beast Into Tame Fox: The Adaptations of *Volpone*," *Studies in the Literary Imagination* 6 (1973), 77.
2. Jonas A. Barish, "Jonson and the Loathed Stage," in *A Celebration of Ben Jonson*, ed. William Blissett, Julian Patrick, and R. W. VanFossen (Toronto: University of Toronto Press, 1973), 38.

3. Stephen J. Greenblatt, "The False Ending in *Volpone*," *Journal of English and Germanic Philology* 75 (1976), 103.
4. This debt is examined by John D. Rea in the preface to his edition of *Volpone*, vol. 59 of *Yale Studies in English* (New Haven: Yale University Press, 1919).
5. Desiderius Erasmus, *The Praise of Folly*, trans. Hoyt Hopewell Hudson (Princeton: Princeton University Press, 1941), 36.
6. Greenblatt, "False Ending in *Volpone*," 90-94.
7. Stephen Gosson, *The Schoole of Abuse*. Reprinted for the Shakespeare Society (London, 1841), 25.
8. As Charles A. Hallett points out in his essay, "Jonson's Celia: A Reinterpretation of *Volpone*," *Studies in Philology* 68 (1971), 50-69, critical response to Celia as silly has a long history. He cites M. C. Bradbrook in *The Growth and Structure of Elizabethan Comedy* (London: Chatto and Windus, 1955), 145; H&S, vol. 2, 63-64; L. C. Knights in *Drama and Society in the Age of Jonson* (London: Chatto and Windus, 1951), 203; John Enck in *Jonson and the Comic Truth* (Madison: University of Wisconsin Press, 1957), 129; and others.
9. One of the insights offered by psychoanalysis is that the impulse to encompass or incorporate can be a destructive one: to incorporate is finally to control or destroy the threatening object. See the entry under "Incorporation" in J. Laplanche and J.-B. Pontalis, *The Language of Psychoanalysis*, trans. Donald Nicholson-Smith (New York: Norton, 1973), 211.
10. Ben Jonson, *Volpone*, ed. Alvin B. Kernan (New Haven: Yale University Press, 1962), 214-16.
11. The point is made nicely, I think, by Volpone at the opening of act 5. Asked by Mosca whether he was "taken" by the courtroom travesty, Volpone replies, "O, more, then if I had enjoy'd the wench:/The pleasure of all woman-kind's not like it." Mosca rejoins, "this is our master-peece" (H&S, vol. 5, 109).
12. H&S, vol. 9, 724.
13. See Freud's essay, "Contributions to the Psychology of Love," especially "The Most Prevalent Form of Degradation in Erotic Life" and "A Special Type of Object Choice Made by Men," vol. 4 of *Collected Papers* (London: Hogarth Press and The Institute of Psycho-Analysis, 1946), 192-216.
14. Carlson, "Judging Spectators," 447.

15. Jonas A. Barish, "The Double Plot in *Volpone*," *Modern Philology* 2 (1953), 83-92. Reprinted in Barish, *Collection of Critical Essays*, 104.
16. For an opposing point of view, see Alvin Kernan's introduction to the Yale edition of the play (Jonson, *Volpone*).
17. Stephen Orgel, *The Jonsonian Masque* (Cambridge: Harvard University Press, 1967), 6.

Chapter Four

1. Northrop Frye, "The Argument of Comedy," *English Institute Essays, 1948, 1949* (New York: Columbia University Press, 1949), 58-73. Reprinted in Leonard F. Dean, ed., *Shakespeare: Modern Essays in Criticism* (New York: Oxford University Press, 1957), 82.
2. My work on *Epicene* owes a great deal to Jonas Barish's analyses of the play in "Ovid, Juvenal, and *The Silent Woman*," *PMLA* 71 (1956), 213-24 and in the chapter entitled "Things of Sense," in Barish, *Language of Prose Comedy*, 142-86.
3. Barish, *Language of Prose Comedy*, 148.
4. Morose offers not once but three times to geld himself in order to preserve the peace and quiet of his life.
5. Edward B. Partridge, *The Broken Compass* (New York: Columbia University Press, 1958), 161-77.
6. Crites himself makes this clear in a speech to Arete:

> O thou, the very power, by which I am,
> And but for which, it were in vaine to be,
> Chiefe next Diana, virgin, heavenly faire,
> Admired Arete (of them admir'd
> Whose soules are not enkindled by the sense)
> Disdaine not my chaste fire, but feede the clame
> Devoted truely to thy gracious name.
>   (V, v, 49-55)

7. H&S, vol. 1, 438.
8. Of course, this is the theory; Jonson's frustrations, revealed in the prologues and epilogues, are the measure of how well the theory works.
9. Barish makes this point, and it is the subject of an essay by Barbara J. Baines and Mary C. Williams, "The Contemporary

and Classical Antifeminist Tradition in Jonson's *Epicœne*," *Renaissance Papers 1977* (Durham, N.C.: Southeastern Renaissance Conference, 1977), 43-58.
10. See chapter 3, n. 13.

CHAPTER FIVE

1. For an extensive analysis of Jonson's poetic use of feasting, see Jonas A. Barish, "Feasting and Judging in Jonsonian Comedy," *Renaissance Drama*, N.S. 5 (1972), 3-35. It has been pointed out to me that there is a further irony in the fact that Face's casting us as guests at a feast does not acknowledge that we have paid for admission.
2. H&S, vol. 8, 64.
3. Enck, *Jonson and the Comic Truth*, 159.
4. A good example is Douglas Brown, ed., *The Alchemist* (New York: Hill and Wang, 1966), xix: "Thus the verdict in which the play comes to rest is an exaltation of Intelligence above virtue, in which the honest Surly is abashed while the impudent Face triumphs." Both F. H. Mares in his Harvard edition of the play (Cambridge: Harvard University Press, 1967) and Herford and Simpson suggest, as a measure of relative wit, that Subtle defeats Surly in the argument in act 2, scene 3. While it is true that Subtle has the last word, it seems clear to me that the situation is saved by Dol's good timing, not by Surly's retreat. She passes in view of Mammon, diverting his attention from the discussion, of course, and allowing Subtle to make a fuss. As so often happens at moments of impending disaster in this play, one of the "venter tripartite," watching from another room, saves the enterprise.
5. Gerald Eades Bentley, *The Profession of Dramatist in Shakespeare's Time: 1596-1642* (Princeton: Princeton University Press, 1971), chapters 1 and 2.
6. Greenblatt, "False Ending in *Volpone*," 103.
7. Roger Bacon, *The Mirror of Alchimy* (London: Richard Olive, 1597), 28.
8. Bacon, *Mirror of Alchimy*, 53, 75-76.
9. Ben Jonson, *The Alchemist*, ed. Alvin B. Kernan (New Haven: Yale University Press, 1978), 11.
10. Walter J. Ong, S.J., *Ramus: Method and the Decay of Dialogue* (Cambridge: Harvard University Press, 1958), 92, 32.

11. H&S, vol. 8, 568.
12. H&S, vol. 8, 570.
13. H&S, vol. 7, 138.
14. H&S, vol. 7, 154.
15. H&S, vol. 7, 409.
16. H&S, vol. 5, 294.
17. H&S, vol. 7, 410.
18. H&S, vol. 7, 412-13.
19. H&S, vol. 7, 413-14.
20. In an odd, parodic way, the "venter tripartite" represents another extension of the Jonsonian drama of oedipal conflict. Instead of the conventional triangle—father, son, wife-mother—*The Alchemist* offers us two males of equal stature, each seeking to establish his superior position in the venture. Since one of the prizes is a night with Dol, she is clearly a disputed love object (in fact, when things nearly get beyond her control, she threatens to take her "part" and leave). She also has a stern, maternal side, functioning as the glue that holds this "family" together. She mediates their dispute, threatening them like two wayward children, insisting that they show some concern for her and for the "republic." While she treats them as equals, she is careful to flatter both Face and Subtle: one is the "general," the other the "sovereign." What strikes me as particularly interesting is that the play should begin with this quarrel, in light of the fact that *Epicene* destroys the notion of oedipal privilege by suggesting that the only victories are Pyrrhic ones. It is as if the question for Jonson has become how to negotiate authority out of such circumstances. The males still need to battle for supremacy, but the background against which the struggle occurs is squalid beyond belief. Each has access to the desired love object, but, while she appears from time to time as the Queen of Fairy, she is really a whore.
21. George Hibbard, "Ben Jonson and Human Nature," in Blissett, Patrick, and VanFossen, *Celebration of Ben Jonson*, 67.

CHAPTER SIX

1. H&S, vol. 2, 132-33.
2. H&S, vol., 5, 291.
3. Two critics who have commented recently on this aspect of the play are Joel Kaplan in "Dramatic and Moral Energy in Ben

Jonson's *Bartholomew Fair*," *Renaissance Drama*, N.S. 3 (1970), 137-56 and George Parfitt in *Public Poet and Private Man*, especially 83-85 and 141.
4. Frye, "Argument of Comedy," 81.
5. William Shakespeare, *The History of Troilus and Cressida*, in *The Riverside Shakespeare*, ed. G. B. Evans (Boston: Houghton Mifflin, 1974), 464. All subsequent citations from Shakespeare in the text are to the *Riverside* edition.
6. Frye, "Argument of Comedy," 85.
7. Frye, "Argument of Comedy," 89.
8. R. B. Parker, "The Themes and Staging of *Bartholomew Fair*," *University of Toronto Quarterly* 39 (1969-70), 293.
9. See Kaplan, "Dramatic and Moral Energy" and Richard Levin, "The Structure of *Bartholomew Fair*," *PMLA* 80 (1965), 172-79.
10. My remarks on *Bartholomew Fair* owe a general debt to Barish's work on the play, both in chapter 5 of *Language of Prose Comedy* and in his article, "*Bartholomew Fair* and Its Puppets," *Modern Language Quarterly* 20 (1959), 3-17.
11. Levin, "Structure of *Bartholomew Fair*," 175.
12. Levin, "Structure of *Bartholomew Fair*," 178.
13. Judith K. Gardiner, "Infantile Sexuality, Adult Critics, and *Bartholomew Fair*," *Literature and Psychology* 24 (1974), 130.
14. Gardiner, "Infantile Sexuality, Adult Critics," 131.
15. H&S, vol. 8, 242.
16. Ben Jonson, *Bartholomew Fair*, ed. Eugene Waith (New Haven: Yale University Press, 1963), 205-17.
17. Edmund Wilson must be credited with the insight that, in Jonson's case, there is a clear link between the control of words and the control of money, although the analogy is one substantiated by psychoanalysis. See Wilson, "Morose Ben Jonson," 63-64.
18. Barish, *Language of Prose Comedy*, 194-95.
19. Knockem: " 'Slood, thou'll not stale without a warrant, shortly" (IV, vi, 5).

CHAPTER SEVEN

1. H&S, vol. 8, 606.
2. H&S, vol. 11, 255. In a note in their commentary on *Discoveries*, Herford and Simpson remark on the peculiar inconsis-

tency of Jonson's treatment of Peniboy: "The curious thing is that this Senecan excerpt, here presented as Jonson's own reflection, is in the play put on the lips of the contemptible miser, Peniboy senior."
3. H&S, vol. 2, 329.
4. Orgel, *Jonsonian Masque*, 97.
5. Orgel, *Jonsonian Masque*, 102.

Conclusion

1. Few writers have dominated the students of their work the way Jonson has, and I think this phenomenon is reflected, directly and indirectly, in Edmund Wilson and his essay "Morose Ben Jonson." I am always surprised at the outrage this essay provokes among scholars, even today. But my own sense is that Wilson is essentially correct, not in his appraisal of Jonson's work but in his description of what goes on in it. I think the critical challenge he poses is to account for his perceptions in a way that is more in line with the historical fact that Jonson continues to be valued as an important writer. Modern criticism generally has felt the need to defend Jonson and has done so by arguing that he has important things to say, that is, on the basis of discursive meaning. While this is certainly an important aspect of his work, what is "said," finally, is more complex than what is transacted at the level of conscious intention and conscious response.
2. W. David Kay, "The Shaping of Ben Jonson's Career," *Modern Philology* 67 (1969-70), 224-37.
3. Barish, "Loathed Stage," 29.
4. The work of Melanie Klein and D. W. Winnicott provides the foundation of this field of study.
5. H&S, vol. 1, 139.
6. H&S, vol. 1, 140.
7. My sense of the masques and their relation to Jonson's drama owes a great deal to Stephen Orgel's work, particularly *The Jonsonian Masque*.
8. Orgel, *Jonsonian Masque*, 6-7.

INDEX

Alchemist, The, 67, 77, 105, 125-56, 157, 160, 180-82, 184, 190, 205, 216, 217; "To the Reader," 146
alchemy, 137-38, 140-47, 150
androgyny, 94

Bacon, Roger, *The Mirror of Alchimy*, 137-38, 140-41
Baines, Barbara J., and Williams, Mary C., 235*n*
Barish, Jonas A., 30, 47, 59-60, 76, 110, 140, 162, 173, 183, 211, 236*n*
Bartholomew Fair, 43, 50, 67, 68, 77, 157-89, 190-91, 196, 218, 219, 221, 227; induction, 4, 128-29, 178-79, 180, 182, 204
Beaumont and Fletcher, *The Knight of the Burning Pestle*, 3, 170
Bentley, Gerald Eades, 135
Bradbrook, M. C., 234*n*
Brown, Douglas, 236*n*
Brustein, Robert, 131

Campbell, Oscar James, 17, 232*n*
Carlson, Peter, 95-96
Case Is Altered, The, 18
Cataline, 64, 170, 205, 218; "To the Reader in Ordinarie," 11, 158, 230-31*n*; "To the Reader Extraordinary," 11, 230-31*n*
Cecil, Sir Robert, 16
Conversations With Drummond, 220
Cook, Ann Jennalie, 229*n*

Cynthia's Revels, 17, 29-35, 42-43, 50, 66, 68, 89, 109, 112, 114, 141, 181, 204, 209, 215, 226-27; prologue, 95

Dekker, Thomas, 15
Devil Is an Ass, The, 191
Discoveries, 141, 150, 194, 212
Drummond, William, 219-20

Eastward Ho!, 15
Elizabeth I, Queen of England, 15, 27, 72
Enck, John, 133-34, 234*n*
Entertainment at Highgate, 142
Entertainment at Theobalds, 142
Epicene, 45, 50, 77, 91, 105-24, 160, 177, 190, 216-17
Epigrammes, 16
Erasmus, Desiderius, 78-79
Every Man In His Humor, 18
Every Man Out of His Humor, 17, 18-29, 33, 68, 78, 84-85, 105, 112, 178, 181, 204, 206, 209, 215, 217, 226; induction, 10, 18-19, 24, 75, 106, 159, 178, 191, 196

female sexuality, 26-28, 62-65, 86-88, 89, 92, 108, 113, 116, 118-20, 163, 175-77, 215-19, 234*n*
Forest, The, 38
Fortunate Isles, 195-204
Freud, Sigmund, 93, 214, 234*n*
Frye, Northrop, 105, 160, 163-64, 187

INDEX

Gardiner, Judith, 174, 188
Gosson, Stephen, *Schoole of Abuse*, 82-83
Greenblatt, Stephen, 76-78
Gunpowder Plot, 16

Hallett, Charles A., 234*n*
Herford and Simpson, 16, 92, 158, 199-200, 232*n*, 238*n*
Heywood, Thomas, *A Woman Killed With Kindness*, 98
Hibbard, George, 155
homosexuality, 91-92, 120
Horace, 37-39

infantile sexuality, 175
"Inviting a Friend to Supper," 127

Jones, Inigo, 15
Jones, Robert, 37
James I, King of England, 15, 142-43, 145-46, 172, 188, 198-99
Juvenal, 193, 195

Kaplan, Joel, 237*n*, 238*n*
Kay, W. David, 210
Kernan, Alvin, 88, 140, 231*n*, 235*n*
Klein, Melanie, 239*n*
Knights, L. C., 234*n*

Laplanche, J. and Pontalis, J.-B., 234*n*
Levin, Richard, 173-74, 238*n*

McPherson, David, 70
Mares, F. H., 236*n*
Marlowe, Christopher, *Hero and Leander*, 170, 172
Marotti, Arthur, 48, 60
Marston, John, 15
masque, 30, 142-46, 179, 195-206, 223-27
Mercury Vindicated, 137, 142, 145
Milton, John, *Comus*, 204

Neptune's Triumph, 195-206

oedipal conflict, 57-58, 61-68, 74, 89-94, 111-16, 120-23, 174, 177, 188, 215-27, 237*n*
Ong, Walter J., S.J., 236*n*
Orgel, Stephen K., 3, 103, 203, 204, 224
Ornstein, Robert, 48
Ovid, 167, 169, 170

Parker, R. B., 172
Parfitt, George, 31, 188, 232*n*, 238*n*
Partridge, Edward, 111
Pearlman, E., 231*n*
Pico della Mirandola, Giovanni, 73
Poetaster, 15, 17, 35-46, 66, 68, 72, 91, 97, 109, 111, 152, 181, 190, 205, 209, 210, 215, 223, 226; Apological Dialogue, 17, 26, 35, 40-41, 75, 150, 210; prologue, 40-42, 132

Ramus, Petrus, 140
Rea, John D., 234*n*

satire, 17, 19, 20, 24, 26-29, 30, 34-39, 42-43, 46, 50, 65-67, 72, 89, 94, 107-15, 123, 148-54, 159-60, 172, 190-91, 195, 208, 222-27
Sejanus, 35-37, 46-69, 72, 79-80, 91, 106, 109, 113, 135, 141, 150, 156, 187, 189, 205, 209, 211, 216, 218
Seneca, 193-94
Shakespeare, William, *A Midsummer Night's Dream*, 161, 164-73, 175, 187-88, 218
Staple of News, The, 191-96, 204

Talbert, Ernest, 36

Vives, Juan Luis, 73

INDEX

Volpone, 35, 37, 46, 50, 67, 70-104, 105, 106, 109, 112, 128, 132-36, 147-48, 150, 152, 154, 156-57, 181-84, 187, 190, 212, 216; dedicatory epistle, 70-71, 103; epilogue, 95, 128

Waith, Eugene, 178, 232*n*

Weimann, Robert, 229*n*
Wickham, Glynne, 229*n*
Wilson, Edmund, 27, 238*n*, 239*n*
Winnicott, D. W., 239*n*
Wycherley, William, *The Country Wife*, 9

Yeats, William Butler, 70, 86, 157

Library of Congress Cataloging in Publication Data

Sweeney, John Gordon, 1950-
　Jonson and the psychology of public theater.

　Includes bibliographical references and index.
　1. Jonson, Ben, 1573?-1637—Criticism and interpretation. 2. Jonson, Ben, 1573?-1637—Biography—Psychology. 3. Theater audiences—England—History—17th century. 4. Authority in literature. 5. Dramatists, English—Early modern, 1500-1700—Biography.
　I. Title.
PR2638.S695　1985　　　822'.3　　　84-42557
ISBN 0-691-06622-1